"*Calming Your Angry Mind* is a wonderful guide to help you transform your anger through mindfulness, understanding, and compassion. It is filled with many practical and hands-on mindfulness practices that you can bring into your everyday life. This book shows you how to live a life with less anger and more peace."

—Bob Stahl, PhD, coauthor of *A Mindfulness-Based Stress Reduction Workbook, Living With Your Heart Wide Open, Calming the Rush of Panic,* and *A Mindfulness-Based Stress Reduction Workbook for Anxiety*

"With compassion, clarity, and skill, Dr. Brantley provides a practical guide to dealing with anger productively and, more broadly, an inspirational introduction to the broader practice of mindfulness."

—Richard M. Jaffe, associate professor in the department of religious studies at Duke University

HILLSBORO PUBLIC LIBRARY
Hillsboro, OR
Member of Washington County
COOPERATIVE LIBRARY SERVICES

calming your angry mind

how mindfulness & compassion can free you from anger & bring peace to your life

JEFFREY BRANTLEY, MD

New Harbinger Publications, Inc.

Publisher's Note

This publication is designed to provide accurate and authoritative information in regard to the subject matter covered. It is sold with the understanding that the publisher is not engaged in rendering psychological, financial, legal, or other professional services. If expert assistance or counseling is needed, the services of a competent professional should be sought.

"Call Me By My True Names" from PEACE IS EVERY STEP: THE PATH OF MINDFULNESS IN EVERYDAY LIFE by Thich Nhat Hahn, copyright © 1991 by Thich Nhat Hanh. Used by permission of Bantam Books, a division of Random House, Inc. Any third party use of this material, outside of this publication, is prohibited. Interested parties must apply directly to Random House, Inc. for permission.

"Everything Is Waiting for You" from EVERYTHING IS WAITING FOR YOU by David Whyte, copyright © 2003 by Many Rivers Press, Langley, Washington. Printed with permission from Many Rivers Press, http://www.davidwhyte.com.

Distributed in Canada by Raincoast Books

Copyright © 2014 by Jeffrey Brantley
          New Harbinger Publications, Inc.
          5674 Shattuck Avenue
          Oakland, CA 94609
          www.newharbinger.com

5413 1668 5/14

Cover design by Amy Shoup
Acquired by Tesilya Hanauer
Edited by Jean Blomquist

All Rights Reserved.

Library of Congress Cataloging-in-Publication Data on file

Printed in the United States of America.

16   15   14

10   9   8   7   6   5   4   3   2   1   First printing

Contents

PART 2
practices for calming your angry mind

PART 3
beyond your angry mind

foreword

You have in Dr. Jeffrey Brantley's latest book a profoundly useful and accessible approach to improving your day-to-day life experiences. Here you can learn and practice simple techniques that will improve your health and your relationships and, perhaps most importantly, provide you with everyday peace of mind.

Anger is something everyone experiences. Indeed, feeling irritated, annoyed, or even outraged is an unavoidable fact of being human. It is vital to know, though, that anger comes with its own blinders and rigid beliefs. It narrows your thinking and pulls you into the blame game. Anger also covers its tracks by making you absolutely certain that your view of the offending situation is 100 percent correct. Making matters worse, any emotion that you feel in this moment slyly works to increase the odds that you'll feel that same emotion in the next moment. With all the insidious ways that anger can control your mind, you can begin to see how it can come to dominate your days, even your life.

Yet even though anger—like any other negative emotion—is to be expected as a normal human experience, the truth is that you need not become a victim of your anger. Psychological science makes it clear that you can choose not to cultivate or prolong your angry experiences. Anger need not become a lifestyle. Science has cataloged the damage done when this challenging state of mind becomes a person's baseline, or first impulse: you can pay a high price in terms of compromised health, strained relationships, and unhappiness.

If anger has come to rule you in ways that you no longer appreciate, rest assured—you can change. This book can help. Drawing equally on ancient wisdom traditions and twenty-first century scientific breakthroughs, Dr. Brantley skillfully weaves practices for calming your angry mind together with vivid success stories that will inspire you to achieve the changes you seek.

You will learn core practices of mindfulness and compassion, plus how and when to deploy them. You will gain wisdom and insight into your own inner workings. You will learn to curb your angry and other negative feelings in ways that will allow you to find more joy, more connection, and more meaning in your days. You will pave the way toward flourishing.

Congratulations on taking the first steps toward understanding your mind and your anger. I wish you every success as you absorb and put into practice the deep wisdom that Dr. Brantley offers here.

—Barbara L. Fredrickson, PhD
Kenan Distinguished Professor of Psychology
University of North Carolina at Chapel Hill
Author of *Positivity* and *Love 2.0*

introduction

Do you ever get tired of being angry?

Do you ever feel weary from the edginess and dreariness that insistent judgments and blaming thoughts bring into your relationships and into your daily life?

Have you ever become concerned about the impact that your irritable and mean words and actions have on others?

If your answer to any of those questions is yes, then this book might help you.

Do you ever wish your life could be happier, or wonder if you might be much more—as a human being—than you feel you are in the burning heat of angry moments?

Have you ever wished that your friendlier, wiser, calmer, and "better" self would more often appear and guide you in your relationships with your loved ones, interactions with coworkers, and your encounters with the joys and challenges of living every day?

If your answer to any of those questions is yes, then perhaps this book can help with that too. This is a simple book for ordinary people, and it could be useful every day of your life.

This is a book about anger and you; and, more importantly, it is about discovering and using the power you already have to change your relationship to anger in any of its many forms and expressions. By learning to free yourself from anger's grip, you can immediately transform your life—and feel greater ease and more happiness more often. You may also be surprised to discover new dimensions of kindness, understanding, and love for yourself and others.

Your innate power to change is based in *mindfulness*, which is another name for awareness. Mindfulness is an energy and quality that all human beings are capable of touching because it is based in our basic human intelligence and is informed by our already present potential for goodness, including our capacity for kindness and compassion.

In *Calming Your Angry Mind*, you will learn practical ways to "grow" your mindfulness and how to rely on it to manage anger and other painful emotions as well as the stress of daily life. You will also find helpful information about mindfulness, anger, and their impact on your health, as well as easy-to-follow instructions for a variety of simple meditations and reflective practices that you can use every day to reclaim your life from the toxic power of anger.

The information and meditation practices you will find here are grounded in knowledge and understanding that come from modern science, psychology, and ancient wisdom about mindfulness, meditation, health, and how your mind and body operate. This accumulated body of knowledge points to benefits that follow from mindfulness meditation, including deepening awareness and insight, and helping you become more compassionate, kind, and loving.

You need no special training or previous experience to take advantage of what is in this book, and you don't have to adopt any particular belief system or hold a unique spiritual or religious view. All that you need to get started is to be interested in doing what you can to help yourself be happier and healthier!

Through this book and the meditation practices of mindfulness, compassion, and wise understanding that it contains, I invite you on a unique journey. On this journey, you'll explore the ever-unfolding, present moment of your life and learn to see it with new eyes. You may also discover that, by mindfully embracing your journey through each and every moment, you come home to yourself and truly connect with your most reliable source for creating more satisfying relationships and experiencing a rich and joyful life. So, if you would like to discover more about yourself and your anger, and learn how not only to gain better control of your anger but also to function more effectively as a force for good for yourself, for others, and for this world, then read on!

THE NATURE OF ANGER

Feelings of anger or tolerance, intense emotions like hatred or love, intentions to make war or to make peace, whatever the feeling, thought, or action, it lives and dies inside each one of us, as a response in each human heart to something we feel, or think, or as a reaction to someone or something around us. Whether or not the emotion is sustained or grows, or fades and dies, depends in large part to how we treat, consciously or unconsciously, the reactive stream of thoughts and emotions that unfolds within and flows constantly through the present moment of our lives.

It's true for all of us. Something happens—a car cuts us off on the freeway, a colleague makes a thoughtless remark, a friend sends a kind note—and suddenly a feeling or an emotion rises up inside us. It could be blame or gratitude, judgment or acceptance, and even feelings of boredom or of interest and engagement. The amazing range of human feelings and emotions begins with some event—a sound, a sensation, or a thought, for example—which then triggers a reaction in mind and body. The emotions can come and go very quickly, or they can linger. How we relate to the emotion makes all the difference in whether they will linger or fade away within us.

The emotion of anger is also like this. How angry you feel or how angry you become in response to any given experience, even whether you become angry at all—it all depends on what happens inside you: what bodily sensations you feel and what you think.

Perhaps you have had the experience of anger (or related feelings such as blaming, judgment, irritation, or rage) taking over your life for a moment or much longer. What did that feel like in your body? What were your thoughts telling you then?

Perhaps someone has told you that anger has become a "problem" for you—at work, as a health issue, in a relationship, or in some other way. Have you been aware of the anger inside of you, or is this surprising news?

Or, perhaps you have, at some time or another, felt that anger "energized" you, and that it helped you get something you wanted. Possibly only afterward did you realize the pain your anger caused, and maybe even then you dismissed it by saying something about "the end justifies the means." Or, equally likely, perhaps you never noticed or truly realized the depth of harm to others that your anger caused.

This is the nature of anger—and of being human; it is a complicated and richly poignant experience. At times, anger happens in your awareness—you know you are angry, you know why, and you know how you express your anger. But at other times, anger happens out of awareness—you may not even know that you are angry, much less why or how your anger affects those around you. Anger arises and is expressed through your ongoing flow of thoughts, body sensations, and the expression and actions that those thoughts and sensations command.

The mental activity and physical reactions that fuel your subjective experience of being angry require a significant amount of energy too. One might say that the expression "burning up with anger" points us to the degree of intense energy present in the emotion of anger. And, because it takes deeply formed habit patterns of connection and communication among your mind, your brain, and your body to produce and sustain anger, I will often use the expression *habit energy* to refer to this energetic and habitual perspective on anger and its related feelings.

What is your personal, subjective experience when anger visits you in the present moment? Where is it "burning you up"? Can you feel the anger in your body, your mind, or your relationship? Does anger erode your sense of well-being and belonging in the world? What does this emotion arise in reaction to? Do you feel disrespected, threatened, or vulnerable perhaps? What relationship do you take to the anger when it comes to you? Do you become angry at the anger, or do you feel that you become the emotion—that you are "just an angry person," for example? What if you could become more aware and discover the answers to these questions? When you think about your responses to your emotions, would you like to respond differently? In short, would you like to be a different kind of person?

The choice we have about our anger is the same choice we have about so many other aspects of our lives: will we turn toward our anger and seek to better understand and manage it, or will we let our habit energy of living, thinking, and acting "in anger" and "from anger" dominate our lives, actions, and the impact we have on others and our world?

In this book, I invite you to turn toward your anger, learn to understand it, and find healthy ways of managing it. I invite you to dive deeply into your personal experience of emotions—especially anger and its related feelings—by accessing your ability to inhabit the present moment mindfully, to become more aware of what happens in your mind and body as you experience particular emotions, and to relate differently to those emotions.

Imagine for a moment that your experience of and behavior around angry feelings could be very different. Imagine that anger, blaming, judgments, irritation, and rage could lessen in intensity and frequency. Imagine that the power anger has in your life and relationships could diminish.

Imagine that you could live your life in a way that acknowledges and experiences anger, but that is not limited or distorted by angry feelings or outbursts. That could be a profound transformation and a radically different life! If your anger were less intense and controlling, maybe you would not feel as isolated or alone, or be plagued by second guessing, or worry about what you have done or need to do because anger hijacked you again.

So how do you get from your life today to the one you just imagined? Mindfulness will help you—and this book will teach you how to use mindfulness to deal with your anger. I frequently teach mindfulness-based stress reduction (MBSR) classes, and I'd like to share one of our core beliefs with you, because you may find it helpful: "No matter how much a person thinks is wrong with them, we believe there is more right than is wrong." The "more right" piece has to do with human intelligence, the capacity to learn and to relate to others, and the ability to know ourselves. It also has a lot to do with the basic human capacity for awareness called "mindfulness," so let's take a closer look at mindfulness now.

WHAT IS MINDFULNESS?

Mindfulness is something you already have, at least as a potential. When you are mindful, you're aware of what is happening now, in this very moment, without judging or getting lost in the thoughts and plans about fixing or changing anything. Mindfulness does not do anything! It simply notices, without judgment.

You can think of mindfulness as a mirror that accurately reflects what appears before it. Mindfulness sees clearly what is present. That is what makes being mindful so important if you want to know what is happening inside your mind and body as well as in the world around you. You can also think of mindfulness as a talent like musical ability. Your ability is innate—it is already there—but for the talent to bloom fully, you have to develop certain skills with your instrument, and you have to practice. This book will introduce the basic mindfulness skills and offer helpful guidance for practicing those skills.

Human beings have literally been practicing mindfulness for thousands of years and have amassed an enormous amount of wisdom about meditation practice and mindfulness. You will be able to draw on this wisdom as you take up the meditations and reflective practices in this book. You will join an ancient tradition of those who seek to cultivate and nurture awareness centered in the present moment. And, as you practice mindfulness, you will also become a scientist because the ancient traditions of mindfulness and meditation are now being embraced and explored by modern science in fascinating and almost unimaginable ways. Let's take a brief look at what science is learning about the brain, stress, and health and their relationship to anger.

NEUROSCIENCE, STRESS, AND HEALTH

Your brain changes depending upon how you use your mind! This is the conclusion of a revolution in brain and medical science over the past several decades. The name for this dynamic and plastic quality of your living brain is *neuroplasticity*.

The implications for having a "neuroplastic" brain are enormous. For example, the mental activities that you deliberately choose (for instance, a positive activity like saying "thank you" or reminding yourself to be grateful or "count your blessings") will result in a stronger brain basis for that activity over time and increase the likelihood that those thoughts and feelings will reemerge. And similarly, because the habit energy of familiar mind patterns is so strong, those patterns associated with feelings like chronic anger, frustration, scorn, and criticism can easily fire. When that happens, they can, in the present moment, evoke within you the energy of deeply held personal views, inner stories, or old memories, any of which can quickly hijack you and drive you into unexpected behaviors.

Anger in its many forms can be like this, an old habit energy suddenly appearing in the present moment with alarming intensity. Given the reality of neuroplasticity, this raises two important questions: Do you "practice" being angry? What would happen if you practiced being mindful?

The way you use your mind changes your brain. In other words, just as you have to exercise your muscles properly in order to stay healthy and for those muscles to do what you ask them to do, you also have to exercise your brain properly in order to cultivate the qualities that are important to you and to let the ones that are not helpful or constructive fade away.

Through the practice of mindfulness, you will have the opportunity to explore your own mind using powerful inner technologies of meditation and reflection. We know now from neuroscientific research that simply using your mind in this contemplative way actually alters how your brain works; and that can have a powerful positive impact by reducing your stress, benefiting your health, and empowering you to better understand and control strong emotions like anger.

And if you wish to become less angry and critical and instead become more positive, joyful, kind, and compassionate, then it helps to know your brain can also change in that direction. Modern science and psychology have made fascinating discoveries that align with the spiritual and wisdom teachings encouraging us to nurture our human potential for kindness and compassion. Let's look more closely at the power and intelligence of the human heart, a theme that we will return to many times throughout this book.

HUMAN INTELLIGENCE AND GOODNESS OF HEART

In the popular film *Saving Private Ryan* (1998), Ryan as an old man visits the grave of a fellow soldier who gave his life to save him during the war. In the scene, Private Ryan pauses and asks the loved ones around him at the gravesite a question: "Did I live a good life?"

What makes a person give his or her life for another? How many times and in how many ways do the acts of others support or even preserve our own lives?

Modern psychologists and health scientists have found that we humans are actually "wired" and evolutionarily "selected" for our capacity to appreciate connections with one another and to nurture that capacity. We have the potential to be extraordinarily sensitive and present to the experience of our own "inner lives" and bodies. And asking questions about the good life, as Private Ryan did, is as old as humanity itself.

As we shall see throughout this book, the focus on positive experience and feelings can be very good for our health and happiness too. The benefits of positive experience and feelings are actually the basis of a branch of modern psychology known as "positive psychology." Much of the science of positive psychology is informed by the work of Barbara Fredrickson. Barbara's work has powerfully demonstrated that practicing meditations based in mindfulness and compassion can help you tap and develop your potential for positive experience and therefore likely improve your health and well-being over time.

As you reflect on these scientific findings, you might recognize a very similar message to the one that spiritual teachers from all traditions—as well as great poets, artists, and writers—have long expressed: as human beings, we possess the capacity and potential for extraordinary wisdom and goodness, right here and right now, in *this* life! The important questions then become this: What does a "good life" really mean to you, how does it relate to your sources of meaning and purpose and to your deepest values, and what keeps you from realizing the possibility for greater well-being in your life? If you think that the anger in your life interferes with your dream of a good life, then perhaps mindfulness practice and meditation can help you understand and control the anger. Perhaps mindfulness practice and meditation can also help you discover the answers to the questions about what a good life means to you.

A MINDFULNESS-BASED APPROACH TO LIVING

In this book, we will explore a mindfulness-based approach to living. That simply means learning to cultivate greater awareness in approaching whatever life brings you. Greater awareness will bring you increased understanding and the ability to manage difficult emotions like anger. The greater awareness that comes from mindfulness practice will also empower you to stay present and connect more deeply with what you value most, as well as offer more effective action in the face of challenging situations.

In my research for this book, in addition to exploring meditative, medical, and psychological sources, I spoke with experts in anger management who work as therapists, educators, and researchers. I told the experts, "You already have some very effective methods for teaching people to better manage their anger and other difficult emotions." Then I asked them a simple question: "What do you think are the biggest challenges and obstacles that prevent people from taking advantage of the successful programs you offer?"

All of the experts gave basically the same answer. They said that the biggest obstacle for people bothered by intense emotional difficulties like anger is that they are not sufficiently aware of those angry feelings and emotions when they are present, and they do not understand the damage that those emotions can cause to their health, relationships, and chances for success and happiness in life.

Being more mindful could result in better control in your life in some very important ways. For example, you could learn to recognize and control your anger rather than letting it control you, and you could take more responsibility for your health, enjoy better health, and be happier about the direction you take and the choices you make every day.

This mindfulness-based approach to life, including mindfully managing emotions like anger, is also often referred to as "contemplative," "meditative," or "reflective" because it uses your capacity to observe what is happening in the here and now and to know by direct observation, instead of thinking. (Just remember how that mirror accurately "reflects" whatever comes in front of it.)

Although you may not be aware of it, this way of living mindfully is very likely something you already have experience with. For example, when you go for a walk and notice the color and shape of a beautiful flower or the pattern of clouds moving in the sky, that direct noticing without (or before) any thoughts is a moment of mindfulness. When you take a sip of cool water and notice the water is colder than you expected, the part of you that knows the direct experience of the coldness is mindfulness.

If you choose a mindfulness-based approach to living, it simply means you commit to cultivating mindfulness—direct observation of all experience—more often in the moments and changing situations of your life. Such direct observation is extremely powerful and always informative. For example, you can read dozens of books about apples, but until you take a bite out of one, pay close attention and notice the crispness, the sweetness, and the juiciness, you don't really *know* the apple!

In the MBSR classes, we also say, "Being informs doing." In other words, if you know clearly what is happening and what is here in this moment, you are more likely to make a better choice for the action you take. For example, let's go back to the apple. After really paying attention to that apple, you might find yourself reaching for another one, or maybe you decide you don't like apples after all. Either way, by paying attention and "being" with the experience of biting and chewing your apple, you make a better decision about "doing" something with apples in the future.

As we consider anger in all of its forms as well as the impact it has on your health and all of your relationships, these three basic statements capture the essence of the mindfulness-based approach to living:

I. No matter how intense it is or what results it brings, your anger is *not* you. It is only a condition or strong energy arising in your mind and body in this moment that results from the temporary coming together of a complex array of other conditions, and it will pass.

2. If you do not fully understand the nature of anger in your life and how it takes control of your life, you will pay a high price in terms of your own health and well-being, as well as in the nature of your relationships and your ultimate degree of satisfaction and happiness in life.

3. According to an intriguing combination of modern neuro-science, health science, and ancient meditative and human wisdom, practicing mindfulness can help you understand and transform not only the emotion and expression of anger in your life, but also the very mind-body foundation that supports anger. This can reduce or eliminate your anger's toxic and "out-of-control" aspects in the future.

As I mentioned earlier, you naturally have the capacity for mindfulness as a human being. And the capacity for being mindful is cultivated and matured by practicing meditation. In the sense we are using it here, the word *meditation* means simply that you direct your attention, in a particular way, for a particular purpose.

Yes, the word *meditation* is often associated with particular religious traditions and groups. Regardless of the faith tradition, if you study the meditation instructions in different traditions and from different teachers, you will probably see that, strictly speaking, those instructions involve some emphasis on directing attention in a particular way for a particular purpose. For example, a person may be directed to place attention on and repeat a phrase in a loving way. Or the person may be instructed to gaze steadily and gently at an icon for the purpose of "quieting the mind" or "being still," in order to feel a deeper connection or come to a greater understanding of a teaching or aspect of that particular faith tradition.

And you do not have to join any particular religious group or take up any specific spiritual view to benefit from the meditations in this book. The meditations are based in two basic human qualities—your innate intelligence and goodness of heart. These qualities are available right now to you and to any human being who chooses to develop them.

It is also very important for you to know that the meditations in this book are *not* the only meditations, mindfulness or otherwise, that can help you to better control your anger and live a happier life. It is a good idea to cultivate a spirit of "skeptical curiosity" about meditation and to trust yourself, including your own intelligence and goodness of heart, to guide you in learning the power of any meditation that can bring more ease and well-being to you.

And, when I speak about "practicing meditation" throughout this book, I do not mean being mechanically repetitive, or practicing to be "perfect," or rehearsing for some performance to come later. No, by *practicing meditation*, I am simply asking you to commit to being present and paying attention in this moment. We "practice" mindfulness and the other meditations in order to better understand who we are and what it means to be a human being. We constantly learn and relearn to show up for our "practice" in a way that embodies the vast dimension of full awareness, and that is supported by the human capacities for calmness, mindfulness, and equanimity, here and now.

WHO THIS BOOK IS FOR

This book is for you if you want to learn better ways to control and manage your anger and other difficult emotions. This book is also for you if, more than just controlling your anger, you would like to discover more authentic and rewarding ways to engage with others, to feel more connected to the beauty around you, and to be more appreciative of the enormous opportunity and potential in your own life.

You don't have to be an expert in anger management to use this book effectively. You don't have to be a meditation guru either. In fact, you don't need *any* previous experience with meditation! Lots of people—from schoolchildren to seniors, from business executives to soldiers, from famous athletes to homemaker athletes, and from people seeking optimal health to those facing terminal illness—practice meditation these days. So, even if you have thought that you are not the meditation "type" (whatever that means), that does not matter. You will see that anyone, even you, can meditate.

The meditative approaches offered here, using contemplative practices to nourish awareness, compassion, and understanding, can be a potent resource if you are motivated and willing to make the commitment to explore them. That is really all you need—motivation and commitment. It helps if you also have some skeptical curiosity. This could mean you are not so sure the meditations can help, but you are curious to see if they can, and you are willing to try.

The approach and the simple, straightforward, easy-to-follow mindfulness-based practices in this book can help you increase self-awareness, discover inner sources of resiliency and capacity, and find more joy. Intentionally bringing even one of these practices into your life could dramatically change your relationship with yourself and others as well as enable you to make better choices and take more effective actions in your life.

A note of caution, however, is in order. This book, these practices, and mindfulness in general are not "magic bullets." They are not substitutes for expert professional health care when that is needed. While there is good evidence that mindfulness practice can help the progress of many treatment approaches, different approaches work for different people at different times. If you need a well-structured anger-management program at some point in your life, then this book and these practices are not meant to be a substitute for that. Please be wise and be kind to yourself: don't hesitate to talk with a therapist, coach, or other professional if you are not certain if you need professional help learning to manage your anger.

HOW TO USE THIS BOOK

This is a book essentially about using meditations based in mindfulness, compassion, and wisdom to better manage anger and other difficult emotions and to enjoy a happier, kinder life. There is no right or wrong way to "do" any of the meditations. In fact, it will help if you stop thinking about "doing" anything (or "fixing" anything, or even "changing" anything) when you practice with any of the meditations. Rather, it really helps if you can relax a bit, engage each meditation with curiosity, and trust yourself to notice what happens as you practice. A good approach with each meditation could be like trying on a new outfit, not knowing what it will actually be like but being curious and willing to give the experience a try.

You will probably "like" some meditations more than others. That is okay. You can experiment with making the ones you like the ones you practice with regularly, say every day or even several times a day. And, at times, it can be very instructive to practice with a meditation or two that you did not like at first. You might find it very interesting if you can stick with some of these for a while and see what changes!

Each time you try a new meditation or go back to a familiar one, trust that you will know the best place to start, Look through the book and start where you find the most interesting material. Trust yourself to know. Begin there. To help you get started, here is a brief summary of the contents of this book and how the information and meditation instructions are organized.

Chapters 1 through 4 offer information about mindfulness, anger, and how to approach anger mindfully as well as practical suggestions for practicing meditation.

Chapters 5, 6, and 7 present specific meditation practices that emphasize mindfulness, compassion, and insight related to working with anger and other difficult emotions. These meditation practices can also help you in many other ways to be happier, more present, and kinder to yourself and others.

In chapter 8, you will find a number of common questions and concerns that arise when people practice meditations based in mindfulness and compassion, and some helpful suggestions in response to those common questions and concerns.

Chapters 9, 10, and 11 contain examples, personal stories, and brief meditations that invite you to consider additional perspectives and possibilities for living more mindfully and compassionately in every moment and any situation.

By exploring the possibilities offered in these meditations and the related examples and stories at your own pace, you can broaden your base of awareness and sustained attention as well as build your capacity for knowing accurately what is happening inside and around you in the present moment and how you can respond most effectively. On this journey of discovery and transformation, you will also very likely gain a deeper perspective and a greater appreciation for your own power to have a positive impact on others and in our world. As you do this, it's likely that you will also transform your relationship to and experience of anger in the process.

SEE FOR YOURSELF

My hope and intention for this book is that it will be a support, an ally, a friend, and perhaps a doorway or even a path for you if you seek to escape from the pain of anger and anger's intrusive presence in your life. Here is the book, but only you can reap the benefits! Only *you* can change you.

Your desire to transform your life into something happier and more positive can be your enduring motivation. Next, form a clear and strong intention to learn what you need to know to become free of the pain and suffering your anger creates. Finally, trust that you already have what you need to change, and commit yourself to exploring mindfulness meditation practices as a way of transforming your life.

PART 1

the foundation

CHAPTER 1

why mindfulness?

Tell me what you pay attention to and I will tell you who you are.

—José Ortega y Gasset

You are not your thoughts, even when they are angry, irritated, blaming, or judging, and you do not have to be ruled by them. Neither are you any of the wide range of unpleasant and strong feelings and emotions that all human beings experience—emotions like rage, anger, frustration, grief, and anxiety—and you do not have to be their prisoner. In fact, as a human being you are much larger, much more amazing and complex; and you hold much more potential than any thought or emotion you may have, even when those thoughts or emotions visit you often or demand your attention in the constantly unfolding present moment of your life.

You already have what you need for practicing mindfulness. You were actually born with the capacity to be mindful. Mindfulness relies on paying attention in the present moment with an open heart, which is something that all human beings can do. *Being mindful simply means that you have paused to pay attention on purpose and without judgment, gently noticing and simply being present with what is here, in this moment.*

Pausing to mindfully notice helps release you from the overidentification and inner momentum associated with constant busyness and incessant doing, fixing, and striving to become something more or someone else. Becoming more mindful does not mean that you have to give up doing things or being busy, but being more mindful does mean that you don't have to be lost in always being busy either. Mindfulness can help you discover new possibilities for living in ways that are not so busy or driven, ways that are more satisfying.

By learning to rest in awareness and to tune in, notice more carefully, and remain present for what is here and now, you will be able to change your relationship to your thoughts and feelings—including angry ones— in remarkable and liberating ways.

By being present and mindfully observing the flow of your inner life and your interactions with the outside world, deeper understanding of your thoughts and emotions inevitably develops. Thoughts and emotions like anger, hostility, scorn, and dislike are not your permanent identity. They are only temporary and depend on each other and many other equally temporary conditions in order to arise and be present in this moment.

Being mindful can also help you develop a more conscious approach to others and to the world around you. Greater self-awareness helps you recognize the triggers in you that fire automatically and spark anger in relationships. Being more aware can empower you to notice your impact on others and to make more effective and positive responses in your relationships.

Now let's take a closer look at the amazing human quality of mindfulness. This critical quality supports you and helps you to be present with awareness in each moment of your life.

WHAT IS MINDFULNESS?

Mindfulness is a potential and a capacity for greater awareness that you already have as a human being. Mindfulness is another name for awareness—awareness that is always in the present moment and that is nonjudging, receptive, and observant of what is present and happening, here and now.

Becoming more mindful opens you to a dimension of stillness and presence that is always near. You can enter this dimension in any moment—indeed, you can be mindful of each breath you take, each step you take, each thought, each sound, sensation, smell, or taste that you experience.

In fact, you have already had "mindful" moments and experiences even if you did not realize it or call them that, because mindfulness is part of you and is already operating (at least to a degree) within you. For example, in that moment when you notice the touch of a cool breeze against your face; or when standing in a line, you notice the smell of food cooking; or when sitting in your home or workplace, you notice the rushing sound of a car or truck passing nearby, in that moment of noticing—before your mind gets busy with its thoughts and ideas about what you noticed—it is the quality of mindfulness that is operating. In the instant when that sensation, smell, or sound makes contact with your skin, nose, or ears, and your brain transfers those signals into consciousness, the knowing of the experience that is happening in that moment is possible because your "natural" mindfulness is operating. Mindfulness notices the changing stream of all sense experience—sounds, thoughts, sensations, smells, and tastes—flowing through the present moment.

So, mindfulness is about being aware—knowing what is happening—in the present moment. It is also about being and not doing—and about not thinking. As we will see throughout this book, because mindfulness is not thinking but is capable of placing any thought (or other experience of mind and body) under the illuminating light of awareness, practicing mindfulness opens a profound path for healing and transformation because it changes your relationship to your thoughts. For example, in a conversation with someone, mindfulness can help you stay present, really hear what that person says, and know your own moment-by-moment feelings and thoughts better.

Now you have an idea of what mindfulness means. To explore this a little further, here is what mindfulness means to some well-known mindfulness meditation teachers.

Joseph Goldstein, one of the founders of the Insight Meditation Society:

> "By mindfulness, I mean the quality of paying full attention to the moment, opening to the truth of change" (2002, 32).

> "Mindfulness is the quality of mind that notices what is present, without judgment, without interference" (2002, 89).

Jon Kabat-Zinn, the creator of mindfulness-based stress reduction:

> Simply put, mindfulness is moment-to-moment awareness. It is cultivated by purposefully paying attention to things we ordinarily never give a moment's thought to. It is a systematic approach to developing new kinds of control and wisdom in our lives, based on our inner capacities for relaxation, paying attention, awareness, and insight (1990, 2).

Thich Nhat Hanh, Zen teacher, peace activist, poet, and author:

> I'll use the term mindfulness to refer to keeping one's consciousness alive to the present reality (1975, 11).

Sharon Salzberg, one of the founders of the Insight Meditation Society:

> Mindfulness helps us get better at seeing the difference between what's happening and the stories we tell ourselves about what's happening, stories that get in the way of direct experience (2011, 13).

MINDFULNESS AND MEDITATION

The territory of awareness that is available to us as human beings is vast. Practicing mindfulness makes that territory available to you. As you practice being mindful, even for a single breath or step, you move more deeply into the present moment and the dimension of awareness. Mindfulness practice offers you a rich opportunity to discover and experience the inner stillness and spaciousness as well as the ease and simplicity in living every day that are our natural heritage as human beings.

Your natural potential and capacity for mindfulness can be richly and deeply developed by practicing a variety of meditation methods that strengthen your intention to be mindful, increase your ability to direct and sustain attention on a focus, and expand your capacity to remain present to any experience with an open and nonjudging attitude. Meditation comes in many different forms, but in this book we will use a very basic definition. *Meditation* is a practice of paying attention in a particular way for a particular purpose. Let's take a closer look at meditation.

What Meditation Is

Meditation—paying attention in a particular way for a particular purpose—is both a skill and an art. The skills of meditation involve intention, attention, and maintaining a nonjudging attitude. Meditation is also an ancient art of self-transformation, practiced by countless human beings in many spiritual traditions. In recent years, many people in health care settings have also become interested in meditation because it is something any person—regardless of faith tradition, ethnicity, economic circumstances, or other distinctions—can learn to do to become happier and healthier as well as to deal more effectively with pain, sorrow, and destructive emotions like anger.

The meditation teacher Christina Feldman (1998, 2) notes several core principles that run through all meditative disciplines:

- *Attention* is "the means of establishing ourselves in the present moment."

- *Awareness* "develops a consciousness that is light, unburdened, sensitive, and clear. It provides an inner environment that is intuitive and still."

- *Understanding* "is born of the direct and immediate perception of our inner and outer worlds." Developing understanding through meditation practice provides "the possibility of traveling new pathways in our lives and is part of the tapestry of deepening wisdom."

- *Compassion* "is a fundamental principle of meditation. Meditation is not a narcissistic, self-interested path."

Thus meditation can be understood as an art and a practice of building skills for directing and sustaining attention, developing awareness that is light and clear, and gaining increased self-understanding and insight into how to live wisely. Meditation is also informed and supported by the basic human qualities of compassion and kindness, which are present in the person who meditates.

There are thousands of ways to practice meditation. One or more of the core principles listed above may be the focus of a particular method of meditation. Learning about the methods and benefits of the various forms of meditation, and how and when to practice different ones is part of the "art" of practicing meditation. And, whatever core principle you select as the focus of a particular method of meditation, you develop your meditation skills of attention, intention, and non-judging every time you practice moment-to-moment awareness.

For example, you may focus attention in meditation very closely on the sensations of breathing, patiently returning attention to the next breath whenever it wanders. Such a practice can be especially helpful in strengthening the skill of focused attention. Or you could focus attention on a quality like compassion or kindness, directing the feelings associated with that quality to yourself or to others, as a way of practicing and strengthening that quality.

Of course, each of the core principles—attention, awareness, understanding, compassion—is present to some extent in any method of meditation you choose. The reason for choosing a particular meditation method is usually more about which of these core principles you choose to explore in your practice.

Mindfulness meditation practices are especially powerful and useful for learning better ways to manage stress and to regain control over destructive emotions like anger. Why? Because they help you deepen your awareness of these emotions and what triggers them whenever they appear in your life.

In chapters 5, 6, and 7, you will find specific meditation practices, all based in mindfulness, to help you explore the different elements and qualities of attention, awareness, understanding, and compassion. In addition, in many of the following chapters you will find brief mindfulness-based meditation practices to help you grow greater awareness and understanding of particular themes and subjects related to establishing and maintaining mindfulness in different situations, especially ones related to anger. In chapter 4, you will find some practical suggestions to help you build your own personal meditation practice, if you choose to do that.

What Meditation Is Not

Now you have a better understanding of what meditation is. But because there are so many ideas circulating about mindfulness and meditation these days, it might also be helpful to consider what meditation is *not*.

Meditation is not "positive thinking." In fact, it is not thinking at all. Instead, it is about developing greater attention and awareness of the presence and nature of your thoughts.

Meditation is not just another relaxation technique. Although you may feel ease and relaxation while practicing meditation, mindfulness meditation is actually about growing awareness. It is important, however, to know that relaxation and ease can support your mindfulness practice and to learn to be self-compassionate and skillful about supporting those important elements in your whole life.

Meditation does not mean going into a trance or "blissing out." In mindfulness meditation, you are not trying to go anywhere! Rather, you are trying to know something about what is here right now and to be present to it.

Meditation does not make you immune from pain and upset. You are alive, and you will continue to experience good times and bad. You cannot stop the waves of life! Practicing meditation and becoming more mindful will help you respond differently, and, as the famous line goes, you will "learn to surf" when life's waves are coming hard and fast.

Meditation does not mean you have to "blank your mind." Rather, mindfulness meditation will help you become disentangled from habits of thinking and reacting because you will be more aware of them, and less prone to overidentifying with them. You will probably find that the thoughts in your mind will actually move on more quickly when you leave them alone.

Meditation is not just for priests, monks, or nuns, and it isn't a religion. Mindfulness and meditation are for anyone who wishes to practice them. You don't have to do or be anything special. Meditation practice is a way of remembering and reconnecting with the basic intelligence and goodness all human beings have. The meditations in this book can be done by people in any faith tradition; and they can be done in a secular way, too, if you do not identify with any religion.

Meditation is not selfish or self-centered. While it is possible to neglect your responsibilities and relationships in the name of meditation, this is a distortion of meditation. *Self-full* might be a better word to describe the changes that come with practicing mindfulness and meditation. This is because as you become more mindful, you will become more present and understanding of yourself and others, and others will probably experience you as more helpful and compassionate.

Mindfulness and Meditation: Important Things to Remember

The capacity for mindfulness is already in you as a potential. Developing skills of intention, attention, and a receptive, nonjudging attitude through meditation practice will help you realize the potential mindfulness offers to inform, enrich, and empower you in every moment of your life. Here is a brief summary to help you remember key points about mindfulness and meditation.

Mindfulness is best understood by experiencing it. Like biting an apple instead of reading or thinking about it gives you unique understanding of that apple, having the direct experience of being mindful is how you really learn about mindfulness. Mindfulness will become stronger if you support it with a regular meditation practice.

The paradox of mindfulness is that, to benefit from it, you have to stop trying to change things or to become someone else. This means not even striving to be a good or better mindfulness meditator!

In fact, you actually have to stop trying to "do" anything and just let things be. We call this practicing "being and not doing." It means that, for once, you can relax and stop working at fixing things. Practicing mindfulness can be a gift you give yourself, the gift of being still and being present with nothing else to do and nowhere else to go, except to inhabit this moment with sensitive attention.

Mindfulness has a dimension some people call "heartfulness." By that, they refer to qualities of friendliness, acceptance, and curiosity about what is being noticed. For example, when you experience a moment of irritation or frustration, the "heartfulness" is expressed as you acknowledge the distressing feeling and choose to welcome it, accept it and let it be present with you, and as you become curious and look more closely at the thoughts and sensations that comprise the feeling. Mindfulness is most definitely not a "head trip," nor is it just about your thoughts. It might be better to say that being mindful is a "whole-person trip," because being mindful means your attention and awareness include and welcome all of your human experience. This means you become mindful of any thoughts, or feelings, or sensations, and even smells and tastes that arise and join you in this moment. When you develop the mindfulness "skill" of a nonjudging attitude, the "heartful" qualities of kindness and compassion are embedded and intertwined in the mindful observing. In this book, you will find meditations and reflective practices to support you in developing the critical heartful qualities of kindness and compassion.

Your "talent" for mindfulness can be developed by meditation practice. By practice, we mean both formal sessions of meditation, and bringing the formal practice forward in any moment of your life. To "practice" simply means to pay attention mindfully more often. For example, if you practice mindfulness of breathing as a formal meditation method, you can bring that practice informally into any moment of your life simply by turning attention to your breath and paying attention mindfully whenever you choose. You might discover how powerful even a single mindful breath can be if you begin to make taking a single mindful breath a practice throughout your day. And when we say "practice," we don't mean practicing to become "perfect" or to become someone other than who you already are. Practicing mindfulness is about being who you already are and knowing something about what that means. (In chapter 4, you will find more information to help you build your meditation practice.)

CORE SKILLS AND ATTITUDES THAT SUPPORT MINDFULNESS

Many mindfulness teachers and researchers like to speak of three main skills you can develop in order to experience the full potential of your natural talent for being mindful: intention, attention, and cultivation of a nonjudging and allowing attitude. You will probably notice that using this language emphasizing skills is another way to speak of the core meditative principles that Christina Feldman pointed us to before.

Three Core Mindfulness Skills

Later in this chapter, you will find a basic mindfulness meditation practice that includes each of the three core mindfulness skills, and throughout this book you will find different, easy-to-follow and easy-to-learn meditation practices based in mindfulness, compassion, and wisdom that you can explore. Adding even one of these practices to your daily routine on a regular basis will help you strengthen these three core skills, experience the core meditative principles directly, and thereby find more peace, joy, and mastery over difficult emotions, including your anger. Now let's take a closer look at each of the core mindfulness skills.

INTENTION

Intention precedes every action you take, even if you didn't notice the preceding intention. Intention is a mindfulness skill because you must intend to be mindful as a way to counteract the deep habits of inattention and absence from the present moment that are also part of our human nature. Knowing that you already have the capacity for mindfulness—as well as knowing reasons based in health science and positive psychology—can be very helpful in supporting your intention to be mindful. And, of course, your own desire to live a happier, more satisfying life might be the greatest motivation for intending to be more mindful in each moment.

ATTENTION

Attention is definitely a skill that you practice and develop in every moment, at least every waking moment! You may have noticed (which indicates that your natural mindfulness is at work) that your attention sometimes moves away from the focus you choose, as when you are in a conversation and realize you did not hear what the other person just said to you. Or, you may have noticed that at times you become so absorbed in your focus that you don't notice anything else, like someone calling you when you are working on a task.

Meditation practices like mindfulness of breathing can help you build attention that remains on its focus longer (is steadier and more sustained and penetrating), and is also more flexible and capable of shifting focus more easily and precisely. Developing an attention that is sustained and flexible is likened to taking a dull knife and sharpening it. The tool becomes much more useful.

ATTITUDE

Having an attitude of nonjudgment and acceptance of whatever arises in the present moment is essential in mindfulness practice. This attitudinal skill means simply that the stance or orientation you take when observing mindfully is to be nonjudging and allowing of whatever arises in the present moment. This attitudinal skill is vital to mindfulness practice because it supports you in "being, not doing" in each moment, breath by breath. Cultivating a nonjudging and accepting attitude as you pay mindful attention to moment-by-moment experience is a skill most people need to practice. The deep mental habits of judging and reactivity arise in mind and body very, very quickly, and they rapidly sweep you away from being and into the busyness of doing or fixing (or blaming, or criticizing, or something else).

This core attitude skill can have many expressions and dimensions, which means you have a variety of possibilities for developing and deepening your skill of being able to rest in awareness and simply "be" present. Jon Kabat-Zinn, the father of mindfulness-based stress reduction (MBSR) summarized seven core attitudes essential for practicing mindfulness in the MBSR model (1990). These attitudes can be very helpful for anyone practicing mindfulness.

Seven Core Attitudes for Mindfulness Practice

1. Nonjudging

2. Nonstriving

3. Trust

4. Patience

5. Acceptance

6. Beginner's mind

7. Letting go

Knowing about these attitudes and learning to rest in them while you practice mindfulness can be a great help. We will refer back to these attitudes throughout this book as we explore different meditation practices based in mindfulness and compassion. Here's a closer look at each one:

Nonjudging. Mindfulness is the awareness that reflects, welcomes, and includes whatever is noticed. Judging separates you from the direct experience of each moment by adding a layer or layers of thinking and blaming concerning what is happening. Practicing nonjudging may be as simple as learning how to notice the habit patterns of judging and letting them go. It could mean you stop judging your own judging too! It can be enough simply to notice when the judging thoughts are there. For example, if a colleague fails to meet a deadline you both agreed to, when the judgments and angry thoughts about that person arise in your mind, just notice the judgments and let them be. Use mindfulness practice to calm and steady yourself, and to become more curious. Why does the missed deadline upset you so much? Can you find out why your colleague missed the deadline without criticizing the person? How would you feel if you learned the deadline was missed because your colleague's child had a medical emergency? Pausing to notice when you have judgmental thoughts broadens your choices beyond anger and criticism for responding to the situation or person. Not judging yourself for having judgmental thoughts is also the practice of nonjudging!

Nonstriving. The habit energy of doing, fixing, and seeking to change how things are can become deeply ingrained in your mind and body. Striving can be felt as a kind of pressure to make things different, or to go someplace else, or to become different yourself. Practicing mindfulness means letting go of this habit of seeking change, truly relaxing into this moment, and allowing whatever is happening to be the way it is, at least for the time of the meditation. Just as nonjudging can be practiced by simply noticing when judging is present, nonstriving can be practiced by noticing the feelings of pressure and urgency to change or escape from what is here and now, and simply allowing them to be.

Trust. You are the best person to know what goes on inside and outside your own skin. As you practice mindfulness, you will develop increasing sensitivity and accuracy in discerning what you think and feel, what is happening in your body, and what is going on around you in each moment. A basic part of learning to meditate is trusting yourself to know what is happening in your mind and your body, which involves not giving in to old habits of self-doubt or self-criticism, but learning to pay closer attention and trust that you will be able to know, if you can keep watching mindfully.

Patience. Patience is the ability to remain calm and present to the difficulty that has arisen in this moment, even if it is inside you—in your own heart, mind, or body. Patience requires connection with your calm inner core, and it benefits from qualities of courage and faith— the courage to stay present to upset and the faith that you will not be harmed by remaining present. Patience draws strength from the wisdom that everything changes eventually, that people and situations have a life of their own with their own changes, and your ego does not call the tune for those changes. Practicing patience can be as basic as recognizing when you feel impatience, turning attention mindfully to those feelings in your body and the angry thoughts in your mind, and then gently watching them.

Acceptance. Acceptance, as we use the term in mindfulness practice, means simply being willing to see things the way they are, in this moment. If you don't like what you see or if you really like what you see, either way, you can practice acceptance by noticing that the feeling of not liking or really liking as just another condition that has (very quickly) arisen in this moment. Practicing acceptance doesn't mean you have to be passive. Quite the opposite. Practicing mindfulness, which also means paying attention with acceptance, means you have taken a deep interest in and focused attention on exactly what is happening with a willingness to let things be just as they are instead of fighting with them or grasping on to them. Acceptance asks you to soften and open to what is here.

Beginner's mind. To practice beginner's mind means to be open to the experience you are having, whatever that might be, as if it is the first time it ever happened to you. This orientation can immediately arouse a sense of curiosity and a feeling of being energized. Perhaps you have noticed the wonder and excitement of a child when she first smells a rose, or feels her first drop of rain, or sees her first dog or cat. That moment of wonder and openness, unfiltered by the layers of thoughts and judgments born in one's past history, that moment is the moment of beginner's mind. You can learn to practice beginner's mind by noticing what is happening directly—a sound, or smell, for example—and also noticing and not becoming lost in the mind's tendency to create thoughts around each experience. You can just let the thoughts be, or let them go, and keep noticing.

Letting go. Nonattaching, or nonclinging, is another way to describe letting go. Most people actually practice clinging and attaching much more than they practice letting go. Often what they cling to most strongly are their ideas and views about themselves, others, and situations. When you really notice your body, this clinging to ideas can be felt as a kind of clinching or gripping in some region, perhaps the jaw or a fist. Such hardening and clinging to ideas and views can lead to many problems, including fueling anger and rage, as we will explore in the next chapter and beyond. You can practice letting go by learning to be mindful when the feeling of clinching and clinging is present in your body and letting it go. For example, if you make a fist with your hand and pay attention, you can probably feel the actual physical sensation of gripping and clinging. If you quickly release the fist, the sensation changes in the physical act of letting go. Can you feel the sensation of release and freedom associated with letting go?

We have been looking at mindfulness, meditation, and the core attitudes that support mindfulness practice. But, you might ask, why would I need or want to practice mindfulness and meditation? For some answers to that question, let's turn to the fascinating and growing body of evidence that practicing mindfulness is good for your health.

THE SCIENCE OF MINDFULNESS

When your anger and hostility are unmanaged or chronically out of control, they can have harmful, even fatal effects. In the next chapter, we will take a closer look at what these toxic effects of anger can be, but what you need to do to better manage anger can be summarized rather simply:

Managing stress is a key element in managing anger.

How you perceive and relate to others and the world is crucial.

The beliefs and attitudes you hold about yourself and others are critical.

Practicing mindfulness can help you improve in each of these areas.

Research with people who practice mindfulness that compares them with people who don't reveals some very encouraging support for practicing mindfulness.

Research Support for Practicing Mindfulness

Research in mindfulness is growing rapidly. A significant body of scientific findings now suggests mindfulness practice can directly and positively impact both the toxic effects and the triggers of anger and other difficult emotions in you. Here are some of those findings.

Mindfulness practice helps reduce the negative impact of stress on your health. Many studies have linked mindfulness meditation training to feeling less stressed, less anxious and depressed, and to reduced overall levels of psychological distress, including less anger and worry (Baer 2003; Brown, Ryan, and Creswell 2007; Grossman et al. 2004). In addition, there is increasing evidence to support the therapeutic effect of mindfulness meditation training on stress-related medical conditions, including psoriasis (Kabat-Zinn et al. 1998), type 2 diabetes (Rosenzweig et al. 2007), fibromyalgia (Grossman et al. 2007), chronic low-back pain (Morone, Greco, and Weiner 2008), and rheumatoid arthritis (Pradhan et al. 2007; Zautra et al. 2008). Mindfulness meditation training has also been shown to reduce symptoms of stress and negative mood states, and to enhance emotional well-being and quality-of-life reports among people with chronic illness (Brown, Ryan, and Creswell 2007; Grossman et al. 2004; Ludwig and Kabat-Zinn 2008), including cancer (Speca et al. 2000; Carlson et al. 2007).

Mindfulness practice helps develop better understanding of others and greater empathy. Research with couples practicing mindfulness has shown significantly improved relationship satisfaction and increased feelings of relatedness and acceptance of the partner (Carson et al. 2004) as well as greater ability to regulate the expression of anger and improved control of emotions (Wachs and Cordova 2007). Research has also found better patient outcomes for psychotherapists who practice mindfulness (Grepmair et al. 2007). Empathy is the ability to share or "feel" another person's thoughts and feelings. It is considered to be a fundamental element in human relationships and crucial to good mental health. Research has demonstrated benefits of mindfulness training in increasing empathy (Shapiro, Schwartz, and Bonner 1998; Shapiro and Izett 2008; Schure, Christopher, and Christopher 2008).

Mindfulness practice helps grow self-awareness of the inner "stories" and habits of thinking that influence your self-concept

and sense of self-worth. Research has found that simply being in a "mindful state" momentarily is associated with a greater sense of well-being (Lau et al. 2006) and that individuals with higher natural levels of mindfulness, irrespective of formal meditation training, report feeling less stressed, less anxious and depressed, and more inspired, hopeful, joyful, vital, and satisfied with life (Baer et al. 2006; Brown and Ryan 2003; Cardaciotto et al. 2008; Feldman et al. 2007; Walach et al. 2006). Other studies have found that mindfulness meditation training helps reduce rumination, which is a cognitive process associated with depression and other mood disorders (Jain et al. 2007; Ramel et al. 2004). Research further suggests that people with higher levels of mindfulness are better able to regulate their sense of well-being by virtue of greater emotional awareness, understanding, and acceptance, and the ability to correct or repair unpleasant mood states (Baer et al. 2008; Brown, Ryan, and Creswell 2007; Feldman et al. 2007). Finally, increases in positive affect and self-compassion can follow from mindfulness meditation training and practice (Shapiro, Brown, and Biegel 2007).

Now you have some general understanding about mindfulness and meditation, and know something of the science that suggests significant health and well-being can follow from practicing mindfulness. Let's turn more attention now to what it means to practice mindfulness.

PRACTICING MINDFULNESS

In this book, you will find a variety of meditation practices to help you bring mindfulness and compassion forward in your life. You will find instructions for using different objects of attention—as mindfulness is not only about your breathing—as well as instructions to explore various aspects of attention, awareness, kindness and compassion, and insights. You may be tempted to read the practices and move on, as you might read a novel or a work of nonfiction, but please don't do that! If you just read the words and instructions and do not practice, you deny yourself the opportunity to experience the power you already hold to change your life through mindfulness and meditation. The following section explains why reading is not enough, and also provides some practical suggestions you can use right away as you practice with any meditation method in this book.

Personal Practice and Experiential Learning

Reading about playing a piano is not the same as putting your hands on the keyboard. Watching an instructional video about putting a golf ball is not the same as holding the club in your hands and stroking the ball. The difference is that a deep understanding about playing the piano or playing golf, like so many things in life, is learned best through direct experience. We call this *experiential learning*.

Exploring the territory of awareness, discovering the positive possibilities waiting for you through meditation, and building the skills of mindfulness are like learning to play the piano or putt a golf ball—they are best learned experientially. Mindfulness and meditation are only truly learned and available to you when you commit to practice and experience the dimensions of awareness and presence for yourself, as they arise directly in your own heart and mind, and each unfolding moment of your life.

Something important and undeniable happens to you when you actually practice and experience *being* mindful. It doesn't happen otherwise. It is in the direct experience of being mindful that the basis of any lasting transformation that comes from practicing mindfulness lies. Reading and thinking about being mindful or meditation are not enough. As is often said about practicing mindfulness, "You don't have to like it; just do it!"

So, what do we mean when we say "practicing mindfulness"? Well, perhaps unlike practicing a piano or practicing your putting, when we talk about meditation and mindfulness practice, we do not mean practicing to get "better," or to be "perfect," or to become someone or something other than who you already are. What we mean by "practicing mindfulness" is that you make a commitment to be present, paying attention nonjudgmentally, in this moment. That's it. When you practice paying attention on purpose in a nonjudging way, with no other agenda than to be present and notice with curiosity and a sense of welcome for your experience, then you *are* "practicing" being mindful. That is enough.

INSTRUCTIONS FOR PRACTICING MINDFULNESS

Here are some easy-to-follow instructions for practicing mindfulness. We will use these general instructions as a basic method to practice mindfulness throughout this book. For example, when you see instructions to "breathe mindfully," you can use these basic instructions by making your breath sensations your primary focus of attention. Refer back to these instructions as often as you like.

A reminder before you begin: Relax! You don't have to "do" anything to be mindful. You already have all that you need to practice being and not doing, and you really cannot make a mistake. Remember this whenever you want to practice mindfulness, and then practice mindfulness by following these instructions:

1. *Stop what you are doing and move your attention out of your thoughts and feelings, into your body, and into this moment.* Allow yourself simply to rest in the noticing of what is happening. Practice letting things be the way they are without trying to fix or change anything, at least for the time of your meditation practice.

2. *Gently set a clear intention to be mindful.* For example, "I am now practicing mindfulness" or "I am discovering what it is like to be more mindful."

3. *Relax as you gather your attention in your body, letting each sensory experience come to you.* This could be as easy as letting your attention rest on sounds and noticing how they sound, or on the feel of sensations flowing through your body and noticing how they feel, or on a particular sensation, like the physical sensations associated with your breath, and noticing as they change when the breath moves into and goes out of your body.

4. *When you notice your attention moves away from this moment to something else, such as your thoughts or memories, just let those thoughts be or let them go, and gently bring your attention back to here, now, choosing a focus on your body sensations, or your breathing, or on sounds, and returning attention patiently to your focus.* When your mind moves away, which it will do many times, it is okay. You have not done anything

wrong or made a mistake. It is just what the mind does, especially when it has not been trained in skills of mindfulness and steady attention.

5. *Let yourself rest in awareness and discover that you can relax, observe, and allow all thoughts, feelings, sounds, and sensations to come and go without becoming lost in thoughts or reactions or attached to them. Practice "being and not doing." Know that you can practice being mindful for one breath, or one step, or one bite, or for as long as you like.*

KEEP IN MIND

- Mindfulness is a basic human capacity. It is a universal possibility for any human being. It is the awareness that notices without judgment and is welcoming—always in the present moment.

- Practicing mindfulness enables you to enter a dimension of life in each moment that provides more choice and real freedom from destructive emotions like anger and the damaging effects of chronic stress. This is why learning to practice mindfulness is so important: mindfulness can help you live a happier, healthier, and more satisfying life.

- Practicing mindfulness can be as easy as relaxing, placing your attention in this moment on a sensory experience, and allowing the experience to come to you as your pay increasingly close and careful attention to the direct experience it offers.

- Modern neuroscience and psychology have demonstrated that, by using your mind to be more "mindful," you actually change your brain in ways that can be better for your mental and physical health and for your relationships. Being more mindful can also broaden and build your capacity to recognize and manage dangerous emotions like anger and the behaviors that result from those emotions.

CHAPTER 2

getting to know your anger

You cannot enter into any world for which you do not know the language.

—*Ludwig Wittgenstein*

We live in the present moment. Our lives unfold in the here and now. What we call the past is a memory that is happening in the present moment; and what we call the future has not yet happened, but is something we imagine or plan now—in the present moment.

Deep and old patterns of angry thinking and feeling require an expenditure of energy by your mind and body in order to appear and to continue. The mind and body connections and circuits over which these energies flow can become increasingly powerful inside of you if anger is allowed to continue unmanaged. You might think of these energies that power the patterns of anger and related feelings in you as *habit energies,* because this pattern of energy flow has become a habit inside of you. If you wish to take back control of your life from the habit energies of anger, irritation, judgments, blame, rage, and even hatred, then it is crucial for you to know accurately the nature of these energies once they arise in the present moment, and to understand what triggers and sustains them when they appear. Mindfulness and meditation can help you. In fact, you can also think of the practice of mindfulness as nurturing more positive habit energies in your mind and body, ones that can support you to better manage anger and other difficult emotions.

Reclaiming your life from anger and other destructive emotions is vitally important, and you can definitely do it, but it can be hard work. As Paul Ekman, a noted researcher of human emotions, observed, "It requires great effort to be able to not respond to anger with anger" (Goleman 2003, 152).

One of the main problems most people have with anger is that it arises so quickly they don't see it coming! Before you know it, the heat of anger, or even rage, is burning in and around you, and you have probably already been driven to act—verbally or physically—by that burning energy, usually in ways that are harmful, either immediately or over time. But, if the sudden rise of anger in your mind and body weren't bad enough, sometimes there is an even bigger obstacle to overcome if you wish to calm your angry mind: basic ignorance about anger.

An experienced anger researcher I spoke with said he had focused a large portion of his research career on anger in order to better understand the consequences chronic anger has for physical and emotional health. He told me that he believed people would be more motivated to change if they better understood these costs.

In his view, too often people simply were not aware that what they were feeling was anger, or that it came at such a high price, especially when they failed repeatedly to recognize or manage it. He wanted his research findings to help change that basic ignorance or not knowing.

Anyone can experience this type of not knowing, which arises out of a basic lack of awareness of the present moment. There may be many different reasons for this lack of awareness, but whatever the reasons for not knowing, they can—with insight—be understood and overcome.

One very important thing to know about anger, for example, is that it always occurs now—that is, in the present moment. When you experience anger, your angry thoughts and sensations of anger in your body always arise and move through the present moment as it unfolds. In this chapter, we will take a closer look at the experience of anger and its many forms, especially as it is expressed intensely and personally in your mind and body.

WHAT IS ANGER?

Human beings experience intense combinations of mental and physical events that we call *emotions*. And, although there is debate about what an emotion actually is as well as what the "basic" human emotions are, the one called "anger" seems to appear on practically every list of basic human emotions. So, anger is something we all experience as human beings. But what if we look more closely? Might we find a better way to free ourselves from anger's power and influence in our lives by learning more about it?

There is wide agreement among emotion researchers and psychologists that an emotion like anger is actually an integrated mind-body experience. That means anger involves both thoughts as well as feelings and sensations in your body.

Joseph LeDoux, a researcher who studies the brain mechanisms underlying emotions, refers to what he calls the "emotional present," and points to the part of your memory system called "working memory" that allows you to know that the here and now is here and is happening now (1996, 282). As LeDoux notes, the emotion or state of mind you feel in this moment is actually emotional information that is entering and being represented in your working memory. Key components of that emotional information streaming into your working memory in each moment are the thoughts in your mind and the sensations or feelings happening in your body. For example, if you feel angry about a conversation you just had with someone, according to this model, the angry feeling is the result of the thoughts you have about the conversation and what it means, as well as the flow of physical sensations through your body. The stream of thoughts and body sensations is the emotional information that fills your working memory and creates the emotional present for you—in this case an experience of anger. Anger management experts agree with this two-part approach—thoughts and body sensations—and usually structure their interventions to help their clients become more focused on the thoughts and the felt bodily experience of their anger.

Interestingly, mindfulness teachers share this understanding that emotions like anger are made up of basic building blocks—including your thoughts and body sensations. In the meditative view, as Joseph Goldstein (2002) notes, "Emotions are more complex, involving feelings in the body, thoughts, or images, and different moods in the mind" (141).

After reviewing psychological research dating back decades, anger authority Ray Rosenman concluded that "it is primarily the perception of an event that determines the emotional response and hence the psychophysiological consequences.... Anger is a cognitive response that is associated with personal appraisal and interpretation" (1985, 105).

In other words, the key to understanding and managing your anger seems to lie in recognizing when a state of bodily arousal is present, what your perception is of a situation, and knowing something about the thoughts or inner narrative you generate about that perception. Depending on the meaning you assign and the thoughts that follow, your unfolding experience of anger either heats up or cools down.

Mindfulness teachers use this wisdom to point to the importance of paying close attention in each moment in order to develop your understanding—through direct observation—of intense and "basic" emotions like anger. For example, consider the words of Joseph Goldstein (2002): "As an experiment in awareness, the next time you feel identified with a strong emotion or reaction or judgment, leave the story line and trace the physical sensation back to the energetic contraction, often felt at the heart center. It may be a sensation of tightness or pressure in the center of the chest" (96).

A critical implication of this thought-plus-sensation perspective on emotions is that you can recognize the powerful role thinking plays in shaping and sustaining your experience of emotions, including anger. If you pause and begin to observe the unfolding experience of anger, noticing thoughts and feelings, as Joseph Goldstein suggests, you will probably also begin to notice other things about anger. As Matthieu Ricard, a trained scientist and Buddhist monk, points out, you may begin to see how anger appears as an "arising emotion" (it arises from some event or stimulus), but what happens from there depends in large part on the "chaining of thoughts" that follows the arising (Goleman 2003, 351–52).

Anger as Thoughts plus Sensations: A Familiar Example

Consider an experience common to many people—you are driving or riding along in your vehicle, or perhaps even walking, when someone suddenly and abruptly cuts in front of you. You probably notice the almost instantaneous arising of an angry or irritated feeling. But what happens to that feeling after the person moves on ahead?

If you focus on the person and the danger or threat they created for you by engaging in an anger-initiated mental story or stream of thinking such as *that so-and-so almost hit me. Just look at them now. They are so rude. I don't know why people don't take more time to be kind. They might have hurt me or any of these other people. I wish the police would stop them. Better yet, I wish they would get some of their own medicine.*

In this scenario, the *chaining of thoughts* (creating and adding more and more thoughts to the original arising emotion of anger) actually feeds the feelings of anger and your internal upset, probably long after the person is out of sight. You might find yourself feeling growing anger, or having feelings of actually wanting to hurt the other person, all as a reaction to the chain of thinking that has fueled the fire of anger in you.

In contrast, imagine that, as the person who cut you off moves ahead, you simply shake your head and say to yourself, *Wow! They sure are in a hurry!* Then you go back to what you were doing before it happened. If you do that, no chaining of thoughts occurs, and then there is no ongoing fuel for your inner fire of anger. Or, as a really interesting experiment, you might intentionally choose to respond with compassion instead of anger when that person cuts you off. It could be as simple as this: first, acknowledge your feeling of anger and then shift your inner story, saying to yourself something like *Wow! That was close. They are really in a hurry. I wonder if they are rushing someplace to help someone, or if they just received some bad news and they are very upset.*

Imagine the peace you can find—within yourself and expressed to others—by learning to uncouple the "thought train" that carries anger on and on, beyond the initial arising angry moment. If you pause to observe, you might find that it is your own "runaway" thought train that actually feeds your angry feeling and sustains the animosity you feel toward another person—much more than what they actually said or did. Here's something to think about: Matthieu Ricard, has noted, "Usually what we call anger is an expression of animosity toward someone" (Goleman 2003, 351).

By developing your capacity to recognize and wisely respond to the sensations *and* thoughts that arise and sustain anger, you can regain control of your life in those intense moments. You will become steady and unshakable in the changing winds of experience blowing through the present moment of your life.

MYTHS ABOUT ANGER

In their book *When Anger Hurts:Quieting the Storm Within*, Matthew McKay, Peter D. Rogers, and Judith McKay (2003) identify several interesting "myths" about anger—ideas, thoughts, and fixed beliefs you may have that can sustain angry behaviors and actions and block your efforts to change them (8). Holding such ideas without examining them only sustains the power of anger to hurt and control your life.

Myth I: Anger is a biochemically determined event.

While certain biological foundations are necessary for anger, particularly the area of the brain known as the "limbic system" (specifically the hypothalamus and amygdala), and specific hormones such as prolactin, testosterone, and norepinephrine play key roles, a long body of fascinating research supports the view that the physiological arousal resulting from these neural and hormonal activities is not alone sufficient to explain the experience of an emotion like anger. Perhaps it is more accurate to say that arousal happens (the freeze-fight-or-flight response or reaction), but perceptions and thoughts play an important role in the arising of anger about the situation that evoked the initial physiological arousal. (For more on the freeze-fight-or-flight response, see "Anger for Protection" and "The Biology of Anger" later in this chapter.)

Myth 2: Anger and aggression are instinctual to humans.

Perhaps it is also more accurate in this case to say that the behaviors we call anger or aggression are not an inevitable response to a situation, but require elements of both instinctual arousal and learned responses. For example, at home one night you hear a loud noise outside your house and you immediately notice the alarm reaction of freeze-flight-or flight arising in you. You're ready for danger, and this is "instinctual." Perhaps your mind races and you remember that your neighbor's car was burglarized recently. You feel more alarm. This increased level of alarm and arousal in mind and body is a "learned response"—in part, at least, because you have learned from experience that sounds late at night outside your home are not "normal" and you should be on guard. If, however, your learned experience of such late-night noises was that your neighbors always made those noises when they came home from working late, then, after the initial alarm reaction, you would probably not become more alarmed. In other words, anger and aggression are complicated!

Although anger and aggression are deeply embedded in our evolutionary past, love and cooperation are also "instinctual," and even more important. Because human children require an extended time period in which they are protected and supported in order to grow and reproduce themselves, the survival of the species required humans to develop biological and neural capacities to generate and sustain connections, attachment, and feelings of affection and love.

Because of this complex relationship between instinctual and learned behavior, and the interaction between each individual and his or her environment, it is an oversimplification to assume humans tend to anger or aggression by instinct. According to many authorities, except in rare pathologies, our human genome does not produce individuals predisposed to violence. Studies have shown that status within a group is achieved by the ability to cooperate, not by increased aggressive behavior.

In 1986, a group of twenty distinguished behavioral scientists gathering in Seville, Spain, issued a statement—the Seville Statement—that was later endorsed by various professional organizations, including the American Psychological Association and the

American Anthropological Association. The conclusion of these scientists about human violence and aggression was "biology does not condemn humanity to war, and that humanity can be freed from the bondage of biological pessimism. Violence is neither in our evolutionary legacy, nor in our genes" (quoted in *Psychology Today*, June, 1988).

Myth 3: Frustration leads to aggression.

This is a myth because frustration does not automatically or inevitably lead to aggression. There are actually many possible responses to internal feelings of frustration. Interestingly, cross-cultural studies have found that different cultures teach their members different responses to internal feelings of frustration (Whitting 1941; Bateson 1941; Dentan 1968).

Anger management courses have demonstrated that angry and aggressive individuals can learn to change their response to feelings of frustration so that aggression no longer follows frustration. For example, Redford and Virginia Williams (2006) offer data from their *LifeSkills* training of the power of their anger management model to change anger-related behavior in employees of their corporate clients.

And, perhaps most basic of all, and repeatedly emphasized by teachers in wisdom and faith traditions worldwide: as human beings we will experience frustration and pain as part of living, no matter who we are. Our learning about ourselves and the human condition actually deepens as we reflect on the inevitability of experiencing pain, frustration, and upset, and how we come to make sense of that—or not.

Myth 4: It is healthy to ventilate.

Neuroscientist Richard Davidson observed, "The amazing fact is through mental activity alone we can intentionally change our own brains" (Davidson 2012, 11). As I mentioned in the introduction, *neuroplasticity* is the technical term for this capacity of your brain to change depending on how you use it. We know that repeating certain thought patterns to yourself (as happens in obsessive ruminations, for example) can actually make particular regions and circuits of connection in your brain more robust. Likewise, not reinforcing those same patterns (by mindfully noticing the thoughts and letting them go or letting them be, for example) will, over time, cause these same circuits of connection to weaken and fade.

In other words, regions and connection patterns (or circuits) in your brain strengthen or weaken depending on how you use or direct your brain. (This also points to the critical role of intention setting.) So, while it is clearly not healthy to suppress strong feelings at any cost, and it can be helpful to acknowledge and give voice to strong feelings at times, it is also not healthy to make a practice of continually ventilating anger and rage.

Carol Tavris (1989) summarized a significant body of research on anger and concluded that people who are most prone to vent their anger actually get angrier. This is probably very much related to the strengthening of brain regions and connections related to anger and hostility through constant "practice" of being angry or hostile.

So, I have a couple of interesting questions for you: What are you practicing—anger or tolerance? What tendencies do you encourage in your heart and mind, moment by moment—hostility or understanding?

Because of the neuroplastic nature of your brain, you *can* change. There is hope. If you have learned to react with anger or violence in a situation, then you have the real possibility—plus the basic human intelligence and goodness of heart, if you choose to apply them—to learn and display a different response besides anger and aggression in any situation.

This is where you will find mindfulness and meditation training to be very helpful. Combined with scientific and psychological knowledge and methods of understanding and managing emotions and behaviors, you can be very confident that you, not your anger, can be in control of your life.

THE FUNCTIONS OF ANGER

So, what does anger do *for* you? Why is it so common and quick to arise in us human beings? The simple answer is that it is very likely that anger has some protective and survival value.

Anger for Survival

For millions of years on our planet, human beings evolved, facing dangers from predators, starvation, and diseases. Our biology evolved also, especially our brain and nervous system functioning. As neuropsychologist and meditation teacher Rick Hanson notes, a driving factor was that, in such harsh and threatening environments, it was "reproductively advantageous for our ancestors to be cooperative within their own band but aggressive toward other bands. Cooperation and aggression evolved synergistically: bands with greater cooperation were more successful at aggression, and aggression between bands demanded cooperation within bands" (Hanson 2009, 30). Furthermore, research supports the view that "much if not most aggression is a response to feeling threatened—which includes even subtle feelings of unease or anxiety" (130).

In other words, we are heavily "wired" and equipped with neural capacities to identify and distinguish between "us" and "them"—especially when there is a real or perceived threat. Why? Because, at times, survival depends upon it. And that brings us to the *protective* function of anger.

Anger for Protection

When you sense danger, your mind and body very, very quickly go into the *freeze-fight-or-flight reaction* to protect you from harm. *Fight or flight* means you are ready to defend yourself by fighting or fleeing from perceived danger. *Freeze* means you may feel paralyzed and frozen, which sometimes also can be the way to avoid being harmed.

Our ancestors had the basic instincts that very quickly aroused them and prepared them to respond to possible threats. When facing a possible threat, they also relied upon what they had learned through their life experience and interactions with others—things like how to distinguish who was "us" and who was "them," and how to act and what to do depending on the discernment between "us" and "them" and the nature of the threatening situation. In these examples, we can perhaps imagine the complex interaction between basic instincts of freeze-fight-or-flight and the influence of learned experience that led to the expression of a wide variety of complex behaviors as interactions with others and the environment.

Freeze, Fight, or Flight and the Power of Your Thoughts: An Example

An everyday example illustrates the power of your thought train to stop or sustain the freeze-fight-or-flight reaction:

Imagine you are in a meeting and a fire alarm goes off. Your first reaction, of course—happening so fast you don't even have to think about it—is that your body hears the alarm and immediately responds with a state of high physiological arousal and increased mental alertness. All of this is intended to help you fight or flee from the perceived immediate danger.

Now, imagine someone opens the door of the meeting room and yells, "Run for your life; the building is on fire!" You will probably experience a flood of panicky thoughts and your body will continue to be immersed in the freeze-fight-or-flight reaction. You might be so frightened that you cannot move—you freeze. Or, you might find yourself already on your feet and heading for the nearest exit, ready to push aside anything in your way. That is the flight and fight piece.

However, what if that person opens the door and says, "Sorry about that. There is no fire. Someone tripped the alarm by accident"? In that case, you would probably breathe a sigh of relief, quickly feel relaxation returning to your body, and over the next few minutes, experience your body returning to the state of normalcy it was in before the alarm sounded.

The important role of perceptions and thinking is evident in this example. Just as thoughts can chain or link together to sustain an angry emotion, thoughts can also chain or proliferate and expand into similar thoughts that sustain the alarm of the freeze-fight-or-flight reaction—the state of arousal that underlies anger and hostility.

Anger as Protection Against Unwanted Thoughts and Feelings

Anger can also function to protect you from other feelings that you don't want to feel. When you experience unpleasant or disturbing thoughts or feelings—pain, fear, or vulnerability, for example—anger can arise to protect you from knowing those thoughts or experiencing those unpleasant feelings. In psychological terms, we would call this type of anger *defensive anger*, because it serves to defend you from experiencing unpleasant or disturbing inner thoughts and feelings.

Such defensive anger can pop up so quickly that you don't even know there are disturbing or unpleasant thoughts and feelings beneath it inside of you. So, you could say the defensive anger is doing an excellent job of defending you from feeling anything else. And just as you do not recognize that you have disturbing or unpleasant thoughts or feelings, you may not even realize you are experiencing defensive anger either.

An experienced psychotherapist once told me that, in her experience, many people who were angry actually did not call it that. Even when it appeared clearly to others that they were feeling angry, instead of naming their own feeling correctly, the angry person used words like "anxious" or "depressed" or even "excited."

This therapist said much of her work with helping these people overcome the problems they came to her about was teaching them to be more self-aware of everything they were feeling. (She was a big fan of mindfulness practice, by the way!) An important piece of that growth in awareness came when her clients learned to recognize and name angry feelings accurately and began to look more deeply at the other feelings and thoughts beneath the anger, instead of protectively denying or mislabeling the painful anger they felt.

Of course, as any wise person or good psychotherapist will tell you, just because you don't let yourself acknowledge the unpleasant thoughts and feelings does not mean you have gotten rid of them or controlled them. Just the opposite—these thoughts and feelings, when denied and suppressed, have a way of getting stronger and coming back with a vengeance, usually when you least want or need them! That was the case for Jake.

• Jake's Story

Jake is a man in his forties with a wife and family. He has become the primary care provider for his mother, who has Alzheimer's disease and lives near Jake in a nursing home. Jake told his mindfulness class that one day he was visiting his mother when they were interrupted by a nurse who needed to take his mother's vital signs. Jake said, "I exploded and told her to leave us alone. I felt terrible after, and apologized to her. I didn't know what had come over me until later, when I told my wife and she said, 'I wonder if you were afraid of something.'" Jake said he realized in that moment that yes, he is afraid. "I am afraid of losing my mother, I am afraid I have let her down, and, worst of all, I beat up on myself and tell myself I am not a good son because she is in that nursing home."

So, if anger that arises repeatedly and intensely in your life is a problem, then it is very likely that it is fueled and maintained by deeper hurts, fears, and beliefs. Learning to practice mindfulness can help you overcome your anger, heal old hurts, and reclaim your life from their influence.

A Response to Obstacles: Anger, Ill Will, and Aversion

An intriguing reflection on the function of anger comes from emotion researcher Paul Ekman, who suggests that the function of anger is to remove some interference we are experiencing. He notes, "What is built into the anger response is the impulse to remove the obstacle that is thwarting us" (Goleman 2003, 152). An interesting and helpful perspective on this "obstacle removal" function of anger occurs in Buddhist teachings, which identify five common obstacles or hindrances to meditation practice. These are worth knowing about so you can recognize and learn from them rather than being harmed by them.

In the Buddhist meditative understanding, these hindrances can be viewed as energies or filters that distort and drive our moment-by-moment relationship to the unfolding experience of our lives. The influence of any hindrance energy quickly extends to our interior experiences of thoughts, feelings, and body sensations; it also colors our perceptions and interactions with others.

The traditional names for the five hindrances are *desire* (for things to be different or for something else), *ill will and aversion* (to what is here, or the way things are), *sloth and torpor* (fatigue, sleepiness, lethargy in the body, and dullness in the mind), *restlessness* (agitation in mind and body), and *doubt* (thoughts about a situation that are flavored with fear or anxiety).

If you think about it, you will probably realize that Buddhists aren't the only human beings who experience these hindrances! You probably already know a lot about desire, ill will and aversion, sleepiness, restlessness, and doubt from your own experience, and you know well how strongly these energies can impact, filter, and distort the activities of your daily life as well as any practice of meditation. It can be very helpful to know about these hindrances, to know their names, and to discover how the power of mindfulness can free you from their power to distort and drive your life experience in each and every moment.

We will look more closely at these five hindrances as a focus for meditation practice in chapter 7, because they offer a powerful insight, based in meditative experience, into the way our minds actually work. But for now, *because it is particularly relevant to anger,* let's focus on the hindrance named *aversion and ill will.*

Aversion is expressed in the action of turning away from someone or something present in this moment in your awareness. It is a feeling of not wanting to be in contact with something or someone. You can feel aversion to things and people around you, and you can also feel aversion to conditions inside of you, like painful sensations or disturbing thoughts. Ill will is antipathy for something or someone. It is the opposite of the feeling of well-wishing, which is generous and compassionate.

You could use other words besides ill will and aversion too—for example, disgust, dislike, resentment, scorn, discrediting, hatred, rejection, discounting, dismissal, and hostility, to name a few. What these have in common is they point to the basic feeling of rejection and the desire to be separated from something or someone present in this moment (including the possibility of eliminating that thing or person). Mindfulness practice can help you to recognize the presence and distorting impact of ill will and aversion and help you to free yourself from the habitual reactions of anger, automatic rejection, and hostility that can be so damaging to you and to others. Let's see how this might play out in your life.

Headaches, Aversion, and Anger: An Example

Consider a headache. You feel pain associated with your head, and you probably say something like "Oh, no! I have a headache, and I hate it!" You may even feel anger toward the headache or yourself, and it probably gets worse after that. But let's take a closer, more "mindful" look at what is happening.

What we commonly call a "headache" is actually a series of unpleasant physical sensations in the area of your head. When you observe your experience mindfully, paying close attention without judgment, you will see that the sensations change, flowing into and out of the present moment. You will likely also notice that these sensations usually evoke an inner narrative of thoughts and memories about similar sensations in your past, or perhaps worries and simulations about imagined future experiences that are similar to this one.

Because they are unpleasant, the physical sensations and the thoughts associated with them evoke feelings of aversion and dislike that are associated with, but not the same as, the actual physical sensations. So, the headache has elements of physical sensation, unpleasant feelings, probably alarming thoughts, and aversion to the physical and mental unpleasantness.

When it is unrecognized, the intensity of the ill will and aversion present generates resistance: you resist the headache and dispute how things are in this moment, which fuels the experiences of fear and ultimately anger. Your natural reaction is to "go to war" with the headache.

This storm of dislike clouds your understanding of, your capacity to connect with, and your ability to skillfully respond to your direct experience in this moment. The actual experience that needs your skillful response is that of the unpleasant physical sensations and, very likely, a series of thoughts that are alarming in their own right: *How long will it last? What is wrong with me? What if I get a migraine?*

Of course, hardly anyone enjoys a headache, but what is useful to know about aversion and ill will is just how extremely common and essentially human they are, and how very quickly they arise in reaction to any unpleasant situation—whether it is inside or outside your skin. It's also helpful to know how effective they can be in hijacking you, steering you into negative emotions and opposition to so much of what is present in this moment.

When the aversion is strong, then the reactive impulse is to resist and fight the situation. Fighting the headache pain adds resistance and multiplies the pain in the situation, and anger actually builds. If you can, notice the aversion, stop the fight ("cease fire!"), and use the basic mindfulness attitude of allowing the experience to be as it is. When you do, ease and the end to aversion and anger is very near. Mindfulness can help you begin to discern the energy of aversion from the experience associated with it.

Remember Paul Ekman's observation that anger is a response to something that is interfering with or thwarting us? Well, the perception of being interfered with or thwarted can certainly be unpleasant, and aversion and ill will toward that unpleasant feeling is also at the heart of the emotion we call "anger." But have you noticed how quickly and easily the anger becomes directed at someone or something "out there"—totally missing the upset and unpleasant experience inside of you in the present moment and perhaps totally missing that the someone or something out there actually has little or nothing to do with you?

Anger's Relatives in the Family of Ill Will and Aversion

As I noted earlier, there are many words in addition to anger to describe aspects of the basic feelings of ill will and aversion—of dislike and rejection—toward the content and experience present in this moment. More examples are the feelings people know as "steaming," "sulking," "brooding," and even "boredom" (which is a powerful way of breaking connection with the present moment by withdrawing attention with an attitude of hostility).

What are some other relatives of anger in the family of ill will? As the Buddhist meditation teacher Joseph Goldstein notes, they can be familiar: "hatred, impatience, and sorrow—all forms of aversion. We can notice the feelings of contraction and hardening of the heart when we get lost in or identified with mind states of ill will. These states of aversion arise when we don't get what we want, or when we do get what we don't want." Goldstein continues in a way that is bit surprising: "Questions often come up about grief and sorrow.... Sorrow and grief arise from loss of some kind. What is our relationship to the experience of loss, which is really another word for change? Is there aversion to it?... Can we experience loss without the attendant sorrow or grief? Perhaps it is acceptance and mindfulness of the feeling of loss that make this possible, and it is nonacceptance that rebounds into grief" (Goldstein 2002, 68–69)

Learning to reclaim your life from the power of anger might be as basic as learning to recognize and name two things: (1) the accurate experience of what is in your thoughts and your body in this moment, here and now, and (2) the presence or absence of an elemental energy of aversion and ill will rejecting whatever is happening and present as you experience this moment. You will be able to explore this possibility yourself using the various meditation practices based in mindfulness and compassion found throughout this book.

THE STRUCTURE OF ANGER

I learned a valuable lesson about my own anger many years ago when I went on one of my earliest intensive mindfulness meditation retreats. The lesson has been very useful in my personal meditation practice and life, and I have found that it resonates with many others with whom I have shared it. And, as you will see, this lesson on what might be called the "structure of anger" also resonates with the research and meditative wisdom pointing to the critical role of perceptions and thoughts, and the distorting power of aversion and ill will interacting with unpleasant and painful feelings and experiences.

On the retreat, I experienced a period of intense angry feelings and hostile fantasies toward a variety of people and things, real and imagined. When I brought this to the teacher and asked for help, he said, very kindly and calmly, "It is okay. It is just your mind at work. Pay closer attention and see what you can discover. Usually, if you look closely enough, you will see that beneath anger is fear, and beneath fear is a fixed belief."

When I followed the teacher's advice, I began to sense in me deep feelings of fear and insecurity about some new relationships in my life. Looking more deeply, I saw beneath that fear some critical self-judgments I repeated frequently to myself about not being a good enough person. Seeing these underlying layers of fear and negative beliefs in myself had an effect of opening up space around the entire experience. Over the course of the retreat, I was able to soften and be more compassionate toward myself, and when I did that, the angry feelings fell away.

This structure of anger may not always be so relevant, but when you approach your anger with this structure in mind, especially when you bring mindfulness to your anger, then you may be surprised at the depth of understanding this model can provide as you look closer and closer. Here are some examples of how it might go:

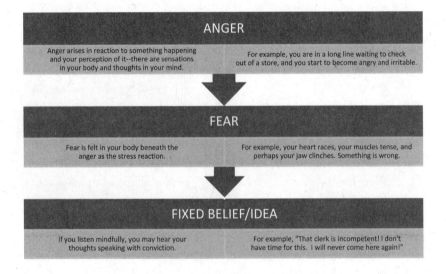

ANGER

Anger arises in reaction to something happening and your perception of it--there are sensations in your body and thoughts in your mind.

For example, you are in a long line waiting to check out of a store, and you start to become angry and irritable.

FEAR

Fear is felt in your body beneath the anger as the stress reaction.

For example, your heart races, your muscles tense, and perhaps your jaw clinches. Something is wrong.

FIXED BELIEF/IDEA

If you listen mindfully, you may hear your thoughts speaking with conviction.

For example, "That clerk is incompetent! I don't have time for this. I will never come here again!"

In this example, if you remain mindful, you will probably notice that so long as your angry thoughts keep their comments going—thoughts like *Look at all these people ahead of me in this line. Doesn't the management know how to staff this store?!*, for example—even though the danger is diminishing (you are moving up in the line, after all) and you are actually physically safe, you will remain angry. Your mind and body will also be caught up in, and very likely add more intensity to, the emotional reaction. Here is another example.

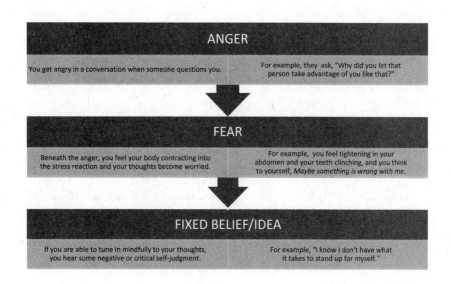

ANGER

You get angry in a conversation when someone questions you.

For example, they ask, "Why did you let that person take advantage of you like that?"

FEAR

Beneath the anger, you feel your body contracting into the stress reaction and your thoughts become worried.

For example, you feel tightening in your abdomen and your teeth clinching, and you think to yourself, *Maybe something is wrong with me.*

FIXED BELIEF/IDEA

If you are able to tune in mindfully to your thoughts, you hear some negative or critical self-judgment.

For example, "I know I don't have what it takes to stand up for myself."

We will refer back to this structural model of anger often in this book. As we do, it will always be in the spirit of being mindful and "seeing for yourself" what might actually be happening in each moment when anger, ill-will, or aversion become dominant and distracting.

THE BIOLOGY OF ANGER

What exactly happens in your mind and body when anger strikes? A good place to begin, if you want a better understanding of what you are feeling in your angry moments, is with the biology of anger.

Human beings are equipped with a protective "alarm system" to combat and evade threats to our survival. In 1929, Walter Cannon, an American physiologist working at the Harvard Medical School, first documented the physiological reactions of different organ systems in animals exposed to threats of all kinds. He found that they suffered the same basic changes and abnormalities no matter what kind of stress they endured. In 1936, Hans Selye, widely regarded as the father of stress theory, named this entire pattern of physiological change in the face of stress the *stress syndrome*. It is also widely known as the freeze-fight-or-flight reaction.

Very simply, when you face an immediate danger, your nervous system detects that danger through one or more of your senses, and the alarm goes off in both your mind and body. This causes a release of hormones and a cascade of other complex reactions throughout your body. The purpose of all of this activity is to increase your odds of survival by enabling you to freeze, fight, or flee. The familiar experiences of tensing muscles, rapid heartbeat, and hyperalertness or mental vigilance are all expressions of this basic reaction. The function of all of this activity in the face of this immediate threat is to help you hear and see more clearly, move faster, run farther and faster, tolerate more pain, and, if necessary, strike back harder.

The survival value of this amazing physiological reaction to an immediate threat or danger may be obvious, but Selye also showed that when this alarm system is activated chronically, there are serious consequences for your health. For example, the freeze-fight-or-flight reaction causes immediate elevations in blood pressure, blood sugar, and heart rate. These changes have a detrimental effect on your health if they occur frequently or are prolonged over time.

The *sympathetic nervous system* is the branch of the autonomic nervous system that is especially concerned with your body's involuntary response to alarm and threat. It is the sympathetic nervous system that is largely responsible for the freeze-fight-or-flight reaction, which is also sometimes called the "stress reaction." More modern research has discovered that, although all strong emotions have a basis in the sympathetic nervous system's stimulating effects on the body during the basic stress reaction, each strong emotion has its own characteristic mix of types, amounts, and balance of the activating hormones; thus, each strong emotion can cause important differences in the body's reactions. For example, an excited person may experience less change in heart and respiration rates than a person who is frightened or distressed, yet each is experiencing a variant of the basic stress reaction. Besides this general foundation, the specific biology of anger has additional interesting features, which we will examine in the next section.

THE PRICE OF ANGER

One obstacle that prevents some people from changing their angry minds is that they believe the expression of anger helps them. But, if you take a closer look, it becomes obvious that the real price of anger far outweighs any short-term benefits you think you gain.

There is a good chance that, if you are reading this book, you already know the price of anger in your life. And, as you begin bringing more mindfulness into your life and into your relationships—including mindfulness of your own inner world of thoughts and feelings—it is very likely you will appreciate that the cost of anger is even greater than you might have imagined. For now, let's review some of the most common and destructive ways anger can exact its toll on you.

The Physical Price of Anger

Anger and hostility have very powerful and characteristic effects of their own, beyond the well-recognized, damaging-to-your-health effects of chronic stress. One of the key factors is that people who react to stress with anger or hostility have been found to excrete much larger amounts of the stress hormones adrenaline and cortisol into their bloodstream (Williams 1999). These hormones have many effects, including increasing heart rate, blood pressure, and blood sugar. The result is that the angry person is then more likely to have a heart attack because the lining of their coronary arteries can be damaged by increases in blood pressure and heart rate; their coronary arteries are also more vulnerable to blockage by higher levels of plaque and cholesterol in the blood. Compared to fear, happiness, and anxiety, anger causes the greatest reaction in the heart and blood vessels and the largest increase in blood pressure (Schwartz, Weinberger, and Singer 1981).

Not only does anger affect your blood pressure if you express it, it also affects your blood pressure if you suppress it. A large body of research supports the finding that people who are filled with anger and hostility and who work to "keep it in" actually have much higher risk for high blood pressure (Gentry 1982). Keeping anger "in" is not the only dangerous anger-coping style. Research has also demonstrated that some people who have high blood pressure are more likely to behave aggressively and to demonstrate hostility than people with lower blood pressure who handle stressful situations in less confrontational ways (Mann 1977).

The stress reaction also impacts the digestive system by interfering with your body's ability to move digested food through the system and by altering acid secretions. The blend of stress hormones that characterizes anger has been found to have considerable negative impact on your digestive system, effects different from depression or fear. For example, anger increases acid secretion in your stomach, which can lead to gastritis and ulcers (Wolff and Wolf 1967). In predisposed people, when anger is held in and suppressed, the colon has been found to become filled with blood and to have more frequent waves of contraction and relaxation, which could increase risk for ulcerative colitis (Lewis and Lewis 1972).

The Emotional Price of Anger

In case you haven't noticed, being angry can stimulate and feed many other unpleasant emotions and feelings. A significant and long-standing body of research reveals much about the emotional price of anger. People who feel chronically angry suffer in multiple ways, including feeling more helpless, alone, and less satisfied with their lives and relationships.

Chronically hostile people suffer from feelings of isolation because they feel less support from family members and less trust in close relationships (Greenglass 1996); they suffer from feelings of low self-esteem and loneliness (Jones, Freeman, and Gasewick 1981); and they tend to engage in more self-defeating and self-destructive behaviors that add to their misery (Deffenbacher et al. 2000).

And chronically angry and hostile people have increased risk for illness, the price of isolation and loneliness (Hansson, Jones, and Carpenter 1984). They also have a higher likelihood of earlier death than their peers (Berkman and Syme 1979; Barefoot, Dahlstrom, and Williams 1983).

If, in response to what you experience in life, you tell yourself things like *I should not feel any pain or hurt, and if I do, it is their fault and they should fix it!* or *It feels like my life is out of control, and I have no control! Someone else is to blame!*, then you'll feel you have few choices in life. With this attitude, the load of stress in your mind and body can increase to damaging levels, and your relationships and behaviors will often be marked by anger.

The Social Price of Anger

Anger and other expressions of ill will and aversion to what unfolds in the present moment have immediate impact on your social environment—the loved ones, coworkers, strangers, children, and even pets and animals around you. How do people react to you when you are angry? At first, they may feel bad or upset themselves. But if they are frequently exposed to your anger, over time they will probably become more distant and less responsive to you or have less empathy with you. Also, they are less likely to want to be around you if you are chronically angry or hostile. Probably because of these interpersonal factors, hostile people often find their social contacts and interactions with others to be less satisfying and of lower quality (Tavris 1989).

Chronic anger and ill will can make a person less tolerant and more rigid in their attitude and behavior toward others (Biaggio 1980). Women with higher hostility scores are more likely to have significantly worse marriages (Weaver and Shaw, reported in Wood 1986). Men with higher scores of anger are more likely to be violent in their marriages (Barbour et al. 1998).

Sadly, the social price and other costs of anger are not limited to adults. Children are especially vulnerable, and, in fact, many angry and hostile adults were victims of childhood abuse—emotional or physical or both—at the hands of angry adults.

In one study, children of angry and punitive mothers were more angry and noncompliant than children of less angry mothers (Crockenberg 1987). Other studies have found that parents who yell or verbally attack their children more often are more likely to become physically violent with their children (Hemenway, Solnick, and Carter 1994; Korbanka and McKay 1995); physical punishment leads to more aggressive behavior by the child (Straus 1994); and physical punishment correlates with increased stealing, truancy, lying, depression, and low self-esteem in children (Herman 1985). McKay, Rogers, and McKay (2003) comment, "For children to learn kindness, they must be treated kindly. For children to discover alternatives to anger and aggression, they have to see those alternatives demonstrated. For children to be considerate of others, their feelings and needs must be treated with consideration" (232).

MINDFULNESS PRACTICE:
Noticing When Anger Is Not Present

It can be very helpful to realize that you are larger and more complex than any single feeling, even anger. As a simple mindfulness practice, set an intention to gently notice for yourself when anger is not present in your life. Stop and take a few mindful breaths from time to time when you are not angry and notice what is present. Include in your noticing how your body feels, and what thoughts are in your mind. How does this feel? Is it pleasant or enjoyable not to feel anger? If you like the feeling of ease and greater peace you notice, let that positive feeling strengthen your motivation to calm your angry mind and to feel peace more often and anger less.

KEEP IN MIND

- If you want to control your anger instead of letting it control you, learn to recognize anger when it is present in your life. It helps to know that your anger can actually take on many faces and can appear as ill will, dislike, aversion to what is present, or even boredom.

- By focusing on your inner life with curiosity and mindfulness when you feel angry, you may begin to see the deeper layers of emotion that act as the foundation for the emergence of your anger. You may begin to recognize and be more mindful of the fear that lies beneath your angry feelings, and if you look even deeper, you may uncover rigid beliefs, opinions, and ideas about who you are or about your own worth or value.

- What you do under the influence of anger has an enormous impact on your own health and happiness as well as the health and happiness of those around you. Your connection with everyone around you is what makes calming your angry mind so crucial. You are not doing it just for your own peace, happiness, and health. When you calm your angry mind, you also bring peace and happiness to others around you and to the whole world. This is your gift to yourself and to them.

CHAPTER 3

approaching anger mindfully and skillfully

The education of attention would be an education par excellence.

—*William James*

The world and everything in it can appear very differently when you become mindful of it. Mindfulness is about becoming more aware; and when you become more aware of what is here and what is happening, it can be as if another dimension has opened in your life. As the process of expanding awareness unfolds, you may find that a totally different—and much more positive— relationship to yourself, others, and life can be yours.

Entering this mindfulness-based dimension will certainly give you more choices. It will also give you a kind of wisdom about yourself that is deeply true, that resonates with your deepest and healthiest values, and that no one can shake. Yet practicing mindfulness can be challenging at times too. To help support you in the actual practice of mindfulness and your explorations using the meditations in this book, in this chapter we will consider what it means to approach anger and other expressions of ill will and aversion mindfully and skillfully.

MINDFULNESS CAN OBSERVE ANYTHING—EVEN YOUR ANGER

From the point of view of mindfulness, *everything* happens in the present moment; and this "everything" includes your sensory experiences, bodily sensations, and the thoughts that make up your inner life. Since anger is an experience that is deeply rooted in your sense of personal identity, which depends on having thoughts, feelings, and sensations, bringing mindfulness to your "inner life" is an excellent place to begin if you want to take back control of your life from anger.

What we call your *inner life* in this book refers to the stream of interior experience—the information flowing in constantly through your senses, sensations in your body, and all of the many kinds of thoughts generated in your mind. This tapestry of sensory texture and mental activity arises and changes moment by moment. It is literally made up of what you are feeling and what seems solid, and what you are thinking_which may not feel solid, but can be compelling and intense, as when thoughts appear as a worry or a memory. All of this richness, solid feeling or not, is the amazing stuff of your particular lived experience in any moment—and all of it can be touched by mindfulness in deep and caring ways.

From the perspective of mindfulness, your inner life includes the moment-by-moment, personal experiences of thinking, emotions like anger (remembering here that "emotion" is a general term that applies to a formation or combination of thoughts and sensations in your body), and the flow of information coming into your senses. From the point of view of mindfulness, all of these experiences, which are usually very personal and intimate, are always changing and are not your permanent identity. In other words, you might feel "angry," but anger is not "you." You can know this about anger because, if you watch closely enough, you will notice anger comes and goes, in and out of the present moment. If it isn't always here, then how can it be "you?"

When you stop and observe, you will discover that you can actually and accurately see for yourself that the true nature of anger is this: it is a temporary condition and not a defining identity. From this view, anger can be understood. It can be controlled. You can learn from it, and perhaps even be healed or be transformed by taking a radically new and powerful relationship to any moment of anger in your life.

So, approaching anger *mindfully* begins when you commit to building a mindful relationship with anger rather than surrendering to the belief that you are a victim of it, or allowing yourself to be unaware of its presence and impact in your life. Approaching anger mindfully will call on you to turn your attention and curiosity toward the intense experience of anger and its various relatives and expressions, learning as you practice to see directly how they arise in your mind and body and also to recognize what factors encourage and sustain them in the unfolding relationships and moments of your life.

Approaching anger *skillfully* means that you develop the skills you will need to be mindful of your anger whenever it appears. These skills include having a strong intention to become more aware and understanding of your anger; the skill of stopping, paying and sustaining attention in each moment, even toward upsetting and distracting emotions; and the skill of keeping a curious, open, and welcoming attitude toward whatever is unfolding in your awareness.

Of course, besides ever-changing emotions like anger, each moment of your life is filled with other conditions that are changing and temporary. The situations, the people, the conditions outside of your skin all change at different speeds and constantly flow into and out of your awareness, forming the uniquely particular—sometimes beautiful, sometimes painful, and always amazing and precious—fabric of your life, breath by breath. As we shall see in later chapters, mindfulness practice can help you connect more deeply with any condition or experience, or any person or situation that has entered the present moment of your life. From this richer connection, you may then enjoy more heartfelt and wiser possibilities for living a richer and more satisfying life—not only on the inside but also in relationship to what is outside of your own skin.

APPROACHING YOUR ANGER MINDFULLY

Imagine this scene.

> You are in a stadium filled with thousands of people. On the field below, there are two teams of players wearing different, brightly colored uniforms. They line up facing each other, with a ball on a tee near the middle of the field, which is divided by lines with numbers assigned to them.
>
> As you watch, a man on one team runs forward and kicks the ball to one end, where a man wearing a jersey of a different color catches it and begins to run forward. The man who caught the ball runs hard and fast, eludes many of the men in the other jerseys, and breaks into the clear, racing toward the other end of the field.
>
> As this happens, you hear people around you cursing and swearing in anger, and you notice people on the other side of the stadium are cheering wildly and jumping up and down excitedly.
>
> When the player carrying the ball reaches the end zone, the stadium erupts in even more noise, and the people around you are even angrier, and some even pick up their belongings and storm away. On the other side of the stadium, the crowd is deliriously happy.

Thousands of people just witnessed the same thing—a man kicked a ball, another man caught it, and ran it back to the other end of the field. Yet half of the people who saw this unfolding action are very happy and the other half are angry and upset. What is going on?

Remember the model of the structure of anger? Beneath anger is fear, and beneath fear is a fixed belief or idea. In this case, could it be that for the thousands of happy people, what happened affirmed a belief or idea they held about what a *good* thing was—their team won the game—and for the thousands of angry people, the exact same series of events was the expression of their idea of a *bad* thing: their team lost the game, and stirred the fear that they would not have a successful season?

Some will be happy for days afterward. Others will be angry for days. And others, on both sides, will move on more quickly. Why are there such differences?

The ability to recognize and embrace intense emotional experiences, and then to release them and move on is actually a skill that can be developed. But, you might say, why would I want to move on from the happy feeling if my team wins? Or, you might say, I wish I could move on when my team loses, but it really sticks with me.

Well, have you ever been able to hang onto any good feeling? Of course not. It may even make you angry because you cannot hold onto the good feeling. And, although the painful ones tend to stick around, they come and go too, pretty much at their own speed—unless you interfere with them, in which case they probably stick around longer! Using mindfulness, you can learn to let them go more easily.

In fact, once the event (the "big game," for example) changes (in this case, when the game ends), and later you have a happy or a painful memory of it, that is all you are having—the memory. We humans are wired selectively to remember the signs and signals associated with a dangerous or alarming situation much more easily than we remember the pleasant and "good" things that happen to us. This selective recall of negative experience is called *negative bias*, and we will look more closely at it in later chapters.

With mindful attention, it becomes clear that the particular situations or conditions that evoke any emotional experience—whether you experience it as "good" or "bad"—are themselves changing and temporary. Practicing mindfulness can help you to be more present when the experience happens, as well as to recognize how it returns to color and shape your life in future moments, and to respond more wisely when the memory of that experience does return.

WAYS TO TAKE A MINDFUL APPROACH

Approaching your anger mindfully can happen in many ways. You might say there is one mindfulness and many methods, each emphasizing a particular meditative or reflective focus as your practice.

Three excellent ways for approaching anger mindfully based in meditation practices are stopping and strengthening attention, activating the energy of kindness and compassion, and being informed by the wisdom and understanding that comes from your own mindfulness practice. These approaches are widely used by meditation teachers and others working with mindfulness-based interventions simply because they are so effective and so easy to learn. Each mindfulness-based direction is both a place to begin and a path for proceeding as you mindfully transform your understanding and experience of anger and other intense emotions.

Begin with Stopping and Seeing

As we have seen, we humans are wired so well for self-defense and protection that the thoughts and sensations in strong emotions like anger arise and sweep us away very, very quickly. Because of that, to help you disentangle from the sticky web of angry emotion, it is crucial to be able to stop and look more closely in order to see what is going on. Consider this example.

• Sue's Story

Sue is in a mindfulness meditation class. She owns and operates her own successful business. She told the class a story of how she was stuck in her car in traffic and late for an important meeting. "I suddenly noticed how hard I was gripping the wheel," she said, "and then I noticed other parts of my body were tensed up too—my neck and shoulders, and especially my jaw. I also noticed I was actually yelling in my head at all the cars around me!"

"What did you do?" someone asked.

"Well," Sue laughed, "I relaxed the grip a lot, and took a few mindful breaths, and noticed that my entire body relaxed some. Then I let go of the angry thoughts in my head and was able to tell myself there was nothing else I could do but wait for the traffic to move. I could relax and stopped being so stressed and angry."

Your first mindful approach to anger could be to become very good at recognizing when you are swept up in thought and feelings, and then *stop* and *observe* what is happening in this moment in your mind and body. So stopping and seeing is the first way to approach your anger.

As you will learn, there are many meditative practices utilizing mindfulness to help you disentangle yourself from overidentification with your interior stream of sensations and thoughts. These practices will help you bring an accurate focus of attention to what is happening. In chapter 5, you will find several different mindfulness practices to help you strengthen your capacity to stop and observe mindfully what is happening in your mind and body.

Include Compassion and Kindness

Have you ever noticed the feeling of having a "hard heart"? Have you ever shut out another person, or a situation, or perhaps even some aspect or dimension of yourself—a physical sensation, a feeling, or a chain of thoughts, for example?

One of the toxic impacts of anger is to make you feel isolated, alone, and disconnected from others. This distorted view can be corrected. You might choose a meditation practice that cultivates the quality of kindness or compassion in order to support or strengthen the mindfulness skill of maintaining a nonjudging and welcoming attitude. Consider this example from a person in a meditation class.

• *Matt's Story*

Matt, a young father of three small children, works as a budget and financial analyst for a large hospital system. He took the mindfulness class after a friend told him that he'd taken the class and found that practicing mindfulness really helps you manage the frustrations and irritations of a stressful job. One afternoon in the class, Matt told this story:

"We are going through a really stressful period at work. I am putting in fifty to sixty hours each week. When I get home, I am exhausted, and usually impatient and irritable. A couple of nights ago I came home like that, and my kids wanted me to play with them. At first, I snapped back at them and said no. Then they looked hurt, and I felt bad, so I said, 'Okay.'"

"What happened next?" someone asked Matt.

"Well, I remembered that we had talked about self-compassion in the mindfulness class, and while I was waiting for the kids to gather their toys, I tuned into my body sensations and noticed how tired and stiff I felt. Instead of beating up on myself for that, plus snapping at my kids, I just breathed mindfully with the sensations, and wished myself well by saying, 'May I take care of myself with ease, and may I be filled with peace.' By the time the kids and I got playing, I was a lot more relaxed and present for them, and felt kinder and better about myself. If I hadn't known about mindfulness and the power of self-compassion, or how to practice them, I hate to think how things would have gone between me and my kids that night!"

Knowing how to approach anger and ill will mindfully by finding and resting in your innate capacity for goodness, and cultivating positive emotions like kindness, compassion, gratitude, and generosity can be enormously helpful, as Matt's story illustrates. In chapter 6, you will find a variety of different meditation practices to help you explore and strengthen your natural qualities of kindness, compassion, and goodness of heart.

Take a Wise View

A third powerful mindful approach you can take toward anger is to take a wise view of what anger actually is. By seeing clearly what anger is and how it functions, you are better equipped to let that wisdom inform how you respond when the intense unpleasantness of an angry emotion storms over you. Consider this example.

• The Rainbow's Story

Have you ever watered your lawn and suddenly noticed a rainbow appearing in the mist over the grass as sunlight, water, and air combined in just the right way? Or perhaps you've seen larger rainbows in the sky after a rainstorm, or possibly you have seen a rainbow around a waterfall in the descending water's mist on a sunny day.

These rainbows are not permanent. They are the result of a momentary coming together of the conditions of air, water, and sunlight. They appear, change, and vanish depending on the changing conditions that support them.

If rainbows are made up of changing conditions, could anger be like that? What if you looked at anger that way?

Well, anger *is* like that, and you *can* approach it that way.

When you observe the experience of anger mindfully, it becomes possible to notice that what you are calling "anger" is actually a complex formation of elements appearing in the present moment. The elements that you can observe mindfully include changing bodily sensations, thoughts in your mind, and (usually but not always) something happening around you or someone else doing something.

If these are basic conditions of the "rainbow" of anger, then what nurtures these conditions? What sustains and strengthens them? More importantly, what nurtures the conditions that form *your* anger?

Remember the structural model of anger that says "beneath anger is fear, and beneath fear is a fixed belief"? You could look at the beliefs as crucial conditions nurturing your anger. How might this model, with the belief at the base, apply when anger appears out of conditions of sensory input, your thoughts, and sensations in your body? What could you do differently if you could learn to "calm your angry mind" (and body), and also more easily identify those fixed beliefs?

Using a wise view approach to anger, you might notice that anger is built on judging thoughts that often are not true. When you notice judging thoughts have returned and if you know they are not true, you will not be grabbed by them with the same power, nor will you get so caught up believing or acting on them.

For instance, you might let an insight that you have gained from being mindful—like knowing that you have a deep fear of failure or of not being "okay"—inform you as you continue to pay attention to your experience. This may help you recognize when something happens to you that evokes your fear of failure or of not being "okay." Then you will be able to see within yourself the structure of anger—how you experience anger, and under that anger you feel fear, and under that fear, you hold a belief that you are a failure or that you're not okay.

So, a third way to approach anger mindfully and regain control when anger hijacks you is to remember and rest in a wise view of anger. Allow that wise view to inform how you relate to the unpleasantness of your angry thoughts and feelings. In chapter 7, you will find a variety of mindfulness-based practices to help you explore your inquiry into the conditions that feed and sustain anger at its roots in your life.

You can approach anger mindfully by using any of these three ways. You can approach anger and gain control over it by stopping and seeing, which enables you to escape absorption or overidentification with your anger; by cultivating feelings of compassion and kindness toward yourself and others; or by taking a wise view, in which you tap into your own wisdom and insight about the actual structure and particular components of your anger. No matter which way you choose, you will probably also discover that those meditations and practices will promote and support access to the other approaches and practices as well.

APPROACHING YOUR ANGER *SKILLFULLY*

In chapter 1, we learned about three core skills helpful in mindfulness practice: adopting an *intention* to be mindful; being able to focus and maintain *attention* on an object of your choosing; and developing an *attitude* that is nonjudging and open to the experience in this moment. Remembering even one of these skills, and having practiced strengthening it, will serve you well in any moment or situation when you feel hijacked by anger, ill will, or aversion. Let's look more carefully at these skills and how they can help you approach your anger skillfully and mindfully.

Intention

Intention is the way your mind directs your brain and body to act. Nothing that you wish for happens without some intention preceding it. When you set your intention, things happen. For example, you don't take a step without a prior intention to move, or you don't take a bite of food without intending to bite. Your mind directs your brain and body to act in these moments.

But do you always know what intention precedes your action, including your thinking? Where did *that* intention come from? Who ordered *that* intention? What if you could know more about these and not go on—or "go off," driven by the "automatic pilot" of reacting without recognizing the crucial elements operating in your inner life in this moment?

Knowing about mindfulness, and how it can help you recognize the elements that make up your feelings (like anger) and not be hijacked by habits of reacting without thinking can be a strong motivation for generating the intention you need to practice mindfulness when you feel stressed, angry, or upset. Here is an example.

• Jane's Story

Jane is a middle-aged woman who came to a mindfulness-based stress reduction class because she wanted to see if being mindful would help her lose weight and keep it off. One evening she told the class this story:

"I was home one night watching television. My kids were playing on the floor, and I was busy eating out of a bag of junk food sitting on my lap. Then I remembered that I was taking a mindfulness class to help me lose weight, and I started to pay attention mindfully to what was going on."

"What did you notice?" someone asked.

"The first thing I noticed," Jane said, "was that I didn't like the taste of the junk food!"

Everyone in the class laughed at that.

"Then," she said, "I noticed I wasn't even hungry. I was just upset."

"What happened next?" someone else asked.

"Well, I put the junk food away, turned off the television, and started playing with my kids. And we had a wonderful evening! I was so glad I knew enough to practice my mindfulness when I did."

According to modern neuroscience, how you use your mind actually shapes and changes your brain. This is the principle of neuroplasticity—your brain builds connections and strengthens its circuits when you use it in one way, and weakens those connections and circuits when you stop using it in other ways.

A very practical example is that if you keep repeating an anger-filled story to yourself about someone you think has hurt you that story will get louder and louder until the very sight of that person will likely evoke the story and an angry, stress-filled reaction in you. In contrast, if you mindfully notice when the story is sounding in your mind and if you don't get caught up in it, or steam and sulk about it, then over time, it will lose its heat. And when you see that person, you are likely not to be so stressed out!

It follows that the intentions you set for yourself actually direct your brain (and ultimately the rest of your body) to "get to work!" So, if intention is a way you can incline your brain and body to emphasize certain streams of information and to let others go, perhaps it is a vitally important principle for you to explore if you wish to live a happier life, a life with less anger and much more joy and generosity.

Rick Hanson, PhD, a neuropsychologist and meditation teacher, describes it like this. He says your brain has three fundamental functions underlying all of its amazing complexity: regulation, learning, and selection:

Your brain regulates itself—and other bodily systems—through a combination of excitatory and inhibitory activity: green lights and red lights. It learns through forming new circuits and strengthening or weakening existing ones. And it selects whatever experience has taught it to value; for example, even an earthworm can be trained to pick a particular path to avoid an electric shock.

These three functions—regulation, learning, and selection—operate at all levels of the nervous system, from the intricate molecular dance at the tip of a synapse to the whole-brain integration of control, competence, and discernment. All three functions are involved in any important mental activity. (Hanson 2009, 14)

Intention could be thought of as the way you "incline" your brain to apply these basic functions to the amazing stream of changing information—which you experience as your life— flowing through the present moment. Once you set your intention, your brain supports the intention, and using its basic functions of regulation, learning, and selection, away you go!

So, in this light of the power of intention, how to become more aware of your intentions and how to set effective intentions become very important and interesting questions. What intentions drive your life? What instructions are you giving to your brain and body—even unconsciously or semiconsciously—because of old habits of mind? Do you ask it to constantly replay scenes and memories when you felt hurt or threatened, along with the inner thoughts and commentary, and mental stories that fill your mind as you remember those scenes? Or do you notice feelings of anger or resentment and ask your brain to draw on different memories—more positive ones, perhaps—and call up inspiring stories and examples of when you or others found within the capacity for better understanding and even forgiveness?

Intention can be understood as the "command" you give your brain to move in a particular direction in response to what happens in the present moment, including what's happening in your mind, body, and the world around you. What follows from that command makes all the difference in what happens next. We see that in Jane's story. When she intended to be more mindful, Jane shifted from an emotional state of upset where she isolated herself by watching TV and soothed herself by eating junk food into much healthier and happier choices: she put the junk food away and played with her children.

Attention

The current scientific understanding of attention is that we humans have the capacity—and the need—to shift our focus of attention. Not only can we shift our focus among different objects—from a red ball to a green ball to a yellow ball—but we can also shift from a narrow focus to a wide focus, from a single object to all objects in our environment. We can, for example, focus on one tree and then shift to a wider focus on the whole forest. The human brain is constructed and "wired" to allow these shifts.

At one end of the spectrum of attention, your brain can enhance a selected stream of information—say, the words of your companion as you converse at dinner—and on the other hand, your brain can inhibit the stream of information from other sources—for example, the surrounding noise in the room. This capacity enables you to have very focused or *selective attention* on a chosen object, in this example, your companion's words.

At the other end of the spectrum of attention, your brain can allow for an inclusive, *open, nonjudgmental awareness* of all that is happening. For example, you can be having dinner with a friend in a restaurant, and during a pause in your conversation, you can notice that your friend seems tense; beside you, you notice that the people at the next table are leaving; and at the same time, you become aware of a strong smoky smell from the kitchen. Your brain can take in all of these things in a moment of open awareness.

Both of these forms of attention—selective and open, non-judgmental awareness—are crucial to our emotional life. Richard J. Davidson (2012), a leading researcher in the area of brain function and emotion, describes the forms of attention like this:

> Selective attention...refers to the conscious decision to selectively focus on certain features of one's environment and ignore others. This capacity is a key building block for other

dimensions of Emotional Style, since the failure to selectively attend can make it impossible to be Self-Aware or Tuned In. Open, nonjudgmental awareness reflects the ability to take in signals from the external environment as well as the thoughts and feelings popping up within our brain, to broaden our attention and sensitively pick up on the often subtle cues that continuously impinge upon us—but to do so without getting stuck on any one stimulus to the detriment of the others (86).

When you practice mindfulness, one of the skills is learning to better control your attention. "Better control" in this case means several things:

- You are able to focus your attention as narrowly or as broadly as you like.

- You are able to keep your attention where you place and focus it.

- You are able to intentionally move attention around reliably and easily (that is, your attention is "flexible").

Many methods of meditation help you train your attention in these different dimensions. As your skills of attention grow with meditation practice, you will very likely begin to notice more and more things. For example, you may discover an increased sensitivity and appreciation of things around you—a flower, a touching word or encounter with another, for example, or the pleasant smell of your favorite food just as you are about to take the first bite.

Christina Feldman is a popular Buddhist meditation teacher and author. Here is a story she tells about her own experience of developing attention.

• Christina's Story

"Some years ago I was invited to teach a retreat in the desert in Arizona. Countless people had spoken to me about the beauty and magnificence of the desert, and I was eager to experience it for myself.... As the sun rose, I looked around and a single disappointed thought arose, 'It's brown.'"

Christina goes on to describe that she went on to teach the retreat, and over the following days took walks and observed the changing conditions of the desert much more closely. Here is how she described what happened with her extended and careful attention.

"I discovered that the more I looked, listened, and felt, the more I saw. The desert was teeming with life. The heat haze shimmered over the ground. . . . Each hour as the sun moved, casting different shadows and light, the desert was changed. It was a wondrous, alive, shifting, changing reality, different in each moment of the day."

And, she concludes this story with the following observation.

"For anything in this world to be alive for us, we are asked to be alive to it. Mindfulness awakens not only our way of seeing, but also everything that is seen" (Feldman 2001, 171).

The beauty and wonder of life is always there and waiting for you to wake up and notice it. Learning better skills of attention, which happens when you practice mindfulness and meditation, thus can be a direct path to sometimes surprising and unexpected sources of great positive experiences.

Attitude

How are you treating life? What relationship do you take to the contents of your own mind and body? To the words and actions of others? To the conditions of the world around you?

The attitude you assume—welcoming or rejecting, for example— toward the thoughts, sensations, and other streams of information flowing through your consciousness in this moment makes all the difference. Cultivating an attitude of open-hearted awareness and inclusiveness toward your experience and inner world does not always come easy, for many reasons. In fact, most people have actually "practiced" meanness and judgmental thoughts and feelings far more than they have "practiced" being kind and compassionate. As you take up mindfulness and meditation practice, it is very important and quite helpful to remember this deeply human tendency to be critical and exclusive toward what is happening, especially when it is something unpleasant.

For most of us, it can still be a daunting idea to consider opening ourselves to and staying present with the difficult experiences in our lives. It can help to realize that accomplished meditation teachers with many years of mindfulness practice have had similar struggles. Joseph Goldstein is a well-respected meditation teacher, author, and Buddhist teacher. Let's hear a story of his about how challenging it can be to develop a skillful attitude in meditation, especially when anger and aversion to what is happening are strong.

• Joseph's Story

"Years ago when I was living and practicing in India, I went to Kashmir for some of the hot summer months. Part of the journey was a very long bus ride—many hours on a hot, crowded Indian bus.... I thought I would just stay with my breath for the whole time, keeping out all unpleasant sensations.... For quite a while, this strategy seemed to work.... But at a certain point, it just became too much effort. I was trying so hard to hold on to the breath and not feel anything else that I was getting exhausted from trying. At that point, there came a mini-awakening. I realized the real struggle was in trying to keep unpleasant things out and what I really needed to do was to let them in. From that moment's understanding, I simply began to open to whatever was arising—the heat, the noise, the uncomfortable feelings in the body, the vibrations, the smells from the engine, all of it. When I could let it all in, the mind relaxed, and the rest of the journey was fine. Things were just as they were; I no longer had to fight with them" (Goldstein 2002, 112).

Your progress along each of these meditation paths of mindfulness, compassion, and wisdom is enhanced by strengthening the three basic skills of intending to be mindful, directing attention and keeping focused on what you selected (for example, the experience in your mind and body of anger in this moment), and cultivating and relying upon an attitude of open-heartedness and acceptance of any experience that is present. Approaching your anger "mindfully and skillfully" is another example of how deeply interconnected these concepts and direct practice experiences actually are!

MINDFULNESS PRACTICE:
Finding Anger in Your Body

This week, whenever you notice any signals that you are angry—in your body, your thoughts, or your actions—stop and pay attention. Give yourself an intention to better understand your experience of anger in this moment. Use some mindful breaths to stabilize your attention and simply notice, without judging, what is happening. Feel the sensations in the different parts of your body, listen and let go of the thoughts, and let the sensations of mindful breathing help you stay present, observant, and disentangled from the stormy stream of anger in your mind and body. If it helps, you could whisper quietly to yourself the name of this experience, saying something like "This is anger" or "Anger is here now in mind and body."

KEEP IN MIND

- When you practice mindfulness, the world and your sense of yourself in it can appear very differently. For most people, as they become more mindful, the world seems more vivid, more interesting, and more alive than perhaps they believed possible. That is exactly why practicing mindfulness is so important to calming your angry mind.

- Ordinary experiences like the big game, or difficult conversations or arguments, can be seen as dependent upon the beliefs and interpretations you place on them. Being mindful of those beliefs can make all the difference if you wish to better understand yourself and to better control your anger and other difficult emotions.

- Approaching anger and its other expressions mindfully means committing to becoming more mindful at all times, and especially when those angry feelings are present. You can become more mindful more often when you learn to stop and pay attention, trust the power of compassion, or adopt a wise view of your experience in the present moment. To do any of those things effectively, it helps to build and strengthen skills of clear intention, steady and flexible attention, and the power of an open and receptive attitude toward your unfolding experience.

CHAPTER 4

preparing to practice

Mindfulness practice means that we commit fully in each moment to being present.

—*Jon Kabat-Zinn*

So far we have been learning a good bit about the power of mindfulness and compassion, and how intentionally cultivating those basic human capacities with meditation can help you transform the experience of anger in its many forms.

We have been suggesting a view of anger that is perhaps very different—even radically different—from how you have approached, thought of, or understood this emotion up to now. This view of anger can be summarized as follows: Anger is not you but is a temporary condition that depends on many other conditions, much like a rainbow or a cloud depends on other conditions in order to appear. Anger does not actually come from "out there" but arises when a stimulus or situation that you meet triggers a complex set of conditions that live in you—conditions such as beliefs, fears, perceptions, and physical reactions. And, by growing more accurate awareness of your anger and its causes, you can broaden and build your resources for choosing to respond to angry feelings with the strength that arises from understanding, compassion, and knowing how to care for any pain that angry feelings mask. Turning toward anger and pain with steady attention that is based in kindness and wisdom can then become your wisest, most trusted, and most effective response whenever anger arises.

By actually practicing mindfulness and training your mind through meditation, you can see for yourself if this view of anger is correct. When—using meditation practice— you learn how to directly observe and investigate anger and other strong emotions, how to watch them closely and touch each with acceptance and compassion as they come and go in your mind and body, then you will be well prepared to decide for yourself if this view of anger as described above is accurate. Only you can actually make that decision, because only you can look within at your own life experience in each moment.

But, while practicing mindfulness, compassion, and related forms of meditation can be simple, practicing meditation is, at times anyway, not easy. When you stop and pay closer attention nonjudgmentally in the present moment, you will probably notice quickly that quite a bit is going on in your mind and body as well as in the ongoing interaction between you and the world around you. There may be moments when you wonder, *What is happening? What is going on, really? Who or what am I, really?*

In this chapter, we will explore a variety of topics to help you prepare to engage the practices in the next three chapters more effectively and powerfully. Specifically, we will look more closely at the paradox of meditation practice; at ways to strengthen your motivation for practice; at practical issues of practice like posture, time, and the elements of a supportive environment for your meditation; and at some common challenges that arise for almost everyone and ways you can successfully meet them.

YOU ARE NOT PRACTICING TO GET ANYWHERE

You have had a taste of mindfulness practice in the previous chapters. The next three chapters offer you a diverse variety of practices based in mindfulness, compassion, and better understanding. Exploring these practices in your own way, while remaining committed to practice, self-discovery, and transformation, is the path now opening before you.

One thing that often happens to people, especially when they are new to meditation, is that they get frustrated because they don't think they are being successful or getting anywhere with their meditation. Of course, this can happen to very experienced meditators too! Let's look more closely at what it means to say "you are not practicing to get anywhere" when you are practicing mindfulness meditation.

The Paradox of Meditation Practice

A basic starting position for your meditation practice involves a great paradox of meditation practice, especially mindfulness practices. That paradox is that the most effective attitude to take when engaging the meditation is to let go of attachment to any outcome. In other words, if you want to calm your angry mind, it will probably go much better toward that goal if you actually stop trying to do anything. Remembering that mindfulness is about "being and not doing" can be very helpful.

Part of the reason this paradox exists is that your thinking and judging mind will continue to operate, even during the meditation— at least at times. So, if your goal is to calm the anger, then your thinking mind will likely be watching and deciding if it is "working" or not. This constant vigilance toward the condition of anger with the goal of getting rid of it will actually maintain a state of arousal and restricted focus. In addition, the underlying attitude of aversion toward (or dislike of) the anger that is present and the desire to be rid of it further feeds the feeling of anger that you are trying to "calm." In other words, being angry at your anger doesn't really help!

So, we say, practice without attachment to outcome. Practice without trying to get anywhere. Just practice with the intention to be present, to notice, and to understand. When you can practice like that, then the rest will take care of itself.

DIFFERENT PRACTICES—THE SAME MINDFULNESS

Because your brain can change its function and its actual structure depending on how you use it (the principle of neuroplasticity, which we discussed in earlier chapters), it is only you, ultimately, who can make the necessary changes happen that will help you heal and transform anger in your life. You have what you need to do your own "inner rewiring" by actually practicing and using the meditations based in mindfulness, compassion, and wisdom.

A point of confusion for some people is how to choose between the practices. People are different, and one person will naturally resonate more with a particular practice—for example, the awareness of breathing—while another may struggle with that practice but feel more comfortable with something else, perhaps walking mindfully or with a practice focused on compassion.

It can help to recall that there is only one mindfulness. Centered in the present moment, reflective, nonjudging awareness operates in each of these practices. The various practices differ in the emphasis on various skills that support the possibility of a more enduring and brighter mindfulness in each moment and in each situation.

In truth, each person is also changing all the time, so it is a good idea not to make too much out of your reaction to a particular practice or to a particular practice session. Your experience will probably be different the next time you practice. It will help you if you don't get lost in beliefs about any particular practice, or let those beliefs keep you from returning to it, or from trying another one.

Be especially careful of deciding if any single practice session was "good" or "bad" just because you felt more relaxed or had an important insight. It is more helpful simply to notice and carefully observe whatever comes up. Another paradox of meditation is that remaining mindful when you are beset by unpleasant experience may actually bring you more long-term benefit than any session where you felt more "at peace" or more "relaxed."

The different practices simply offer you a variety of ways to utilize mindfulness and compassion to investigate your own life and the experience of strong emotions like anger. Remember—many practices, one mindfulness.

GETTING AND STAYING MOTIVATED TO PRACTICE

Remember that intention is one of the mindfulness skills. Well, when you don't feel like doing mindfulness practice for any reason—your mind will generate lots of reasons!—it can be extremely useful to draw support for forming a strong intention by reflecting on the motivations that can help you overcome the resistance you may be feeling to practice in that moment.

Here are some motivations that could be very useful for you. Feel free to add more of your own to the list at any time.

Motivation: Remember You Have What It Takes

It can be a great motivator to know you can actually accomplish something, anything, to better manage your anger and strong emotions. From that point of view—that you can calm your angry mind because you already have what you need—let's look at some of the ways human beings are equipped for calming and controlling their anger.

As a human being, each of us, through mind and body connections, is wired to go very quickly into the stress reaction for basic survival reasons. The really good news is that humans also have control mechanisms for rebalancing and controlling the stress reaction and therefore for better managing negative emotions like anger and fear.

These mechanisms operate from higher brain centers down to lower ones, and from the body and lower brain regions upward as well. Also, very importantly, the functioning process of your operating brain, using all inputs, is now known to be a "distributed" process, which means that it does not require or operate using a central coordinator.

Different areas of the brain are constantly in contact, interacting with each other moment by moment to create the contents of conscious experience in each of us. In other words, your brain leaves nothing out and operates out of the wholeness and richness of your total life experience—both remembered and happening anew in this moment. Here's more about these mechanisms you already have for calming your angry mind.

TOP-DOWN MECHANISMS

As we have seen, once this stress reaction begins, your brain begins a process of analysis and understanding that recruits memories and associations from different times and places in your life. The activity at the "top"—in your brain, especially in the area called the neocortex—can have a sustaining or inhibiting effect on the stress reaction in your body. And, if the activity at the top draws on memories that give specific meaning to experience unfolding in the present moment, then strong emotion is very likely to be present as well.

The top-down approach involves your prefrontal cortex (PFC) and related regions in your neocortex. The *neocortex* is literally the youngest region of your brain from an evolutionary perspective, and it literally sits on top of the older regions of your brain, those subcortical and brainstem areas and structures associated with emotions and the basic reflexes and bodily functions that keep you alive.

Your *prefrontal cortex* (PFC) is involved in executive functions such as setting goals, making plans, and directing action. Through its rich network of connections to other brain regions, it can impact emotions by sometimes inhibiting and sometimes stimulating the limbic system, which is nearby and "below" the neocortex.

Your *limbic system* is actually a collection of parts that together are central to emotions and motivation. The limbic system includes structures like the *basal ganglia,* which is associated with rewards, stimulation seeking, and movement; the *hippocampus,* which is associated with forming new memories and detecting threats; the *amygdala,* which responds to stimuli associated with danger and plays a central role in activating the freeze-fight-or-flight reaction and conditioning the fear reaction.

One powerful example of how your PFC operates is in the thoughts that you have about what is happening. For example, if someone interrupts and cuts you off in a conversation or in an important meeting, you probably feel some irritation, perhaps even anger. If you begin talking to yourself with thoughts like *They had it in for me. I should teach them a lesson*, then you will probably continue to feel anger, and it may even escalate into rage or an urge to do harm to the other person. On the other hand, if, as you feel the anger when they interrupt you, you tell yourself, *They are really stressed out and they don't mean anything by it. I can help them out if I keep quiet, leave them alone, or offer to help them*, then you will probably find that your anger will soon diminish, and the encounter will go much better too.

In this example, you actively engage your PFC with skillful use of thoughts. This will help the PFC begin to exert its calming effects on the parts of your brain and body that are in hyperarousal.

BOTTOM-UP MECHANISMS

We are creatures of mind *and* body. The "bottom-up" mechanism for controlling your anger starts with attention to your body and knowing how to help it naturally grow in ease and relaxation.

There are many ways to signal your body to "relax," and they all involve activating your parasympathetic nervous system (PNS). The *parasympathetic nervous system* is the branch of your autonomic nervous system responsible for maintaining many routine bodily functions in daily life. The PNS is also critical for signaling muscles to relax, helping heart rate and blood pressure to resume resting levels, and restoring a more general and relaxed feeling of balance in your body following the hyperarousal and vigilance of the freeze-flight-or fight reaction in the face of stress and threat. The sense of relaxation you can feel when muscles soften and breathing slows has been called "the relaxation response," and it is the direct result of the action of the parasympathetic nervous system. Paying attention in a nonjudging way or paying attention to a neutral object—something that is not particularly pleasant or unpleasant, in other words—is a very effective way to activate the "relaxation response" (Benson 1975). One of the best ways is to bring attention into your body, allowing the sensations of the body to be a focus for attention. This is exactly what you do when you practice mindfulness of your body.

So, the bottom-up approach can be as simple as when you notice you are in a storm of anger, you bring attention to your body, repeatedly if necessary, and simply observe the sensations of breathing or moving. In chapter 5, you will learn some specific mindfulness practices to help you build your capacity to inhabit your body with awareness and to invoke both the bottom-up and the top-down approaches to controlling anger.

Mindfulness can help you utilize each of these mechanisms—top down or bottom up—in a wide variety of ways, as we will see. But a word of caution: remember that you are not practicing to get anywhere! Trying to make yourself relax is the surest way to get in the way of that actually happening. Instead, just practice bringing attention that is kind, curious, and compassionate, and simply notice what is happening. Your brain and body will do the rest.

THE DISTRIBUTED NATURE OF CONSCIOUSNESS: IT'S ALL YOU!

Neuroscientists now know that your brain works as a whole system, with connections and circuits firing or remaining silent throughout your brain many times each second. To say that a particular function (like planning a trip, or feeling sad or happy, or creating stories of blame and revenge, or stories of gratitude and appreciation) belongs to only one part of the brain is incorrect in the current understanding of brain function. Indeed, as one authority puts it, what we call the "mind" interacts so profoundly with the brain, the body, and the world that mind and brain are best understood "as a single, codependent, mind/brain system" (Hanson 2009, 7).

Working in a highly distributed way as a whole system, your brain does not have a single place where "you" are. That sense of "you" or "I" can feel momentarily very solid and secure, but it is, in fact, dependent on many activities in many parts of the brain.

Wolf Singer, MD, PhD, is the director of the Max Planck Institute for Brain Research in Frankfurt, Germany. Here is how he summarizes modern research on the function of the human brain:

> Different brain areas deal with very different inputs—from the eye, from the ear, and from the touch senses—and are also connected to areas belonging to the limbic system, which attach

emotional connotations to the contents of conscious experience. There is no single place in the brain where an observer could be located, a command structure could be implemented, or the self could have its seat. It is a highly distributed system in which many functions occur simultaneously and there is no coordinator. They self-organize (quoted in Kabat-Zinn and Davidson 2011, 67).

According to this view, you might think of your brain as a processor for many streams of information coming from outside your body, through your senses (like hearing or seeing), and from inside your body (like the function of your beating heart, or the thought stream of memories about a particular event, or the ideas and deeply held opinions from your culture or upbringing). These many streams of information come together, change, and go apart—breath by breath, and step by step—to form your experience. The experience of "you" in each moment includes your emotional experience with all of its richness and poignancy, and this experience is most definitely made up of the input coming from all of your senses, from your entire body, and from all the sensory sources and directions information can flow from to be available to you as an embodied being. This amazing process of consciousness is simply what your brain is built to do to create the experience of "you" so you can live and contribute your gifts to others and our world as a human being with all of your beautiful and amazing particularity and common humanity.

Recognizing this immensity of who we are as human beings has long been the subject of poets and artists. The poet Walt Whitman once wrote, "I am large, I contain multitudes."

So, another motivation for practice can be to reflect on the complexity and ingenuity of our human brains and bodies, including the top-down mechanisms for thoughts and perceptions to impact the body, and the bottom-up mechanisms for the body to impact the cognitive dimension of our being. Motivation might also come from a sense of wonder and mystery that the long body of your life story is with you and is constantly being woven into this moment's experience as part of the profound miracle of being human that appears in each moment of our lives.

Motivation: Be Happier, Healthier, and Wiser

Besides knowing you are powerfully "wired" and interconnected in mind, brain, and body so that you actually can do something about your anger, and knowing a bit about how that might work as "top down" and "bottom up" in your mind and body, more strong motivations for practice can be that the meditative experience of mindfulness, kindness, and compassion can have important positive effects on your health and well-being.

For example, positive feelings can result in a stronger immune system (Fredrickson 2009) and a cardiovascular system that is less reactive to the harmful effects of stress (Fredrickson and Levenson 1998). Positive feelings can also increase your sense of optimism and resourcefulness and your resistance against the damaging effects from painful experiences, including trauma (Fredrickson 2001; Fredrickson et al. 2000). And, very importantly, the positive experiences we are talking about here are *interior* experiences—unfolding in your own heart, mind, and body, moment by moment.

Barbara Fredrickson, a leading researcher in the field of positive emotions, identifies from her research the ten most common positive emotions: joy, gratitude, serenity, interest, hope, pride, amusement, inspiration, awe, and love (2009). Fredrickson has also found in her research that cultivating mindfulness can "sever the link between negative thoughts and negative emotions" (2009, 167.) In addition, cultivating the heartful qualities of kindness and compassion through meditation can help generate and promote many positive benefits such as increased self-acceptance, positive meaning, and greater trust of others (Fredrickson 2009, 197).

So, a motivation for your meditation could be that there is research support to suggest that meditation can help you grow and experience all the benefits increased positivity can bring to your life.

Motivation: Remember Why You Practice

To gain relief from pain and suffering and to connect with one's deep sense of meaning and purpose are two very common and excellent reasons to take up meditation and to continue a practice. Reflecting on these two important motivations can be a real help in those times of difficulty and doubt that come to anyone who meditates. Here is more about these motivations:

REMEMBER THE PAIN

When you don't want to practice a meditation or don't like something that is happening, it can be helpful simply to pause and remember why you are meditating in the first place. Perhaps beginning a meditation session with a brief, quiet, inner review of your motivation for practice could help. If you are experiencing suffering, or your anger is creating problems for you, a short acknowledgment of that and an expression of your desire to be free of this pain can be a powerful ally.

REFLECT MORE DEEPLY

Do you wish to be more present, or more loving, or more aware? Perhaps you wish to feel more peace, or be more generous, or to experience the wonder and awe present in so many moments in life. Recalling these aspirations that link to your deeper hopes and dreams about who and what you are and how you wish to be in your life can be a powerful support and inspiration to carry you through any difficult times you experience in your meditation journey.

HELPFUL TIPS FOR PRACTICING MINDFULNESS

When you begin to practice mindfulness, your experience of yourself and others will likely become very different. Sometimes this different experience can be shocking, but usually it is both a big relief and exciting. The relief and excitement come when you realize and experience directly the dimension of awareness available in this very moment, and the possibilities for more peace and a happier, more satisfying life that arise as you live more intentionally with increased awareness.

Here is a more detailed orientation—things you might notice and encounter—when inhabiting the dimension of mindfulness and compassion. I also provide some practical suggestions for building and sustaining a practice of meditation to help you dwell in that dimension more securely.

Things You Might Notice When Practicing Mindfulness

Mindfulness is not about doing anything. It is about "being, not doing," as we say in mindfulness-based stress reduction classes.

In this moment, practicing mindfulness simply means that you relax and pay attention without any agenda except to see, to know, and to better understand whatever you observe. Because we are all so used to doing things—planning, fixing, moving ahead, not stopping, and so on and so forth, the very idea of "being" and not "doing" may sound strange, even unappealing at first. Doing things is important certainly, but you have probably noticed how exhausting a lifestyle of constant busyness and doing can be.

So, it may help to remember that practicing mindfulness means you can relax and trust that what you need is already here. You can drop the agenda of having to fix anything, even yourself or your anger. In fact, when you are being mindful, you can drop any opinions you have about yourself (you don't have to uphold them, either!), and just observe what is happening in your mind and body, breath by breath.

When you begin to approach your experience mindfully, you will probably notice some very interesting things. In particular, you may become more aware of sensations and thoughts.

NOTICING SENSATIONS

Becoming mindful of emotions like anger can be as simple as paying closer attention to your body and noticing the sensations that are both present and changing in this moment. The practice here is to notice the *direct experience* of the sensation, not your thoughts and opinions about it.

For example, if you take a moment to notice the sensations of your body as you sit while reading this book, you will probably feel some points of contact, perhaps where your feet touch the floor or where your back rests against the chair. Or you may feel some sensations of heaviness, or vibration, or warmth or coolness in parts of your body.

Noticing sensations can be as simple as that. Just bring your attention back to the direct experience of sensation in your body. When you practice mindful breathing, for example, you let the sensations of your breath be the primary focus for your attention.

NOTICING THOUGHTS

Thoughts are just thoughts. This is a liberating revelation when you begin to practice mindfulness. Thoughts are not you, and they are not permanent. If your thoughts were all you were, then who would you be when the thoughts change? When those fans left the game and began thinking about their plans for the next day, if their identity was only what they thought about their team, then who was making the plans? Mindfulness is something you already have. Because of this natural mindfulness, you have very likely already experienced the fact that you can actually observe or know that you are having thoughts, at least some thoughts.

When you practice mindfulness, it is good to remember that thoughts are not your enemy. When practicing mindfulness, you treat thoughts just like anything else you notice—they are not more important and they are not less important. You don't have to control them in any way. It is enough to observe them, let them be, and let them go—just as you mindfully observe any other experience that appears in your awareness and flows into and out of the present moment.

NOTICING THAT EVERYTHING HAPPENS IN
THE PRESENT MOMENT

The present moment is where everything actually happens. The past is just a memory (either wanted or unwanted) that returns to visit in the present moment, and the future is just a simulation or imagined experience. Even when it is carefully plotted and planned, the future still has not happened yet.

When you practice mindfulness, you inhabit the vast territory of awareness, which is always here in the present moment. When you are being mindful, one of the new ways you discover of experiencing your life and seeing with new eyes things that are very familiar (like your breath sensations or angry feelings) is that you very quickly notice how these experiences, sensations, and thoughts are all changing and temporary. From the point of view of observing mindfully, everything you observe can be seen to be arising, changing, and passing out of the present moment.

Many people today have noticed they are not present for the important moments of their lives, often because they are distracted and absorbed into memories of the past or plans and worries about the future. Practicing mindfulness is a wonderful way to return to the present moment and to become totally available for all of the richness that is happening in the here and now.

When you are able to experience a deep shift in your own understanding about anger because you have actually watched angry feelings mindfully, seen them change, and observed how they move through and exit your field of awareness, always in the present moment, then the power of anger over you will be shaken deeply and permanently.

Some Practical Suggestions for Practicing Meditation

To help you get started, here are a few suggestions about practicing mindfulness meditation. You can use these anytime and anywhere—whether it is for a single breath or for much longer.

Posture: Take a comfortable position that supports your body and is upright and dignified, not slouching. Please remember, you are practicing to wake up, not go to (or remain) asleep!

Try to sit still, but if you have to reposition yourself, that is okay. Just pay careful attention as you change position, feeling the changing sensations in your body, and resume your original focus of attention when you are settled again. You can lie down too, if you need to.

You can be mindful as you move too. In that case, let the focus of your attention be on a repeating sensation, like the sensations in your feet as you walk or run, or in your arms if you are swimming.

Eyes: Your eyes can be open or closed. If you prefer to meditate with them open, I suggest you pick a focus and fix your gaze there, perhaps on a spot on the floor a few feet ahead of you. The main point is not to get caught up in looking around and distracting yourself. Of course, you can also practice with eyes closed.

Hands: Do something comfortable with your hands. It can help to let them rest, either with one holding the other gently or each resting on your lap.

Music, candles, and other "aids": I suggest you practice without these. It is too easy to be distracted by them, tranquilized by them, or to think they are essential to your mindfulness practice. They are not.

Drugs, alcohol, and prescribed medications: I suggest you refrain from taking any mind- or mood-altering chemicals that might affect your meditation practice, at least for the time you are practicing. If you take prescribed medications, try to schedule your meditation practice when the side effects of your medications are not likely to interfere. If you think you need recreational drugs or alcohol to "relax" to help you meditate, you are wrong. They will only delay or block the real benefits of mindfulness and meditation practice.

How long to practice and when: How long you make your formal session of meditation practice is really up to you. Just start where you are with the amount of time you can devote to the practice. It is important to make a commitment and to have some discipline. Aim for several formal meditation sessions each week. Most people find that beginning with fifteen or twenty minutes daily, or every other day, is a good place to start. You can extend the time or add more sessions as you like. When to practice usually depends on when you feel some energy and when you can have the time you need and not be interrupted. It can vary. Be flexible.

How to decide which practice to do each day: It is good to develop a practice routine that involves each of these elements: steadying attention on a particular focus; attention to your body and sense experience in addition to your thoughts; practices that help deepen the heartful qualities of compassion and kindness; and regular reflection on the insights your meditation has brought to you. It is also important, always, to practice without attachment to outcome.

So, a routine could be to focus on a practice that emphasizes a particular one of these elements—say kindness and compassion—for a period of time, say a week or a month, and then move to a different practice after that. Or, you could practice with briefer forms of two or more of the meditations during the same session of formal meditation. This might go like this: begin with a few minutes of a kindness or compassion meditation and move to a practice of mindfulness of breathing or mindful walking in the same thirty- or forty-five-minute meditation session. The time you work with a particular practice is up to you. Be sure to give yourself plenty of time for each practice, though, without judging anything. For example, you might stay with a particular routine of brief practices in each formal meditation session daily for one month and see what happens. Trust your own intelligence to guide you as you go.

Finding ongoing support for your practice: Most people find that having support for their practice is very important. Support can come in the form of other people to practice with, becoming part of a meditation community, using instructional or inspirational material from books or the Internet, and taking support from the fact that you have joined an ancient and rich community of human beings who have used meditation as a path to greater happiness and wisdom.

MEETING COMMON CHALLENGES IN MEDITATION

The take-home message so far, from ancient contemplative traditions and from modern health and neuroscience research, is simple: the deepest and most long-lasting benefits from meditation and mindfulness practices come only when you do the practice yourself. But when you actually sit down to practice and explore mindfulness and meditation, challenges will arise. It can help to know something in advance about what to expect from common challenges, doubts, and frustrations that are a part of everyone's meditation practice.

Recognize the Influence and Power of Negative Bias

Human beings are wired to selectively notice and remember threats. Scientists believe we are wired to remember negative experiences more easily than positive ones because it bestows an evolutionary advantage. For example, if you don't know the rustling sound in the bushes is a saber-toothed tiger, you could keep walking and that tiger might eat you. But if you managed to get away, there is a very good chance that the next time you hear the rustling sound, you will remember the tiger, and you definitely will not wait to see if it is something besides a tiger moving through those same bushes! You *will* remember the danger from your past experience. This selective preference for recognizing and remembering the negative or threatening experiences in our lives is called *negative bias*. Here are some modern, everyday examples of negative bias, also based in research:

- Learned feelings of helplessness, like when you think you have no control over a situation, are easy to gain but hard to undo (Seligman 2006).

- People will do more to avoid losing something than they will to gain something of similar worth (Baumeister et al. 2001).

- Learning something bad about someone carries more weight than good information about that person (Peeters and Czapinski 1990).

Because of the power of negative bias, it is very important for people who wish to control their anger and other strong emotions to learn to recognize when the negativity is present. It is also important to know it can happen quite often.

When negativity is present—as a feeling of fear or alarm, perhaps—it often appears as a memory of a threatening experience from the past, or a misperception that something happening now is like a threatening experience or situation from the past. When you notice the negativity that is present, that can be a very good time to ask yourself this question: Is it is only a memory, or is there something actually threatening me in this moment?

Not reacting or overidentifying with the negative thoughts and feelings can be a challenge when you practice mindfulness. But you don't have to become discouraged if, at times, you notice there seem to be more negative thoughts or memories than positive ones. If that happens, just notice the thoughts, sensations, and memories. Know the experience in that moment will eventually change. Whatever the thoughts or memories are, they are not your permanent identity.

Of course, no one can avoid losses or painful and difficult experiences in this life. They happen to everyone. It is the meaning we assign to them and the relationship we take to them as life continues to unfold that determines the power of the difficulties in our lives and the role they play in the intensity and frequency of our feelings of anger, ill will, and aversion.

Psychologists and other health scientists now recognize that the best remedy for managing negativity is not to try and forget it or to always distract ourselves from it. Instead, the best remedy is actually to be mindful of the negative and to turn toward those thoughts, feelings, or sensations with awareness and compassion. It also helps if you intentionally cultivate positive emotions like joy, gratitude, serenity, interest, awe, hope, pride, amusement, inspiration, and love—in your heart, mind, and in your actions—so that these experiences become part of you, right down to the circuits in your brain.

Notice with Compassion and Confidence When You're Angry

When practicing mindfulness, you can expect to notice very clearly the intense upset you feel when you are angry. In mindfulness-based stress reduction classes, we say, "It will probably get more stressful before it gets less stressful." Knowing in advance that any upset you feel could seem to be stronger or more intense as you become more mindful is very helpful as you begin to use the power of mindfulness to reclaim your life from the toxic impact of anger, ill will, and aversion.

Whenever you feel angry, it is actually okay, especially if you can be more mindful about having the feeling. It is not a failure if you feel angry. It is not a failure or a form of weakness if you feel uncomfortable or upset. And it is not a failure if you don't feel anything at all. It is just the way it is. Can you notice that? Whatever "that" is? Can you practice bringing the attitudes of patience and nonjudgment and kindness and compassion to yourself no matter what you are feeling?

Understanding exactly how deep the habit energy of anger and judgment is can help you. Noticing if you tend to be critical of just about everything from how your boss treats you to the clothes your kids choose to wear to the color of your neighbor's fence could be a signal to pause. Noticing when anger and irritation are present is a vital step to transforming these feelings and finding more peace and happiness in your life.

The more often you notice the presence and disturbance of anger, the more often you are likely to be able to do something to transform the disturbing emotions. And the more often you notice anger in yourself, the more likely you are to notice it in others and be able to offer them compassion and understanding, instead of more angry judgments.

Cultivate a Sense of Safety as You Practice

One of the most challenging aspects of mindfulness practice can be meeting and overcoming the old habits of fear in mind and body. Because these habits are so deep (aided by the natural tendency toward negative bias), having some practical ways to nurture and strengthen a sense of safety in and around you as you practice can be extraordinarily helpful.

Without realizing it, you could be operating in the world from a deep perspective of not feeling safe, or of not trusting that you could be safe. In some of my classes, people have told me they have never felt safe in their lives, and they don't want to get "too relaxed" because they believe they will be too vulnerable.

If they look more deeply at the question "What are you afraid of?" they frequently find they are afraid of not being in control. The next helpful question is why do you need to be in control? When they listen more deeply to their inner wisdom about that, they often touch some stored, perhaps long-carried, sense of danger or hurt that is now awake in the present moment and is close by, easily coloring the present-moment experience.

Learning to bring mindfulness, kindness, and compassion to interior experiences of danger or nonsafety is very important. What is revealed in mindful attention can also help you take practical steps to feel safer in your life, in your daily routines, and in your relationships.

It is also very helpful if you let your growing awareness of any sense of danger energize your curiosity about what is happening inside of you, and use your learning to move beyond the deeply held sense of danger. For example, being mindful and turning toward any felt sense of inner unease or danger, you might ask yourself questions like these: "What am I afraid of if I meditate?" "What am I afraid of in my life?" "Is this really something I should be afraid of?" "Am I in danger in this moment?"

Don't get too analytical. Just ask your question and listen mindfully for your own inner voice to respond. You could be surprised by what it has to say! And, if you are truly in danger, protect yourself.

Expect Your Mind to Wander

This challenge is easily met if you begin your meditation already knowing your mind will wander, and not fighting it or criticizing yourself when your mind does move away from your chosen focus for attention. Instead, you might be grateful when you notice your mind has wandered or filled with thoughts, and be grateful you could notice that and that you have a mind at all! It helps if you can remember that mindfulness practice is not about controlling your thoughts. Instead, it is about knowing something about what your thoughts are as well as what else is happening in your mind and body in this moment.

Meet Desire with Wisdom

It is human nature to want things to be different when some part of us doesn't like how they are. Practicing mindfulness has a very practical side to it. If what is here causes you harm or puts you in danger, definitely do what you can to be safe. But this is usually not the case for most people. What is more likely is that they are experiencing some discomfort or upset, in their body or their thoughts or a combination, and a part of their mind demands that they change things.

A common challenge in mindfulness practice is to recognize this inner demand for changing what is here ("If those noisy people next door would just be quiet, I could meditate!") or for indulging the inner plan to make things better ("If I just got up and got something to eat, it would be better!")—and to let it be. Just watch the demanding thoughts, without fighting them or yielding to them. Just watch, and see how they change. What happens next? They will change. You may find that you don't have to change the world, but you can change your reactions to the world—and that is where you can find peace and ease.

KEEP IN MIND

- As you actually experience mindfulness through personal practice, and taste for yourself the accessibility and richness of meditation, you will give yourself the direct experience—and the understanding and wisdom that follows—that various meditation teachers and modern research point to.

- You can see for yourself, by practicing meditations that nurture mindfulness, kindness, and compassion, that you do have the power to radically alter your view of yourself and others, and to empower yourself to heal and transform your life in ways that align much more closely with your deepest values and purpose.

practices for calming

your angry mind

CHAPTER 5

calming your angry mind by stabilizing mind and body

Look deeply. Don't miss the inherent quality and value of everything.

—*Marcus Aurelius*

Taking a view from the present moment can be very helpful if you wish to learn better ways to control anger and other strong emotions. This view, centered in the present moment, begins with recognizing that anything that happens, happens in the present moment. Your thoughts, the sensations and feelings in your body, even intense emotions like anger—which is a combination of thoughts and bodily sensations—always arise, unfold, and fade into and out of the present moment. Even when you are remembering or "reliving" the past, or planning for the future, those thoughts, associations, and emotions arise, change, and move into and out of this moment, enabled by the ever-changing neural activity and patterns in your brain and the related physical responses in your body.

The fate of anger, like the fate of your thoughts and other experiences of mind and body, depends directly upon other conditions in the present moment that either sustain the angry feelings or not. For example, if you are waiting in line and become impatient with the speed of the check-out person, your anger is likely to grow and continue in direct proportion to the degree that you keep sulking and judging inside, repeating the tirade of angry thoughts and words about each person around you. Fueled by such angry thoughts, your upset and suffering will grow even as you advance steadily toward the check-out counter.

Mindfulness of the entire melodrama of anger that your ego-mind unfolds during the check-out process can help you realize a basic truth: in any situation, you will remain angry for as long as you remain caught in the river of angry thoughts and sensations and continue to feed them with more angry thoughts and feelings. And, since it is so easy at times to be swept away by the stream of physical reactions and reactive angry thinking that follows even the slightest provocation, learning to recognize the presence of angry energy in your body and mind, and knowing how to step out of the stream of reactions and disentangle yourself from your old mind-body habits of thinking and acting in ways that keep anger going becomes a crucial, even life-saving, skill.

The five meditation practices in this chapter are designed to help you build and strengthen the skills you need to pause, steady yourself, and rest in your natural capacity for awareness and equanimity even when the storm of anger threatens to carry you away. For each practice, you will find instructions for a brief version and for more extended ones. You will see that these meditations can easily be done for longer periods of time as formal meditations, and they can also be integrated in the flow of your daily life and its unfolding situations in easy and practical ways.

What "brief" means and what "extended" means is entirely up to you. For example, you could give yourself fifteen or twenty minutes to practice—or maybe thirty minutes, or forty-five or more, if you like. There is no "best" length of time. Every practice period can be fruitful, even if it doesn't seem that way at first. See for yourself.

You cannot make a mistake or do anything "wrong" in these meditations. Try them out, and try them on. If you sincerely wish better control over the anger in your life, then the only mistake you could possibly make would be not to experience the practices at all!

MEDITATION PRACTICE #1:
Using the Brake of Mindfulness

Your natural capacity for noticing—what we could call your "natural" mindfulness—is always there for you, and it can be a powerful "brake" on the runaway train of anger.

We often long for a simpler life, and to rest in the space and stillness that allows us to touch and know our inner rhythms and the world around us more intimately and more authentically. Uncontrolled anger can frustrate us and keep us from realizing this deep longing for peace and ease as well as from the experience of a deeper connection with ourselves and the world.

Bringing this practice into your life could help you rediscover the vast landscape of awareness always waiting to add a new dimension to living. Perhaps your entry into this dimension is as close as your next mindful moment.

BRIEF PRACTICE #1

When you notice that you feel angry, irritable, or upset in any way, remember to stop and step back. Trust yourself to recognize what is happening, and trust that your own mindfulness is already here and ready to help you. You don't have to judge yourself for having the feeling, whatever it is. Instead you can practice the qualities of patience and nonjudging toward yourself and any feelings of anger or upset.

Remember that bringing mindfulness to what is happening can literally mean stepping out of (or away from) the situation you are in for a few moments. Or it can simply mean shifting your attention on purpose—without leaving the situation—to your own body, to breath sensations or to sounds, and taking a few mindful moments for yourself.

Trust yourself to know how to proceed, and shift your attention mindfully into this moment. Relaxing, pausing, and gently observing. Watching and knowing the feeling of sensations in your body, watching and knowing you are hearing sounds, watching and listening to any thoughts you are having. Watching and knowing they are happening, and—with patience and generosity of spirit—letting all of these experiences and sensory impressions simply be, and letting them go, at least for a few mindful breaths.

Pay careful attention, gently and patiently, as you observe—perhaps noticing how the thoughts and feelings are constantly changing, allowing yourself to notice any changes in your sense of connection or how you feel when you bring your attention back to the situation and context you began with.

EXTENDED PRACTICE #1

As a Longer Formal Meditation

Use longer periods of meditation practice to build your skills of intention, attention, and the attitude of welcoming and letting things be as they are.

Commit to practice mindfulness every day for a few minutes or longer when you will not be disturbed, and begin by choosing a focus for your attention and resting there. Your focus could be sounds, or the changing sensations of your body, or your changing breath sensations.

For the time of your meditation, relax and allow yourself to simply notice your experience without having to fix anything or make anything happen. Cultivate increasing sensitivity and careful observation of anything that happens, also noticing how the sounds, sensations, thoughts, and feelings—indeed, everything coming through your senses—is here for a while and moves on, and how the next experience replaces it.

Anytime you feel lost or confused, or nothing much is happening, gently return attention to your chosen focus.

Let your observing be supported and infused with the qualities of friendliness to what you notice and of patience whenever your mind comments or something distracts you. Remember that the comments of your mind are only more thoughts that are changing, and in this meditation, you can watch or listen to them without adding anything new. Let them be, and let them go, like everything else.

Into Daily Life

At different times throughout your day, take a few minutes to pause and be still. Relax and remember you don't have to do anything in those minutes. Your practice is simply being present and noticing what is happening. It could be as simple as pausing for a single mindful breath and noticing how that feels moving in and out of your body—or noticing sensations in another part of your body, or sounds around you, or the play of light and color as you look around.

It can be challenging, but also especially rewarding, to pause and notice when the situation is intense or when you are feeling angry, irritable, or upset in some way.

If it helps, in challenging or stressful moments, put your attention on a specific focus, like sounds or your body sensations, or your breathing sensations, remembering that this is an awareness practice—not a breathing exercise. Trust your body to breathe naturally as you watch and feel each sensation, not having to control your breathing in any way.

When you notice something has pulled your attention off of your focus—a feeling or a distracting thought or judgment for instance—it is okay. You have not made a mistake. Keep watching. If you feel lost or if nothing else seems to be calling you, gently return your attention to your chosen focus. Let patience and trust, and a sense of curiosity and respect for and about your life, energize you as you pause and notice mindfully throughout the day.

MEDITATION PRACTICE #2:
Experience Presence and Well-Being with Mindful Breathing

Your mind and body are very smart, and they work together beautifully because they are actually not separated but deeply interconnected and dynamically interactive, moment by moment.

Together your mind and body know how to generate feelings of ease and well-being to balance the physical and mental intensities of the freeze-fight-or-flight stress reaction. An important skill for self-care and for personal stress management is knowing how to signal your mind and body to shift into feelings of ease and well-being, to relax and calm down. From the foundation of greater ease, your capacity for seeing clearly and experiencing a greater degree of presence in each moment greatly increases.

And, when practicing or beginning a session of meditation, it can help to remind yourself of those core attitudes of mindfulness practice—not striving and not judging. When practicing to promote ease and well-being, and to experience greater awareness and presence, the paradox is that it will go much better if you stop trying to "make yourself relax" or "do" anything. Simply stopping and noticing, being mindful, and allowing what is happening to happen will be the clearest signal to your mind and body that they can generate ease and well-being on their own.

Mindful breathing is not only about ease. It is, perhaps more importantly, about being present, about experiencing presence—awake, open, aware, sensing, and unshakably here, now. Let this meditation—mindful breathing—help you discover these dimensions of ease and presence.

BRIEF PRACTICE #2

Whenever you like, stop and take a few moments to be still and to be mindful.

You can begin by setting a kind intention—saying something to yourself like "With this meditation, I am practicing stopping, relaxing, and being present with awareness."

Then, taking a comfortable position, pause, letting yourself drop into awareness, and gently place your attention on the changing sensations of your body. Not getting caught up in thoughts or names of the regions of the body or the parts of your body, just relaxing and feeling the experience of being in your body.

As you gather awareness in your body, when you are ready, sharpen your attention more precisely to a focus on the sensations of your body breathing. Trusting that your body knows how to breathe, let it continue its life-sustaining in-breaths and out-breaths as you bring a sharper focus of attention to the place or places where you are able to feel the breath sensations most easily.

Your focus for attention on your breath could be at the tip of your nose or your mouth, or the places where your chest expands and contracts, or the changing sensations as your abdomen rises and falls. There is no right or wrong way to pay attention to your breath. Wherever you can feel your own breath most easily as it comes and goes is the place to relax and rest your attention.

When your mind wanders, it is okay. You have not made a mistake. Noticing that your mind is caught up in thinking, just smile, letting the thoughts be, letting them go, and patiently bring your attention back to this breath—unfolding now. What is here? Is it the in-breath or the out-breath, or the space between?

Letting the breath come to you, letting the meditation support you, practice this mindful breathing for as long as you like. Noticing the experience in mind and body that arises as your practice, allow that to support and inform you as well.

EXTENDED PRACTICE #2

As a Longer Formal Meditation

You may wish to explore the power of mindful breathing using longer periods of formal meditation.

In these longer sessions, remember that you are practicing "being, not doing" and that when something distracts or thoughts become upset or demanding, it helps to let all of that be, just noticing, and bringing attention back to the breath sensations in your body. Letting the breath sensations be a kind of anchor, or safe harbor to return to, time and again, to rest your attention and to notice what is present.

It is also very helpful to remember that everything that is happening, actually flows into, through, and out of the present moment. As you establish mindfulness by paying attention to your breathing and by returning to the sensations of the breathing softly and with patience, you may find yourself noticing more acutely this ever-changing flow of experience through the present moment.

Into Daily Life

It can be very helpful and informative to extend mindful breathing practices into the different moments and situations of your daily life.

This can be as simple as remembering or reminding yourself to take a mindful breath (or several!) at different times throughout the day.

For example, sitting in a vehicle as driver or passenger, come back to breathing mindfully at a stoplight or traffic snarl. Or, before opening your email or answering a phone call, take a single mindful breath, or maybe two. Or, before speaking in a meeting, or in a conversation, pause and breathe mindfully for a few breaths. Or, between bites of your food at a meal, or before taking the first bite, pause and take a mindful breath.

The opportunities for mindful breathing are as diverse and numerous as the moments and situations arising daily. You breathe anyway, so why not become more mindful of it? What might happen differently and what might you notice if you add some mindful breathing each day to the unfolding tapestry that is your life?

MEDITATION PRACTICE #3: *Discover and Embrace Embodiment with Mindfulness*

While your body is always living in the present moment, your mind may be spending a lot of its time someplace else. Perhaps it is occupied with remembering or regretting the past, or planning, worrying, or even feeling angry about something that might happen in the future. By learning to return your attention to and sustain mindful attention on your body in a kind and curious way, you can regain access to the present moment anytime your attention has moved away from here and now.

Noticing where your mind has gone, and returning to the present moment can be very useful for you too, if you wish to calm your angry mind. For example, instead of becoming lost in angry or upsetting thoughts and worries, or continuing a battle with your body and criticizing it (how it looks or what condition it's in) and then voicing negative judgments about all of that, you can choose instead to practice mindfulness of your body, just as it is right now.

You will find that you can practice mindfulness of your body in any activity. You can practice mindfulness of your body when it is still or moving, in any position, and in any situation.

Becoming more mindful of your body immediately changes your relationship with your body and the experience of living in a body. You might even find that learning to inhabit your body with awareness is an important element for overall healing and self-care, for growing emotional intelligence, and for building a richer and happier life. Bring the simple meditation on mindfulness of your body (below) into your life, and see for yourself.

BRIEF PRACTICE #3

Take a few minutes to pause and bring attention directly to the sensations and feelings arising in your body.

Helpful attitudes you might bring to this noticing are nonjudging and nonstriving—not trying to fix or change anything. The helpful attitudes include a sense of curiosity and patience for what you notice, and trust in yourself that you are actually capable of noticing what is happening.

As your attention on your body sensations and the parts and regions of your body becomes more steady, allow your attention to be suffused with feelings of friendliness and perhaps even gratitude that your body functions as well as it does—whatever that may be. Let your attention be flexible enough and big enough to include all of the sensations coming to you, ever-changing and flowing into and out of this moment.

Your focus of attention could be wide and include all the sensations in all the parts and regions of your body, noticing how different parts and regions feel and sensations shift, breath by breath and moment by moment, and how the sensations come and go from the different places in your body.

Or you could narrow your focus of attention to a particular part or region of your body, and look more deeply at the nature of sensations right there. Is there a feeling of solidness or heaviness? Is there warmth or coolness? Is the sensation contracted or gripping, or expansive and softening? How long is the sensation here? How does the sensation you are feeling change?

When your body is moving—walking, for example—what do you feel? Where are the strongest sensations? In your feet? Your legs? Where?

What are you feeling, and where is that sensation, when you are sitting? When you are lying down? When you are standing?

When your thoughts about your body (or anything else) become loud, just smile and let them go or let them be. Patiently return attention to the direct experience of the sensations you are feeling in your body, and follow the coming and going of the sensations, of what you are feeling in your body, as the feelings are happening.

EXTENDED PRACTICE #3

As a Longer Formal Meditation

Give yourself a longer period of formal meditation to discover the depth of embodiment and the power of mindfulness more fully.

Take a comfortable position in a place where and when you will probably not be disturbed for the time of your meditation, and relax as you drop into awareness.

If you like, begin by choosing a region of your body, perhaps the top of your head and, every few breaths, move your attention systematically—pausing, noticing, and breathing mindfully in each region—as you proceed from your head down through the rest of your body. Move from the head to the neck and shoulders, the back and arms, the chest, and on through your abdomen, pelvis, legs, and feet, just noticing more systematically the sensations in each region of your body. No matter what is happening, observe and let it go, and then, after a few breaths, move onto the next region, noticing, welcoming, and allowing whatever sensations are there simply to be. In this practice, keep moving your attention into and out of each region—lingering and observing for several breaths, then moving on.

When you have moved mindfully through your entire body, you can end your meditation, or you can go back through some or all of the regions again.

Alternatively, as a longer formal meditation on embodiment, you can choose walking meditation. One way to do mindful walking meditation is to place your focus on the changing sensations in your feet as you walk. It can be helpful, at least at first, to walk slowly so that you can focus more easily on the changing sensations, keeping attention receptive and open to the changing stream of feelings and sensations as you lift, step, and place each foot with each step in your walking meditation. Notice and let go of any thoughts that come as well, and gently return attention to the focus on the flow of sensations in your feet whenever your attention goes someplace else. You can practice formal walking meditation by going back and forth on an outdoor path several steps long, or in a room in your house or office, walking slowly and mindfully across the room and back. Pause at the end of the path, wherever you are walking, and notice the sensations of standing. When you are ready, turn and step mindfully forward.

How you practice is totally up to you. See for yourself what each approach reveals. You can practice and explore either approach—the steady noticing of each and all sensations in walking meditation, or the more systematic approach of deliberately moving attention through your body at rest and observing sensations in particular regions.

Into Daily Life

Practice extending mindfulness of your body into daily life by noticing what is happening in your body throughout the day and night, and in different situations and activities.

Tuning mindfully and steadily into the flow of sensations as you are moving or walking, or tuning in to a particular part or region of your body when you notice sensations there—either of these approaches can be as simple as paying attention on purpose, and be willing to observe and allow what you are feeling, for at least a few breaths, before you move or act on the sensations you feel.

It can be interesting and rewarding to practice walking mindfully anytime you walk to get someplace. You don't have to slow down; just place attention on the sensations of walking as you feel them in your body, and let yourself notice what happens when you come out of the busy mind (or the angry mind!) and connect with what is happening and present in this moment of your life.

Practice whenever you like, you don't even need much time. In any moment, there is power in mindfully tuning into your experience of embodiment—even for the time of a single mindful step or a single mindful breath.

And in those times of angry mind, of ill will and aversion, connecting with the sensations and feelings in your body when you feel upset, angry, or irritated can be especially revealing and grounding, and can help you disentangle from those challenging emotions and reactions.

MEDITATION PRACTICE #4:
Finding the Courage to Let It Be

As human beings, we are wired so powerfully to survive that experiencing painful thoughts or sensations in our bodies can activate strong reactions of aversion and a burning desire to escape from or to change what is happening in this moment. Of course, you should change what you can when you are able and when there is a real threat. But how often is that urge to change something so strong that the urge itself causes irritation and upset? And many times your ability to change things is very limited or even nonexistent.

This meditation offers a way to step out of that very rapid and reactive cycle of aversion and frustration in your mind and body that often arises when you realize there is nothing more you can do to change a situation. In meditation, by drawing on your natural capacity for mindfulness, and resting upon the heartful qualities of courage and acceptance, you can access your capacity for equanimity, the capacity to allow things to be the way they are, at least for the time of the meditation.

It can take some real courage and faith that you won't be harmed or destroyed if you stop resisting and make room, notice, look deeper, and allow the pain and upset present in a given moment to be as it is. And be prepared—your doubting mind uses fear and memories of past pain, failures, and disappointments to try and scare you away from stopping and looking deeply.

But by trusting yourself and having faith that you have what it takes, as you rest in the stillness and pause moment by moment in mindful noticing, you can find that it actually is possible to feel the strength of courage, acceptance, and equanimity supporting your entire being. Quite possibly you can find support for both the faith that you will not be destroyed by angry or fearful thoughts and feelings—and the realization that your faith has been rewarded. The empowerment you gain from that realization cannot be taken from you.

BRIEF PRACTICE #4

If you find yourself in the midst of angry feelings or caught in an inner narrative of angry thoughts—steaming, sulking, judgmental—about anyone or anything, take a moment to pause and step back. Immediately take a few mindful breaths where you are or take some mindful steps as you walk. Notice the thoughts and sensations in your body, including doubts and fears, and trust—have faith— that you have all you need to stay present with the upset and notice it mindfully.

When you are able, give yourself some protected time and space, and set an intention to use these feelings of anger and ill will to help you grow and nourish the positive qualities of wisdom, strength, and courage, remembering that courage does not always mean the absence of fear but can be the capacity to stand firm in the face of fear.

Take a comfortable position and bring attention mindfully into your body. Focus mindful attention on your breathing for a few breaths.

Allow any angry thoughts or painful memories to return, and notice them as you breathe mindfully. Practice patience and acceptance, trusting yourself.

Remember as you practice that peace does not always mean the absence of unpleasant or unwanted thoughts or experiences. Instead, it relies on the qualities of mind and heart that can make room for, rather than reject, those very experiences here with you in this moment. Trust that you have what you need already.

And, as you continue to breathe mindfully and to notice and include your thoughts, feelings, and body sensations, remember as you practice that nonjudging can be as simple as noticing when judgments are present, and noticing how your body feels in that moment, and allowing what you are noticing to be just as it is.

Breathe mindfully and notice inner resistance of any kind—kindly and patiently making room for it, knowing that the resistance is also a form of suffering, breathing mindfully and compassionately. Perhaps observing directly that the resistance you feel is only a combination of thoughts and the body sensations that arise with those thoughts. Noticing any sense of gripping or hardening in your body, breathe mindfully and observe. Can you feel when that gripping and hardening begins to soften? Keep watching. Notice and allow yourself to feel the qualities of mindfulness, the strength of courage, and the deepening of faith in your capacity to hold and understand even the most difficult inner experiences.

EXTENDED PRACTICE #4

As a Longer Formal Meditation

Give yourself a longer period of protected time and space to practice mindfulness and explore the qualities of courage, acceptance, and equanimity.

Begin by taking a comfortable position and putting attention on the sensations of your breathing. Practice relaxing and trusting—trusting your body to breathe naturally and relaxing into your innate capacity to notice mindfully the unfolding experience in mind and body, breath by breath.

Just rest in the noticing, breathing mindfully and including all thoughts, feelings, and sensations in awareness. Allowing every thought, every feeling, and every sensation to appear, to reveal itself, and to come and go in its own time. No need to do anything about any of them. Nothing to fix. Nothing that needs changing or improving. Just letting all of your experience come and go, with each in-breath and each out-breath.

With each breath and each rise and release of sensations, thoughts, and feelings, let yourself know that your inner wisdom and courage, and your capacity to experience these depths of intelligence and heart, are not imaginary but can become realized in direct experience, in this moment.

Into Daily Life

Pause for a few moments from time to time to be still and notice your inner life.

If it helps, steady yourself in the present moment with a few mindful breaths.

Practice noticing, including, and patiently allowing whatever is happening in your body sensations or your thoughts, especially if it is painful, upsetting, or unpleasant. Breathing mindfully with it, and watching and listening deeply, even for a few breaths. Explore and rely upon the qualities of courage and faith that you will not be harmed by these experiences, breathe with the contents present in each moment mindfully and look more closely, allowing yourself to relax and soften as you observe. Can you notice how everything changes? Do you see any connections between the thoughts in your mind and the sensations arising and changing in your body?

Trust that you have what it takes to create a different relationship—in this very moment—to any pain and difficult feelings and thoughts that inevitably arise in your inner life, and to befriend and transform them.

MEDITATION PRACTICE #5:
The Antidote to Fear

As we have seen, beneath anger is very often a strong and unpleasant feeling of fear. Once you know this about the essential structure of anger, you can learn to address the feeling of fear much more directly.

One powerful meditation practice to balance feelings of fear is loving-kindness meditation. Loving-kindness meditation is basically the practice of resting in your natural human capacity for kindness, friendliness, and compassion, and using that as the foundation for shifting out of your isolating and painful mental tendencies to live in "stories" of judgment, criticism, and ill will.

Legend has it that the Buddha taught loving-kindness meditation to his monks and nuns as the "antidote to fear." Modern psychology, especially the field of positive psychology, has shown a correlation between meditation practices based in loving-kindness and better outcomes of health, happiness, and overall well-being.

There are many different meditation practices for cultivating loving-kindness and compassion. They are universal qualities, available to each human being. Use this meditation to explore loving-kindness (sometimes also called "great friendliness") practice for yourself, especially as a means of stabilizing yourself in the present moment during a storm of anger or rage, or facing the challenges of a fearful situation or frightening person.

BRIEF PRACTICE #5

Take some time for a brief formal meditation period—it could be less than a minute, or longer if you like.

Take a comfortable position that supports your body and promotes awakening and alertness, and put your attention on your breathing for a few mindful breaths.

When you are ready, imagine that you are surrounded by one or more of those who love you. They could be people or animals who love you. Or, if you prefer, you could imagine that you are surrounded by nature's wonder and beauty, such as witnessing a gorgeous sunset, walking in a field of summer flowers, standing by a waterfall, or gazing upon a majestic mountain.

Let the warm feelings and power of the beauty you feel in your image fill you. Allow yourself to feel and rest in any feelings of love and affection your image offers you. You do not have to worry about how much love you feel, or get caught in the story of the people or animals in the image. Just rest in the image you have chosen, feel what you feel, and trust that you already have everything you need for this meditation.

If it is easier, another approach into the feelings of loving-kindness is to remember a time when a loved one or dear friend was leaving on a trip and you wished your dear one well with these same feelings of kindness and love. "Have a safe trip," you might have said. "Enjoy yourself!" "Have a great time!"

Continuing to rest in the feelings of love, beauty, and affection from either of these images, now imagine speaking to yourself with the same great friendliness and well-wishing you gave to your friend before his or her trip, or the same feelings you had being seen and surrounded by loved ones or nature's beauty.

Open yourself to the possibility that you can be your own best friend and can wish yourself well. Practice befriending and wishing yourself well by gently repeating a kind and compassionate phrase or phrases to yourself. You might say something like "May I be safe. May I be happy. May I live with ease. May I be filled with peace. May I take care of my anger and fear with compassion and ease."

Relax and breathe mindfully with your phrases and any feelings or thoughts that come up. When your mind wanders, gently bring it back and return to the loving-kindness phrase or phrases that resonate most deeply and truly for you.

Notice and include any feelings or thoughts that arise in this meditation—even upsetting ones—and hold them with kindness and compassion as well, maintaining gentleness and patience with yourself.

EXTENDED PRACTICE #5

As a Longer Formal Meditation

Give yourself a longer time period and one protected from interruption, and take a comfortable position.

Begin by gathering attention in your body and breathing mindfully for a few breaths.

When you are ready, shift attention to a loved one and wish that one well, using phrases that resonate, phrases that wish happiness, peace, health and well-being, and safety. Feel free to develop your own phrases, and pay attention to the ones that resonate most deeply and truly for you. Pausing for a few breaths between phrases, and breathing mindfully, let yourself feel the energy of loving-kindness present within you.

Explore what it is like to send loving-kindness to different types of people during your meditation. Send loving-kindness to teachers and mentors, to loved ones, to those you don't know well, and to those you don't even like! Keep watching and including any reactions. In this meditation, you don't have to "feel good." And the other person doesn't have to "feel good" either. You have no control over others or how they feel. This meditation is about cultivating an open and generous heart, and feelings of friendliness in yourself. It is not about controlling anything or anyone.

What is important is to have the intention and to cultivate the feelings of loving-kindness. You will probably find that with different types of people you will notice a variety of different feelings arising. No problem! Just continue sending each one kindness with the phrases you have chosen. When you are ready, move to the next type of person—a mentor or teacher, loved one, friend, one you don't know well, or a difficult person.

Try expanding your vision and focus to include others far and wide. Whatever makes sense to you is worth trying. It could be everyone in your town. Or all those living in your country or in the world. It could include all animals, or all plants, or the earth, or any living thing you like. Relax and let yourself be surprised at the depth and breadth of your own heart.

Don't forget to include yourself. Experiment with beginning the meditation with yourself and with ending with yourself. Notice any feelings of sadness or unworthiness, or anger or guilt, or anything else, and have compassion and kindness for the pain. Remember that you are just as worthy of being loved as anyone or anything else.

Into Daily Life

In different situations, quietly focus your attention on another person and send that person loving-kindness using your favorite phrase or phrases. Remember, you cannot control the fate or happiness of others. This meditation is about changing your heart and mind and how you are in ongoing relationship to others and to the world.

KEEP IN MIND

- The five meditation practices in this chapter are designed to help you build and strengthen the skills you need to pause, steady yourself, and rest in your natural capacity for awareness and equanimity even when the storm of anger threatens to carry you away. They are not the only meditations that can help you this way, but they are a good place to begin.

- Practicing mindfulness can help you apply the brakes to anger, find ease and more peace, discover the miracle of embodiment, realize your courage and strength, and unlock your unlimited capacity for understanding through kindness and compassion.

- You can practice these meditations in brief forms, as longer formal meditations, and by extending them into the changing moments and situations of your daily life and relationships. You already have all you need to practice these meditations because you already have the foundation of human intelligence and goodness in you—even if you don't always feel intelligent or good! So, you can relax and try these meditations on and try them out. See for yourself what power they hold for helping to your calm your angry mind and to transform your life!

CHAPTER 6

calming your angry mind with compassion

In this life we cannot do great things. We can only do small things with great love.

—*Mother Teresa*

Have you ever had the experience of witnessing the pain of a perfect stranger and feeling moved to help them? Most people have. Or, most certainly you have had the experience of hearing about the pain of a loved one or a friend and rushing immediately to do something to help. *Compassion* is the human quality, part of that innate goodness of heart we all have, that recognizes the pain of another and gives rise to the urge to do something to relieve that pain.

THE SCIENCE OF COMPASSION

Interestingly enough, we human beings have brains and nervous systems that are selectively "wired" for this quality of compassion. We have "circuits" formed by connections between specific neurons and regions in our brains that support a key dimension of our emotional life known as "social intuition" (Davidson 2012). We also evolved neural and psychological systems as human beings in order to nurture children, bond with mates, and hold together in community with others (Goetz, Keltner, and Simon-Thomas 2010). And, research reveals a core network of connections in the middle and lower regions of our brains that appear to integrate multiple social and emotional capabilities, and this network is stimulated by the emotional tone of important relationships (Siegel 2007).

But it is just as important to be compassionate toward yourself as it is toward others. Extending compassion to yourself by practicing "self-compassion" is very good for your physical and mental health because it can lower stress hormones, strengthen resilience, and reduce toxic self-criticism (Neff 2011).

The meditations in this chapter are devoted to helping you explore your innate capacity to access, experience, and nurture compassion. Compassion is not a quality to idealize or project into some future moment, rather compassion can be a response in any moment to the pain, confusion, and suffering in another or in you.

Turning to compassion can be relatively simple, and it does not require you to become a saint or to become somehow better than you already are. As you approach the meditations focused on compassion, it can be very helpful to have faith and to remember that you already have all you need to be compassionate. Compassion is a basic human quality that can be developed, nurtured, and refined. These meditations, even when practiced as a mindful and compassionate moment or a single phrase of well-wishing, have the power to nurture and deepen the process of growing compassion in your life.

Nurturing compassion—the heart's response of steadiness and embrace of pain, including anger, fear, and hurt arising in others or ourselves—can be challenging. Choosing compassion as a response in the present moment, although difficult at times, is definitely possible, and is usually a matter of learning to penetrate or let go of any confusion that keeps you from feeling and reconnecting with the powerful force of compassion already within.

We are focusing on compassion practices as a crucial resource for you to use to control your anger because the practice of compassion has been recognized by ancient meditation and spiritual teachings as well as modern science as a profound vehicle for transformation and enjoyment of healthier, happier lives. By practicing compassion, you actually activate systems in your brain and body that help you move from old habit energies and patterns of self-centeredness, isolation, and loneliness (all of which act to fuel feelings of anger, and in turn are fueled by that anger) to a more expanded, and more accurate, perception of your connections with others, and related feelings of well-being arising from those connections. This expanded view and more generous feeling within you serves to broaden and build your capacity and resources for staying present with less anger and rejection, a more open heart, and more mercy for the pain of others and the world.

The five meditation practices in this chapter are designed to help you explore the power and strength of a heart enlivened by compassion, a heart that is becoming more tender and merciful. Just as in the previous chapter, for each of these meditation practices, you will find instructions for a brief version and for more extended versions. You will see that these meditations can easily be extended for longer periods of time as formal meditations, and they can also be extended in easy and practical ways to help you explore the dimension of kindness and compassion in the flow of your daily life with its changing relationships and situations.

MEDITATION PRACTICE #6:
Discover the Power of Self-Compassion

In exploring meditative practices focused on compassion, we will begin with self-compassion simply because many researchers and psychologists agree that most people tend to be their own worst critics. Tendencies to be self-critical not only are harmful to your health, they also contribute to inaccurate and distorted views of yourself as not worthy or valuable. Views that deny your inherent goodness and worth as a human being can be ripe ground to grow and sustain chronic and destructive feelings of anger and fear as well as distorted perceptions of others.

In her pioneering research, Dr. Kristin Neff has established self-compassion as a field of study and the practice of self-compassion as crucial to living a happier and more productive life. Dr. Neff describes self-compassion as being composed of three core components: *self-kindness*, which involves actively comforting ourselves when we feel pain; *common humanity*, which is the recognition of our connection with others—including the reality that all living things experience pain, aging, sickness, and death; and *mindfulness*, which she emphasizes is the capacity to "hold our experience in balanced awareness, rather than ignoring our pain or exaggerating it" (2011, 41).

You can investigate the experience of compassion for yourself with this meditation practice. Remember, you already have all you need (even if you don't think you do or don't believe you are worthy of compassion!), and you cannot make a mistake. All you need is to try, remain mindful, and let yourself be open and learn from anything that happens from the practice. Let whatever you notice guide and inform you.

BRIEF PRACTICE #6

When you notice you are experiencing unpleasant feelings—perhaps in your body, as painful sensations; in your mind, as worried or anxiously repeating thoughts; or in your heart, as the heaviness of sorrow or the heat of anger—when you notice these, or any other pain or distress within, as soon as you can, pause and give yourself a few minutes protected from outside interruptions.

Taking a comfortable position and putting aside distractions, let yourself drop into awareness. If it helps, put your attention on the sensations of your body or on your breath, and let your attention rest there for a few mindful breaths. Just notice the coming and going of the sensations, and allow any thoughts to come and go as well, gently keeping or returning attention to your chosen focus—your body sensations or breath sensations—with patience and kindness.

When you begin to notice the feelings of pain or upset have returned, put your mindful attention on that part of the body where the feeling is most intense. For worried or anxious thoughts, put attention on the place in your body where you feel the worry or fear, where you feel the tightness or gripping. Perhaps it is your jaw, or your hands, or your abdomen or shoulders. For feelings of sadness, or anger, or other strong emotions, looking closely, find and mindfully place your attention precisely where you feel the sensations of that emotion in your body. Remember to allow the feelings to simply be just as they are, noticing how they change, and continue to breathe mindfully in and out, just observing and allowing each sensation.

As you observe a strong, unpleasant, or painful feeling in your body, stay attentive and present, and experiment with extending compassion to yourself. This could be as simple as offering yourself goodwill and comfort by gently repeating one or two quiet phrases to yourself as a whisper in your heart and mind: "May I find the resources to care for myself with compassion" *or* "May I care for my own pain just as I care for the pain of others." *Kindly observe whatever arises in you as you repeat your phrase, and let it be included in awareness and released freely with compassion when it moves on.*

You can use any phrase or phrases that resonate for you. Softly whisper your phrase to yourself like a lullaby you might sing to an infant. You will probably find that the most powerful phrases for self-compassion will change over time and in different circumstances. It can help to settle on just one or two phrases in a particular practice period. Practice for as long as you like and whenever you like. Practice without trying to "fix" anything, even your pain. Rather, practice with the intention of seeking to better understand, to offer comfort, and to remain open and friendly to yourself and your experience as it changes in each moment.

EXTENDED PRACTICE #6

As a Longer Formal Meditation

As a longer meditation, try taking an entire formal period to practice self-compassion, kindness, and gratitude with a focus on your own body. Begin by taking a comfortable position in a place where you won't likely be disturbed, drop into awareness, and bring attention to the sensations in your body.

When you are ready, with mindful attention on the sensations in your body, pick a place to start—perhaps your head or your feet—and pausing, with attention focused on that area, offer it compassion and kindness using any phrase or phrases you choose.

You might say, "These are my eyes. May they be safe and protected" *or* "This is my hand that does so many things to support my life. May it be healthy." *Use words and wishes for compassion and gratitude that resonate with you.*

After a few breaths and phrases in that part, move attention to another area nearby, pausing and breathing, noticing and feeling the sensations, whispering your phrases of kindness and compassion to that part. And after a few breaths and phrases there, move on someplace else. Keep practicing this way until you have touched as many of the parts and regions of your body as you like with awareness and kindness.

You don't have to know all the names or even all the parts or regions. Just use the body names you know, and put your attention on the part and places you choose. While you are on any part, breathe mindfully and connect more deeply by noticing any sensations. Then try sending kindness and compassion to that part using any phrases you like. They might be ones from the brief practice above, or they could be different ones like these: "May you be safe and well." "May you be at ease." "May you be protected."

It may be interesting to experiment with gratitude for your body as well—perhaps by being grateful for your body and that the different parts work as well as they do. Imagine speaking more explicitly to any part or region and offering it thanks. For example, "Thank you, my lungs, for the breath of life that keeps me alive" *or* "Thank you, my feet, for carrying me around this life" *or* "Thank you, my eyes, for the gift of sight and the knowledge of the beauty to be seen in this life."

You can also use this practice as a smaller part of any formal meditation practice period. For example, you could begin any formal meditation practice period with a few minutes of preliminary practice with your phrases of kindness and compassion, or you might end any formal practice period with a few phrases of kindness and compassion for yourself or for others.

Into Daily Life

Extend the practice of self-compassion and kindness into your daily life by remembering to meet any pain or upset you feel—in heart, mind, or body—with a few mindful breaths and one or two of the phrases of self-compassion that resonate with you. Taking even one mindful breath or repeating a single phrase to remain open and caring for your own suffering may make all the difference in determining whether your next response to the pain will be healing or more damaging.

MEDITATION PRACTICE #7:
My Pain Is Your Pain

Buddhist psychology identifies anger and fear as "near enemies" of compassion. One possible meaning of this is that feelings of anger or fear arising within you in any moment can block you from (that is, be the enemy of) feeling compassion for the pain of another. One result of such interference with your capacity to respond to pain with compassion is an interior experience of feeling separate and perhaps alienated from the person and from the situation. Such interference by anger and fear can, and often does, happen to practically everyone.

There are many ways to view this complex expression of inter-connectedness around pain and compassion that we share with other human beings. The meditation teacher Sharon Salzberg points to the critical importance of acknowledging, not denying, the truth and the causes of any suffering and pain we experience in ourselves.

By our willingness to turn toward our own pain and to seek to understand it, we find a path for discovering a different relationship to the pain marked by the fact that we can safely include such pain in awareness and embrace it with self-compassion. And when we realize that the pain in us has the same causes and qualities as the pain we can observe in anyone, that insight can bring us to experience greater compassion for others as well (Salzberg 1995, 106–7).

Use this meditation to explore the power of acknowledging your own pain, turning toward and holding it in awareness, and touching the possibility for compassion to grow in your life, and benefit yourself and others.

BRIEF PRACTICE #7

Any time you feel isolated or disconnected from someone or several others, you might choose to pause and take a few moments to acknowledge and investigate those feelings with compassionate and mindful attention.

If it helps, find a place where you can be undisturbed for a few minutes, and take a comfortable position for meditation.

Bring mindful attention into your body and kindly notice the sensations that are flowing through your body in this moment. Are they feelings of heaviness or gripping? Where are they most intense? Pay particular attention to your jaw (is it clenched?), to your hands (are they in fists?), and to any place where the muscles are tightening and tense. Your neck, shoulders, someplace else? Notice and breathe mindfully with each part or region of your body.

Quietly repeating one or two phrases, gently and intentionally send yourself compassion and kindness. You might breathe in mindfully, and on the out-breath, quietly whisper to yourself a phrase like "May I be free from pain and upset. May I meet my pain with kindness and mercy."

As you remain present, include any feelings of isolation or alienation. Also include in your awareness any angry, blaming, and judgmental thoughts directed at others or yourself. Breathe mindfully with the thoughts, allowing them to be as they are. You don't have to be angry at the angry thoughts or blame yourself for having blaming thoughts. Your practice is simply to notice them, and let them be. Touch them with mindful attention, looking deeply, softening enough to allow yourself to feel any pain and to hear any judgments or blame. Breathe in mindfully, and on the out-breath offer a compassionate wish for yourself: "May I be free from so much anger and blame" or "May I find the resources to understand and not judge myself or others harshly."

Conclude your meditation by breathing mindfully, and stating briefly and quietly to yourself any insight you may have gained from this meditation.

EXTENDED PRACTICE #7

As a Longer Formal Meditation

You may make this meditation a longer practice of wise reflection on the shared truth of pain and suffering in your life and the lives of others. It can be helpful to remember that mindfulness and the qualities of kindness and compassion are unique and powerful allies you already possess. To support you, it could also help to recall the teaching that says, "The awareness of pain is not in pain." "The awareness of fear is not afraid." "The awareness of anger is not angry."

Whenever you would like to explore this reflection on pain, compassion, and awareness, settle in a place where you will not be disturbed for a period of longer meditation, and take a comfortable position. As you begin your meditation period, it may help to remind yourself that your intention is not to "fix" any pain or to magically escape from it, but rather, as in all mindfulness practice, to seek to better understand the causes and conditions that give rise to and sustain the pain you are investigating. Healing and transformation of any pain are more likely to come out of actions generated by understanding than in actions driven by anger, fear, and ill will.

Begin by putting attention mindfully on the sensations flowing through your body or on the sensations of your breath. Allow your body to relax, and let your attention become steady.

When you are ready, deliberately recall something painful in your life. It could be physical, emotional, psychological, or based in a relationship. As soon as you notice the painful thoughts and feelings are present, put your attention on the place in your body where you can most easily feel the pain. Even if it has a psychological or relationship source, the pain will also be someplace in your body. Continue breathing mindfully as you notice, look more deeply, and allow the sensations be just as they are in that part of your body.

Now, widen your attention and include any thoughts you having. Notice if you are repeating some phrases or reliving some scenes from a situation or moment. Keep noticing and breathing mindfully, including the thoughts, not feeding them or fighting them but just noticing and allowing them. It may be helpful to ask a question quietly from time to time—"Is there fear?" "What is the fear?"—and listen for the answers in the next few thoughts. Or ask, "Who is afraid in this moment?" "What is there to be afraid of?" To each of these questions, listen mindfully without judgment to any thoughts that arise in response. Breathe mindfully for a few breaths and steady yourself from time to time, if it helps.

When you are ready to end your meditation, put attention back on your breath for a few more mindful breaths. Reflect on your meditation. What did you notice? What have you learned about the nature of pain and suffering in you? About the relationship of body sensations to thoughts and memories? About the contribution of fear and feelings of vulnerability and being out of control? You don't have to overanalyze it; just reflect on what you have noticed in yourself during this meditation.

Finish with a question to yourself about others. Could their actions be driven by similar feelings of anger and pain? Could you begin to understand them and their actions better if you looked closely at anything they did or said as being driven by pain burning in them in that moment?

Into Daily Life

Compassion meditations are a powerful way to transform your relationship to any pain and suffering in your life. When you notice a reaction to any pain—in yourself or another—a reaction that might be angry, sad, afraid, agitated, or even bored, pause and name it: "I am aware of painful feelings of anger (or sadness, fear, agitation, boredom, for instance) in me now." Bring attention into your body and breathe mindfully. Look deeply and listen for the louder angry and blaming interior voices, and for the deeper, usually quieter fearful voices, all of which are feeling out of control and vulnerable. Touch them all with kind and compassionate attention. Offer them support with one or two phrases like "May I care for my own pain and suffering just as I care for the pain of others" or "May I understand and accept all of my feelings, thoughts, and experiences in this life."

MEDITATION PRACTICE #8:
Your Pain Is My Pain

When facing the pain associated with another person or with a disturbing situation, many responses are possible. The voice of despair might say, "This is unfair!" The voice of blame and agitation might say, "This is all your fault!" The voice of guilt and an overblown sense of personal responsibility might say, "This is all my fault!"

It is very easy to fall victim to these voices and their "stories," and believing them, of course, only adds to the misery. If you become blindly reactive and absorbed in desperate efforts driven by those voices and stories to alter, modify, fix, or escape the situation, you can easily generate more avoidance and pain—and, as a result, you will not be of much comfort to those who are in pain and may need you.

Rather than becoming lost in a reaction of denial or aversion to another's pain, a wiser approach—ultimately much more healing and more transformative—may be, first, to pause, which will help you to remain present and receptive. Then, become curious and investigate the situation, choosing a mindful and compassionate exploration of what is happening in the moment when pain arises and for the time it is present. When informed by the wisdom that follows mindful observation and compassionate exploration, your response to the pain of another person, or in any situation, is much more likely to be constructive and helpful.

Try this meditation to help you remain present and nurture compassionate understanding for the pain of others, even when they are hurtful or critical of you. This meditation can also be helpful if you are in a disturbing or unsettling situation.

BRIEF PRACTICE #8

To find yourself present to pain in another person or the pain in a disturbing situation, when you notice yourself caught up in anger or fear or an urge to escape, pause and bring attention back to your body and breathe mindfully for a few breaths.

Always remember to protect yourself first. If you can, and if it would help, withdraw to a safe place for a few minutes to move more deeply into this meditation. If you cannot separate from the situation, protect yourself as best you can, and let mindful attention to your body and your breath be the anchor that helps you stay present and grounded.

Kindly and patiently begin by acknowledging any pain you feel or any pain you have taken on in responding to another's pain in this moment. Breathing mindfully for a few breaths, extend compassion to yourself with one or two phrases: "May I live in peace, and free from pain and sorrow." "May I take care of my pain with kindness and mercy." "May I be safe and protected." "May I live with ease."

After a few moments of mindfully breathing and offering yourself compassion, quietly shift your focus to the other person, or people, and their pain. Continue to breathe mindfully and, on the out-breath, whisper quietly—in your own heart and mind—one or two of the same phrases to offer them your compassion: "May you be free of pain and anger." "May you be safe and take care of yourself with ease." "May you find relief from your suffering."

As you practice, remember that sending the other person kindness and compassion does not mean you are making yourself vulnerable or that you cannot protect yourself. Nor does it mean that you condone any hurtful actions or words from that person. Offering the person kindness and compassion also relies on the understanding that the person is the owner of his or her pain, and that you cannot control that pain or take responsibility for it.

Allow this understanding to support and strengthen you.

As you continue to practice, breath mindfully as you look more deeply at the other person or people in pain. Can you remain present, seeing and hearing more fully the nature of their suffering? Trusting the depth and strength of your own heart, let it support you to remain present for the others. Looking deeply, breathing mindfully, perhaps you can sense the possibility that you too have felt or could feel such pain.

Continue your practice, offering others your good wishes for freedom from pain and suffering, knowing they could be you: "May all living beings be free of sorrow and fear." "May all living beings find joy and live with ease."

EXTENDED PRACTICE #8

As a Longer Formal Meditation

If you like, you can make this a longer formal meditation. Pause and take some time when you won't be disturbed, and breathe mindfully for a few minutes.

When you feel ready, choose someone in your life who is in pain, and use one or two phrases to send them compassion: "May you live with ease." "May you be free of pain and suffering." "May you find the resources to truly heal."

You might begin with someone you care for; then, if you wish, explore sending compassion to others. You could send compassion to loved ones; to people you don't know well; or to groups of people, like all cancer patients or all the people in a war-torn country. You could even include animals or any living thing that makes sense to you. You could explore sending compassion to difficult people in your life, those you know, and those you don't know but have strong feelings about.

Between the categories or people you send your compassionate phrases to, pause and breathe mindfully. Relax and take your time. Stay present and notice any and all reactions you experience. You cannot make a mistake. Practicing compassion meditation is a way of exploring and changing your relationship to pain and suffering. Remember to include yourself.

Into Daily Life

Compassion practice is concerned with bringing stillness to the upset, fear, and agitation arising in our hearts as a reaction to pain in others and in the world. This practice can be an immediate response if we train ourselves to turn to it.

When you see pain unfolding in the life of another person or in a particular situation, if you can help, of course, do so wisely. So often, unfortunately, we are limited in how much we can do to relieve the pain of others or change their situation. This fact of our own limitations can obscure compassion and generate doubts and feelings of hopelessness as we face of others' pain, especially overwhelming pain or fear.

In any moment in daily life, when you encounter pain in others, gently notice and bring attention to yourself first. Wish yourself protection and safety, freedom and ease. Then, breathing mindfully, shift attention to the others and wish them safety, relief, and ease. Experiment with gently repeating a single phrase of kindness and compassion for even a few breaths. Knowing you do not have control over the pain of others or the events of the world, letting yourself soften, breathing mindfully, let the phrase support you. Remember that the well-wishing includes you: "May all beings everywhere be safe and filled with peace."

MEDITATION PRACTICE #9:
Three Directions of Forgiveness

Resentment is the sense of hurt or indignation that arises from feeling injured or offended. The Latin roots of the word *resentment* could be translated as "to feel again." To be *indignant* means to feel anger or scorn, especially at someone or something that is deemed unjust, mean, or ungrateful. The roots of the word *indignant* mean literally "not worthy."

Resentment and indignation can be toxic fuel for chronic feelings of anger and blame. And, for most of us human beings, it is inevitable that events in our lives and relationships will indeed arouse feelings of resentment and indignation. We are only human.

Interestingly, when you think about it, the hurt we experience in life or in relationships can come when someone intends harm toward us, but, possibly more often, hurt comes to us from the unintentional (but still hurtful) acts of others or ourselves. Intentional or unintentional, the acts that cause us hurt can easily fuel the feelings of resentment, and we definitely "feel again" that hurt when we are reminded of it by something in the present moment. As a memory from some past hurt or offense, intentional or unintentional, unmanaged and chronically carried resentment and indignation need little encouragement to explode into the present moment and distort our experience of all that is here.

Of course, it is common to feel resentment and indignation toward others, but how often do we recognize or acknowledge that our actions, intentional or unintentional, have hurt someone else, and may lead them to feel resentment and indignation toward us? And what of the hurt we cause ourselves when our own inner critics berate us with resentful and indignant self-judgments and blame?

The really good news is that there is a powerful remedy to resentment and indignation. It is forgiveness.

Forgiveness can be defined many ways, but a very useful definition is also very simple. *Forgiveness* is the end of resentment.

As a meditation practice, mindfulness can help us to be increasingly present and available to work with the painful and toxic energies of resentment and indignation in our lives. Being present offers us the opportunity to use phrases in support of ending resentment, just as we can cultivate qualities of kindness and compassion meditatively, using mindfulness and phrases linked to those qualities.

Try these meditations to work with any negative energies of resentment and indignation in your life. The "three directions of forgiveness" are to offer forgiveness to another, to ask for their forgiveness, and always to remember to offer forgiveness to yourself.

BRIEF PRACTICE #9

At or near the end of your day, pause and set aside some time for meditation. Taking even a few minutes for this practice may help you experience greater feelings of peace and ease. Set your intention to work deliberately with any feelings of hurt, resentment, or indignation that you are carrying from your day or from some earlier time. Know from the start that you don't have to "fix" anything or "clear the slate" completely, but that the very act of turning toward such feelings with awareness and compassion, forming an intention to acknowledge and heal any hurt and to release any associated resentment, can be enormously helpful, revealing, and healing.

Taking a comfortable position, breathe mindfully for several minutes. When you feel settled, more at ease, and present, shift attention to your meditative practice of forgiveness.

Begin by bringing to mind someone who has hurt or offended you. It does not have to be your archenemy. The hurt could be something minor or just irritating. Breathing mindfully, imagine speaking kindly to this person, quietly in your own heart and mind: "For any hurt you have caused me, intentional or unintentional, I offer you forgiveness." *Repeat this phrase quietly and without expectations. Remain open to any feelings or thoughts you notice in yourself and let them be, let them go. If you feel angry or afraid, gently come back to your body, and practice mindful breathing. When you feel steady again, gently resume offering your forgiveness phrase.*

When you like, you can shift the focus to someone you have hurt, even unintentionally. Breathing mindfully, imagine speaking quietly to this person: "For any pain I may have caused you, intentional or unintentional, I ask your forgiveness." *Remain present and mindful of any feelings or thoughts this brings up in you. Meet those feelings with mindful breaths and with self-compassion.*

Complete your forgiveness meditation session by shifting your attention to yourself: "For any harm I may have caused, intentional or unintentional, to myself or to others, I offer myself forgiveness."

Remember that forgiveness can only be offered. This offer is an expression of the intention to release any resentment or indignation you hold—toward another or toward yourself. Practicing this intention is what counts. Meeting whatever comes up as a result with mindfulness and self-compassion can take your practice even deeper.

EXTENDED PRACTICE #9

As a Longer Formal Meditation

You can make a longer formal meditation out of this practice by spending more time (repeating your phrases more slowly or more times, or trying different phrases) with each person you choose to practice forgiveness with. Or you can extend this practice by focusing on additional different people in the first two directions—offering forgiveness to them and asking forgiveness from them—and always spending time in the third direction—offering forgiveness to yourself.

It can also be fruitful, after working with the phrases, to pause and allow yourself time to reflect upon anything that comes up for you in the meditation. This could be as simple as letting go of the phrases, returning to silence, and sitting and breathing mindfully as you notice any memories and feelings as they come and go. Pay especially close attention and remain receptive and open to the thoughts, memories, and feelings associated with particular people you focused your meditation on. Let what you notice guide, inform, and heal you.

Into Daily Life

Practice extending forgiveness meditation into daily life by pausing when you are aware of feeling hurt or offended, and quietly acknowledge the feelings as you breathe mindfully for a few moments. Then use your silent phrases to offer forgiveness quietly in your own heart and mind to the one who hurt you. Explore adding the direction of silently asking that person to forgive you for any hurt you may have caused, intentional or unintentional, and observe any thoughts or feelings you might have. End by offering yourself forgiveness for any hurt, intentional or unintentional, that you may have caused anyone, including yourself. If your meditation and wisdom guide you to do so, consider speaking or writing to the other person regarding any hurt between you.

MEDITATION PRACTICE #10:
Sorrow, Kindness, and Equanimity

What do you do when the great pain of fear, sorrow, and loss visits you in this moment—again? What is your response when the pain in yourself, or in another, or in a situation, seems too much to bear, and you feel helpless to soothe or end it?

Such pain, coupled to the feelings of helplessness and vulnerability associated with it, can easily summon fear and anger. In turn, those energies can take us away from this moment and obscure the tender response of compassion within us, reinforcing the habitual response of anger when any pain is present. But the choice to respond to any pain—not with anger, but with kindness and compassion—is always there, and the capacity to make that better choice can be cultivated and strengthened.

Equanimity, as Sharon Salzberg has noted, is "a spacious stillness of the mind, a radiant calm that allows us to be present fully with all the different changing experiences that constitute our world and our lives." She goes on to say that "equanimity deepens as we learn to accept the truth of change, and develop our ability to let go" (1995, 139).

Roshi Joan Halifax has devoted many years to caring for dying people, and offers valuable lessons about equanimity and compassion in the service of helping others and ourselves. In her book *Being with Dying: Cultivating Compassion and Fearlessness in the Presence of Death*, Roshi Joan observes, "In the experience of giving care, there is a delicate balance between opening our heart endlessly (compassion) and accepting the limits of what we can do and how we and others feel (equanimity). Most of us need to cultivate this balance between compassion—the tenderness of the heart in response to suffering—and equanimity—the spacious stillness that accepts things as they are" (2008, 99–100).

By learning to balance the open heart of compassion with the unshakable, wisdom-based strength of equanimity, you can remain present for and deeply touch any pain and sorrow you face. Wisely and dependably present for sorrow, you can truly feel and respond with kindness—not anger. Such a response brings with it profound positive consequences for everyone involved.

Phrases that acknowledge limits, promote peacefulness, and encourage acceptance can be used as a meditation practice to cultivate the quality of equanimity. Such phrases point to "that spacious stillness that accepts things as they are," as Roshi Joan Halifax put it. In the meditation below, explore these phrases just as you have worked previously with phrases to cultivate qualities of kindness and compassion. The phrases in this meditation are inspired by the work of Roshi Joan Halifax and Sharon Salzberg. If you like, you can create your own phrases.

BRIEF PRACTICE #10

When you notice you are feeling distressed or overwhelmed, and seem unable to ease the pain of another or pain in the world, pause for a brief meditation period in a place that offers some privacy.

Take a comfortable position, even lying down if you need to, give yourself some time, steadying attention and encouraging ease in mind and body with mindful breathing or by placing mindful attention on your body or on sounds.

When you are ready, shift attention to the disturbing or painful situation. Notice any thoughts and feelings of responsibility or frustration you have at how the situation is going. Breathe mindfully as you notice and allow all of these thoughts and feelings, and notice and allow the sensations in your body also.

When you are ready, gently and softly whisper your phrase of equanimity to yourself: "May I remain in peace, and see my limits with compassion." "May I show you my love and concern, knowing I cannot control your pain or make your choices for you." "May I find the resources to remain present and help in this situation, and may this experience help me understand the true nature of life."

The phrases are expressions of well-wishing and great friendliness for yourself as you bear the pain present in this situation. Continue breathing mindfully between your phrases, or repeat your phrase with the rhythm of your breath. You can use one phrase, or all of them, or any combination. Or you can use a phrase or phrases that you create yourself. Practice without trying to make anything happen, and without attachment to any outcome, even to that of feeling more equanimity.

Remember to relax and notice mindfully any feelings or thoughts that arise during your meditation. Let them go, let them be. Come back patiently to your breath, and let your phrases of equanimity be like a gentle lullaby that you sing to yourself. Let the phrases support you. Let the meditation support you.

Practice for as long or as briefly as you like. End your meditation by sitting quietly and breathing mindfully for a few more breaths. What do you notice?

EXTENDED PRACTICE #10

As a Longer Formal Meditation

You can make this a longer meditation by pausing and perhaps taking several mindful breaths between each phrase or between different phrases. In the stillness of noticing and breathing mindfully, include and make room for all thoughts and feelings, simply letting them be or letting them go.

You can also extend this as a formal meditation by repeating each phrase several more times before moving to another phrase, or by adding additional phrases of your own choosing.

Into Daily Life

In the moment, any moment, when you feel frustrated or overwhelmed by the pain of another or the difficulty you experience as you try to help others, pause, stay where you are, and breathe mindfully for a few breaths.

Choose one or more of your favorite equanimity phrases. Repeat it quietly in your heart, breathing mindfully, as you slowly repeat your phrase. Let the breathing and the phrase support you in this moment and in this situation: "I care about your pain, but I cannot control it." "I wish you ease and well-being, and I cannot make your choices for you." "May this situation help me to know and accept my limits with compassion. May it open me to the true nature of life."

KEEP IN MIND

- Anger, fear, vulnerability, and related feelings feed the illusion of separation and isolation as well as feelings of alienation and impatience with ourselves, others, and the world.

- By engaging meditative practices focused on the qualities of kindness, compassion, and equanimity, you can reconnect with the goodness of heart that resides in every human being, including you! Remembering and reexperiencing the strength of your goodness will broaden and build your resources and capacities to manage anger and fear and to enjoy a happier life.

CHAPTER 7

calming your angry mind with wisdom and understanding

If we look deeply into the flower, we see a cloud because we know without the cloud there would be no rain and this flower could not manifest.

—*Thich Nhat Hanh*

If you are piloting a hot-air balloon, and you want to use only the currents of the wind to direct and carry you, then you have to be aware that at different altitudes the currents are blowing in different directions. Depending on the particular conditions at a given altitude, the air currents at that altitude, like great rivers in the sky, will flow in a specific direction. If you are in that current, it will carry you in the direction it is blowing.

Of course, the air currents don't always blow in the same direction. The way the wind blows at any altitude is dictated by changing conditions of pressure, temperature, moisture, and other factors in the atmosphere. So, good balloonists remain constantly alert and aware, watchful and observant, as they are flying. They learn to change altitude, going up or down in their balloon in order to enter or leave a particular air current and go where they want, or escape when they are swept away.

As a human being, in your busy life, you might sometimes feel like that balloonist. Only instead of high-altitude air currents, you could find yourself being carried away by strong and changing inner currents of thoughts, strong emotions like anger, or intense body sensations like those associated with pain or injury. Each of those inner currents is itself the result of a number of conditions, constantly changing in the present moment, just like the air currents are produced and vary depending on the diverse and particular atmospheric conditions coming together for a time in the present moment.

Your inner atmospheric conditions of mind and body include your physical status, cognitions like your perceptions and inner narrative, and the constant stream of information through your senses as you interact with others and the world around you. As these elements combine, they form powerful inner currents. You can find yourself being carried forward by them into more thoughts, emotions, and even actions, breath by breath, just as when conditions in the atmosphere above create those great air streams blowing everything—including balloons— through the sky.

In the span of a few breaths, or even a single breath, watching closely and mindfully, you might observe as body sensations form around thoughts and memories, or watch inner reactions to a sound or smell from the world outside of your skin evoke memories and judgments that in turn activate strong reactive sensations in your body and demanding thoughts in your mind. And those conditions can change very quickly. The flow of experience through mind and body shifts, and you can find your perceptions and ways of relating to the world around you also shift with the changing flow of experience.

For example, walking down a street, have you ever experienced a warm feeling toward a perfect stranger and realized you were feeling happy and at ease in the moments before you encountered that person? Or, if you continue walking, and worried or angry thoughts arise about someone or something and fill your mind, have you noticed how the other people around you, especially strangers, can suddenly seem to be more threatening?

Developing greater awareness and more accurate understanding of the changing and interrelated nature of life as we experience it in these human forms and conditions can be immensely valuable to you if you wish to live a happier, more satisfying life—and one less dominated by the toxicity of chronic anger and hostility.

Anger and other strong emotions are a natural part of our experience as human beings. We are not somehow failures when these emotions come to us. They will arise often, at least for most of us. How aware we are of that strong emotion, what meaning we assign to it, and the relationship we take to it makes all the difference in how we respond—and depends directly on growing our understanding of the nature of the emotion.

Meditation teacher and psychotherapist Sylvia Boorstein recalls a story about His Holiness, the Dalai Lama (Boorstein 2007, 111). He was speaking to a large group on the day after he was awarded the Nobel Peace Prize, and someone asked him, "Do you ever get angry?" "Of course," he responded laughing. "Something happens. It isn't what you expected. Anger arises. But, you know, it doesn't have to be a problem." And he laughed some more.

The practices in this chapter focus on helping you change your experience of anger in all of its forms by using the wisdom and understanding available through meditative practice. Meditation helps you view anger and its causes and sustaining conditions differently. As you identify anger's supporting conditions and learn how to stop feeding them—in your mind and in your body—the mental and emotional habits sustaining anger, blame, fear, scorn, hostility, and related feelings will lose much of their power over you.

Just as in the previous two chapters, for each of the practices in this chapter, you will find instructions for a brief version and for more extended versions. You will see that these meditations can easily be extended for longer periods of time as formal meditations, and they can also be extended in easy and practical ways into the flow of your daily life with its unfolding relationships and situations. In either brief or extended forms, these meditations can help you understand and explore the atmospheric conditions that create anger in any situation.

MEDITATION PRACTICE #11:
Seeing Anger as a Temporary Condition

An easy way to drown in the river of angry emotions is to forget that anger, like all emotions, is not a permanent condition. Anger is not an unchanging character trait or a fixed character flaw. It is only a condition that arises when the other non-anger elements that make it up are present.

By focusing mindful attention on anger when it is present, and noticing how it changes and leaves, and by making the times when anger is not present also a focus for mindful attention, you can soon see the truth of anger's impermanence for yourself. That understanding about anger—that it is temporary—can then become a source of strength for you when anger appears again in a future moment. Simply remembering, even in the heat of anger, that *this is not permanent* and learning to quietly repeat phrases like *This will pass* or *My anger will pass* will support you in calming your angry mind.

Practice this meditation and let it help you remember you are not your anger, and your anger is temporary and not you.

BRIEF PRACTICE #11

Pause during the day or evening and take some time for yourself for meditation.

Begin by taking a comfortable position and reducing distractions as best you can, as you put your tasks down for the time of your meditation. Settle into your body and relax into awareness as you remember that you already have all you need for this meditation.

Choose a focus—body sensations or breathing. Place your attention purposely and more closely on the sensations flowing in your body or on the sensations of your body breathing. Allow yourself to feel the sensations deeply as they come and go through your awareness. No need to fight with them, or hurry them along, or try to change them. Relaxed and observing, patiently let the sensations come to you—and gently, freely allow them to go, in their own time.

When you notice any other experiences—thoughts, sounds, smells, or tastes, for example—remain relaxed and watchful, observing and allowing each condition to be as it comes and goes. Practice for as long as you like, just watching and allowing these changing conditions to come to you and to go.

As you mindfully observe, can you notice how every condition—every sensation, every thought, every sound, taste, and smell—changes at its own speed? Let yourself be curious. Perhaps look more closely at how many different speeds there are, and how each thing you notice changes and vanishes, sometimes quickly, and sometimes slowly, but always it vanishes eventually. Not one is permanent.

When you notice a strong emotion has appeared, watch closely how thoughts and body sensations come together to form it. Can you see them changing? Do the sensations or the thoughts vanish first? What else do you notice?

If you like, end your meditation by reflecting briefly on the fact that you have been watching closely, and things really are changing and impermanent. What does that mean for you? What are the implications for your life?

EXTENDED PRACTICE #11

As a Longer Formal Meditation Practice

You can extend this brief practice into a longer formal meditation, and return to it over time in many formal meditation sessions. It can be a great help, when facing intense emotions like anger, to know surely and deeply that the emotion is only temporary, and it will pass.

You can practice in formal meditation by making the quality of change your primary object of attention. Let your attention include the arising, the changing, and the disappearing of any experience as you sit or walk in your formal meditation period.

For example, if you are practicing awareness of your breathing, when you feel more focused and relaxed, and your attention rests more steadily on your breath sensations, put your attention on the beginning of the sensation—of in-breath or out-breath—and notice how that sensation changes into a different sensation as the middle of the breath appears and how those sensations change again at the end, and how the breath sensations themselves vanish into stillness before the next in-breath sensations come to you. With practice, you will probably be able to stay present for most or even all of a full breath cycle of changing sensations, and know they truly are changing. This breath is not the last breath or the next breath. Each breath is unique, and each one is only here for a short while.

If you like, you can choose a different focus to explore the truth of change in your meditation. In any meditation period, you can choose to place attention on sounds or other bodily sensations, or even thoughts, as experiences that arise, change, and vanish—perhaps noticing simply when a particular phenomenon is here, present, and as you observe gently without interference, seeing it change or simply noticing that it is gone. Practice for as long as you like, relaxed and watchful of the constantly changing field of experience and conditions moving through your awareness.

Into Daily Life

Extend this practice into daily life by pausing at times throughout your day and evening and tuning in mindfully to what is happening. Pay particular attention to your inner conditions. What do you notice? What is changing?

Gently name or note what you notice without judgment—just noticing, relaxed, and observing.

Notice when you feel energetic or tired. Notice feelings of happiness, or any feelings of irritation and annoyance. Notice thoughts of urgency, planning, judging, and worry. Notice whatever is here, now. How long does it last?

Breathe mindfully with what is here. Relaxed and watchful, can you notice how it changes? Can you notice how the feelings of this moment have changed from just a while ago? Notice how angry feelings can be here, and how later they are gone. Like everything else, anger is temporary.

Finish with a phrase of wisdom and understanding, perhaps reminding yourself of what you've observed by saying something like "Yes, this is here now, but it will change."

MEDITATION PRACTICE #12:
The Cloud of Anger

Most people look at clouds all the time, but how many ever pause to consider that a cloud is made of conditions and elements that are not clouds?

Clouds of all kinds appear, but they only appear when conditions arise that support them. The conditions that make up a cloud include moisture, temperature, light, and pressure. None of these conditions is, by itself, a cloud. They all have to be present together to form the cloud. When the proper conditions are present, the cloud appears. When they are not present, there is no cloud—nothing to see. Clouds arise when *noncloud* elements come together in just the right way.

"Shoe" is the name we assign to something that is a combination of materials having qualities of color, feel, durability, shape, and size, and which serves one or many functions. You might say that the shoe is made up of *nonshoe* elements, because none of the constituent elements that make up the final product is, by itself, what we call a shoe.

When you stop and think about it, just about everything is like that.

Isn't vanilla ice cream made up of non-vanilla-ice-cream elements? Not one of ingredients or conditions—the sugar, cream, vanilla, other specific flavorings and ingredients, or elements of cold, and the energy involved in blending the different elements by itself is vanilla ice cream! Vanilla ice cream takes all of these. Without one of them, it is not vanilla ice cream.

Knowing something about the different elements that make up anything we give a name to can help us to better understand and better manage, enhance, or (if we choose) disentangle from that thing—whatever it is. It can be a wise and radical shift to view your anger, or any strong emotion, like this. Anger—like the cloud, the shoe, or the ice cream—is a temporary coming together of required and particular conditions. In other words, the condition or emotion that we call "anger" is made up of *"non-anger"* elements.

Let this meditation practice help you look more deeply and see the different conditions and elements that are necessary for the cloud of anger to appear in you. Getting to know those conditions better will help you uncouple, deidentify, and escape from any angry feelings that otherwise can hijack you so easily.

BRIEF PRACTICE #12

When you notice yourself feeling angry, take a few moments to pause and take a few mindful breaths.

If you cannot separate from the situation where you feel angry, first make sure you are as safe and as comfortable as you can be, and continue breathing mindfully. Silently name and acknowledge what is happening around you, or what has just happened, if you are no longer in the situation.

As you breathe mindfully, look more deeply and notice the sensations in your body. Wherever you notice uncomfortable tension or tightness, you might gently name that as suffering or as an unpleasant feeling. Breathe compassionately into the feeling. Notice how the sensations change as you watch them.

If you wish, look even more deeply as you breathe mindfully. See if you can touch with kindness and compassion any deeper sense of fear, insecurity, or vulnerability within. Is there any disappointment, hurt, or sadness at this deeper level? Allow yourself to open as much as you can and feel safe. Notice any of these difficult feelings and breath mindfully and kindly with them. Can you acknowledge and remain open to any pain they hold, seeing it wisely as another of the conditions and causes of your anger?

Continuing to breathe mindfully and to acknowledge the suffering in your own body, mind, and heart, notice any thoughts you are having. What is your mind telling you? Let any thoughts you notice just be, or let them go, and continue mindful breathing.

Finish your meditation by reviewing what you have found. What happened? What are the causes and conditions that created this cloud of anger in you? What and where were the bodily sensations? What were the complex and difficult feelings deeper down in you? What thoughts or stories did your mind spin to uphold and promote those feelings?

Can you see how your anger is temporary, and how it depends on particular conditions happening around and inside of you? How could you begin to change those conditions?

EXTENDED PRACTICE #12

As a Longer Formal Meditation Practice

To make this a longer formal meditation practice, take some time in a formal practice session to reflect on the non-anger causes and conditions that form the cloud of anger in you.

One way to do this is to sit quietly and practice mindful breathing for a while. Practice without striving, trying to fix anything, or trying to make anything happen. Just relax and allow yourself to be open and receptive to each breath as the sensations come to you and depart.

When you feel relaxed and ready, and your attention is stable and steady on the breath, recall a situation or time when something happened and you felt angry or annoyed or irritated.

Continue breathing mindfully as the memories of that situation or time come to you. Notice the different elements present in the angry memory—the pictures or words in your mind, the tone of voice of any thoughts, the sensations in your body. Practice meeting all with kindness and compassion, allowing them to be just as they are.

As you look and listen more deeply, as you continue breathing mindfully, allow yourself to open, more willing to touch any feelings of hurt or sadness or fear and vulnerability that may be present. Notice any thoughts that come with those feelings. Notice any tendency to shift attention or avoid what is happening. Gently acknowledge any pain and suffering that you feel. Keep noticing and breathing mindfully, opening to, and allowing your experience to reveal itself, unfolding in its own time and its own way.

Recognize that it is not always easy to stay present or to be compassionate, especially with yourself. Be patient with yourself no matter what happens, do the best you can, and trust that you will notice what is important for you in this meditation. You don't have to worry about the next meditation, or the last one. This meditation is here for you now.

Finish your meditation by reflecting on what you have witnessed and learned about the cloud of anger in your life. What conditions are required for the cloud to form? What were those conditions in the situation you reflected upon? What can you do about those conditions to heal and transform the experience of anger in your life?

Into Daily Life

Extend your inquiry about the cloud of anger into daily life by bringing mindfulness to any moment when you feel anger, hatred, boredom, irritation, annoyance, or other expressions of ill will and aversion. Let yourself be curious and kind. When you notice the angry feelings, pause and acknowledge that suffering is present in you. Breathe mindfully and notice where in your body the feelings are strongest. Breathe mindfully and touch and care for any feelings of fear or hurt. Breathing mindfully, listen for the voices of despair and upset, meeting them all with kindness. Remembering that you don't have to fix anything or change anything in this moment, you can relax, being curious and allowing your experience to unfold; and you can simply notice what is happening inside of you—even for a few breaths.

What happens when you bring mindfulness and compassionate attention more often to feelings of anger when they appear during your day? What non-anger elements make up your cloud of anger?

MEDITATION PRACTICE #13:
Stop Fueling Your Anger

If you take the view that anger is like a cloud and only appears when certain conditions are present, perhaps, by being mindful, you have actually seen this happen or even identified some of the conditions. If that is the case, then a useful approach to calming your angry mind could be to identify and take away some of the necessary conditions, to remove some of the fuel, that sustains your anger.

So, the next question might be "What fuels your anger?" A quick, usually easy, and not-so-helpful response could be to blame someone or some situation for "making" you angry. Besides being an incorrect understanding, this response is not usually that helpful because we have limited control over others and over most situations. How much better, really, does it make you feel to say, "If so-and-so would not say such-and-such or do this-and-that, I would not be so angry"? How long will you have to remain angry or irritated waiting for so-and-so or this-and-that to change?

Blame can be a form of resistance to our own pain or to the way the world appears to us, and it can, and often is, unconscious. We may not realize how much we protest and push back against what we feel or what happens in this moment, inside of us or in the world outside of our skin. With mindfulness, you can observe pain and your resistance to it. You will be able to see for yourself if this statement is true: pain is inevitable in this human life, but the suffering we experience—how we make the pain worse—depends directly on our own resistance when pain arises.

So, although blame and resistance to pain that we cannot manage can fuel anger, there is another important source of fuel for anger. That fuel is lack of self-awareness.

A hermit living quietly and simply in a cave may suffer through countless moments dreaming of a better life. A wealthy person may steam and struggle internally every day in his or her large, comfortable home replaying some old, familiar story of resentment. Outer change, in others or in our own particular situation, carries no guarantee of inner change—or of peace of mind or of being at ease and comfortable in our own skin. The pain in our lives lies not so much in the circumstances we face, but in the relationship and response we take to what is happening. Growing self-awareness of the relationship we take to what is happening—how we treat life, you might say, in each moment—is another powerful ally for you in calming your angry mind.

Use this meditation to explore, become more aware, and work more wisely with any resistance or other fuels of your anger: judgments, concepts, hurts, and blame—and their companions, doubt, fear, and vulnerability. Explore the power of your own intelligence and goodness to help you drop the resistance, to acknowledge and include any feeling or experience in your awareness, and to heal. In the process of dropping resistance to anger and its fuel, you could perhaps find yourself eliminating some of that fuel and cooling the fires within.

BRIEF PRACTICE #13

Upon noticing that anger, boredom, resentment, or another expression of ill will and aversion is present in you, take a few moments for a brief meditation when you can.

Take a comfortable position or, if you prefer, move or stand mindfully for the time of this meditation. Drop into awareness, and bring mindful attention to the flow of sensations in your body, or to the sensations of your breathing coming and going, in and out.

If any of the angry or upset feelings are still present, bring mindful attention to them. Allow yourself to soften and open, looking and listening more deeply as you breathe mindfully with the difficult feeling. Name the feeling, if you can: "Anger, anger, anger..." "Resentment, resentment, resentment..." "Annoyed, annoyed, annoyed..." *Also notice:* "Fear, fear, fear..." "Worry, worry, worry..." "Feeling vulnerable and exposed, vulnerable and exposed..."

As you breathe mindfully with the painful feeling, after quietly naming it, add a simple yes after each naming: "Anger—yes," "resentment—yes," "annoyance—yes," "fear—yes," *and so on.*

Remember that for the time of the meditation, you don't have to fix anything or make anything change or go away. Saying yes helps you drop any resistance and simply allow the feeling to be present in the kind, caring light of mindfulness. Without judging, continue breathing mindfully and noticing what follows after you whisper, "Yes."

Breathing mindfully with the feeling and adding yes, look and listen, especially to any thoughts or beliefs that may be fueling resistance, or feeding the fear, upset, and anger you feel. Name the thought and say yes to each of these, also: "This is crazy—doubting thought! Yes." "I am afraid it's not helping—fearful thought!—Yes." "I hate feeling this way—hostile thought. Yes."

Can you soften and acknowledge any pain you may be feeling in this moment and offer yourself compassion? Can you recognize how resisting this painful feeling adds to your suffering around the pain? "May I recognize my own suffering with compassion." "May I be safe and protected." "May I find the resources to live in peace."

EXTENDED PRACTICE #13

As a Longer Formal Meditation Practice

In each moment in your longer formal meditation sessions, you can also explore the power of resistance to add to your suffering and the power of saying yes to cool that resistance and protest.

Choose any mindfulness meditation practice you like for a period of formal meditation and begin your practice. When you notice any sense of unpleasantness, distress, or upset in mind or body, gently name it and whisper "Yes" as you watch mindfully: "Ache in the neck—yes." "Racing thoughts—yes." "Feeling sleepy— yes." "Angry thoughts—yes."

Resting in awareness, let yourself soften and open to whatever you notice in your mindfulness practice. Make the intentional turn of heart to open and say yes to it all—at least for the time of the meditation.

You might use the "yes" when you are noticing a sense of tension or struggle and straining within. You can relax and explore how it feels to drop resistance, even briefly or a little bit. Be awake and explore how dropping resistance can help you open more fully to the vast territory of awareness and more brightly illuminate what is here now, flowing through this moment.

As you become familiar with any repeating patterns of thinking and feeling appearing in your mind and body, let what you are learning about them become the basis for deeper understanding to guide, protect, heal, and transform you.

Into Daily Life

In the flow of moments and situations in daily life, when you notice yourself feeling anger, irritation, pain, or any kind of upset, pause and, breathing mindfully with it, acknowledge it, name it, and whisper, "Yes." If you need to, continue this practice over several breaths or a few minutes or longer. Remember to embrace this practice with a sense of curiosity and without attachment to outcome. Be careful about trying to "fix" or "get rid of" the painful experience with this practice. Dropping resistance and saying yes means being willing to stay present when the pain has not departed. Can you make room and keep watching, saying yes even to this?

MEDITATION PRACTICE #14:
Meet the Hindrances

Many people have the idea that they want freedom for their body. Freedom to come and go, freedom to do what they like, freedom to take in and experience what they want with their bodies. Many people value freedom of activity for their bodies.

What idea of freedom do they have for their minds? How does freedom of activity apply to one's mind? What do you think freedom means in your mind?

Of course, most people already experience times when their minds do not feel free. Here are some examples.

Have you ever been busily doing a task when suddenly your mind fills with *desire* for something else more pleasant and that desire diminishes your effectiveness doing the task?

Or have you have noticed you can be in a situation alone or with someone and suddenly your mind fills with *dislike and aversion* for what is happening. You urgently want to get away or to push the moment (or the person or situation) away.

Perhaps you have had the experience of feeling *fatigue in your body and dullness in your mind* and seen how they can cloud and distort any efforts you make to accomplish something.

Freedom in your mind can be lost to feelings of *restlessness*, perhaps in the form of agitation in mind and body. Has restlessness ever kept you from settling into something you are trying to do?

And, there is *doubt*. Have you ever noticed how persuasive and intimidating doubting thoughts—and the feelings of anxiety and worry in your mind and body they stimulate—can be? Have you noticed how doubt can literally cause you to hesitate or even abandon an activity or job that feels very important?

You might say these energies—desire for something else, aversion, fatigue and dullness, restlessness, and doubt—*hinder* or block you in living freely and happily because they can take over your mind and influence your body very easily. In the case of ill will and aversion, they feed angry feelings and thoughts directly. And, for most of us, they are very, very common visitors in our lives.

These same hindrances often arise in meditation practice as well. When they arise in meditation, it helps if you view them not as an enemy but simply as another set of causes and conditions worthy of your curiosity and attention. By placing mindful attention directly onto the hindrance and observing it as an object of your meditation, the hindrance changes from hindering to being instructive to you.

Those five mental states have the same simple names in meditation as we used in the examples above. Knowing their names and learning something about each one through mindful attention can definitely help you recognize them in all the moments of your life, whether you are meditating or not. The common names you might use to label these energies—when they appear in meditation practice or in life— are *sense desire, ill will and aversion, lethargy and dullness (or sleepiness), restlessness, and doubt.*

A simple and powerful mindfulness practice is simply to name the hindrance when it is present. Illuminating it with awareness by naming it makes you more mindful and immediately shifts your relationship to the hindrance energy.

Use this meditation to develop your awareness of these five mental states and see how, with greater awareness, you can begin to remove them as obstacles to the natural freedom that is possible for your mind—and, by extension, the freedom that is waiting for you in your life.

BRIEF PRACTICE #14

Take some time for a brief meditation at some point during your day or evening. Assume a comfortable position in a place where you will have some privacy and relax as you drop into awareness.

Put your attention on a focus that is easy for you to notice and return to when your attention moves away. It could be your breath sensations, or the sensations flowing in your body, or sounds around you, for example.

As your attention settles on your focus and your meditation unfolds, allow yourself to be watchful for and welcoming of any of the hindrances when they appear. Let yourself be curious.

Be relaxed, curious, and present, allowing each changing condition to be and simply noticing any thoughts or feelings that arise related to wishing for sensory pleasures. They could be pictures in your mind, or words or phrases like these: "I wish I had something to eat" "Wouldn't some relaxing music be nice?" "I want a different chair to sit in." *Notice any thought, daydream, or fantasy about more pleasant circumstances and gently name it—*"Desire, desire, desire"*—as long as it is present. Remember that you have not made a mistake. Know that it is okay to have the desire. You don't have to fight the desiring thoughts. This practice is about learning to recognize desire and each of the other hindrances too.*

Continuing your mindful attention on your primary focus, notice when any of the other hindrances appear.

Notice, name, and observe any expression of ill will and aversion. Perhaps it appears in phrases like "I hate this" *or* "I am so bored." *Or it may appear as a reaction when an uncomfortable or unpleasant feeling or memory appears, such as the aversion in a phrase like* "Oh no! I have a headache. I hate my headaches." *Breathing mindfully, notice the sensation, or the thought, and also notice the unpleasantness and the feeling of dislike and aversion for the experience that is present. For a few breaths, simply name the hindrance—*"Aversion is here. Feelings of aversion and dislike, aversion, aversion, aversion"*—not getting lost in the feeling but remaining aware and watchful.*

Remaining present with mindful attention, notice sleepiness in the same way. Be open and curious. Where is it in your body? What happens in your mind? Keep watching and naming—"Sleepiness, sleepiness, sleepiness, sleepiness"—*letting it go, not fighting it, but looking more closely and allowing it to reveal itself.*

Include and welcome restlessness in your practice when it visits. It is not necessary to fix or change any of these hindrances. Observing, breathing, allowing each thought and sensation to be, let yourself notice and remain curious. Where does restlessness live in your body? What happens in your thoughts when restlessness is here? Allow it to reveal itself, letting the meditation support you.

Breathing mindfully, acknowledge doubt when it comes. Doubt is only a combination of worried thoughts and sensations in your body. Bring mindful attention more closely to thoughts and sensations. Breathing mindfully with the feelings and thoughts of doubt, patiently listen: "This is doubt. Doubt feels and sounds like this. Doubting mind, doubting mind, doubt, doubt, doubt..."

What happens when you deliberately make the hindrance the focus of mindful and compassionate attention? Do you notice how sometimes the hindrances work together? Sleepiness or desire lead into doubt or restlessness or aversion, for example.

Finish your meditation and reflect on what you have learned about the hindrances. Let that learning inform you in times of meditation and beyond.

EXTENDED PRACTICE #14

As a Longer Formal Meditation Practice

Knowing about the hindrances, you can include mindfulness of the hindrances in any longer period of formal meditation. As you become more familiar with each hindrance, you may find you recognize it sooner. There is no need to change the hindrance or fix it. Relaxed and present, allow yourself to gently notice any time one or more of the hindrances appear during any formal meditation session—perhaps naming the hindrance, and allowing desire, or aversion, or sleepiness, or restlessness, or doubt to reveal themselves to you.

Into Daily Life

Extend your learning and awareness into daily life by deciding to notice one or more of the hindrances during one or more of your usual daily activities. Or extend the practice of being mindful of the hindrances into daily life by selecting a particular hindrance and reminding yourself to be mindful of it whenever it arises during the course of a day, or a week, or longer. Let yourself be playful and curious about the hindrances. There are many ways to become more mindful of them in daily life. Trust your intelligence to guide you. Desire, ill will, sleepiness, restlessness, and doubt will not hinder you so much or be such obstacles if you can become more conscious of them when they enter the present moment and when you are able to treat them not as enemies but as teachers who bring lessons about the true nature of life.

MEDITATION PRACTICE #15:
Broaden and Build Your Resilience and Your Response Capacity to Anger and Other Strong Emotions

When life presents you with difficulty in the form of challenges, annoyances, irritations, or other unpleasant experiences, it can be difficult but also empowering to radically shift your perspective. Try to respond by turning toward the moment with interest and kindness, allowing yourself to be open to a new perspective.

Research in positive psychology has demonstrated powerful benefits from the intentional cultivation of positivity. Barbara Fredrickson has focused especially on ten positive emotions: joy, gratitude, serenity, interest, hope, pride, amusement, inspiration, awe, and love (Fredrickson 2009, 2013). Her research points convincingly to how nourishing positivity in yourself can help you broaden and build your inner resources to cope more effectively and resist the pull of difficulty and upset, including the upset of strong emotions like anger. Nourishing positivity will also help you strengthen your capacity to meet any difficult moment mindfully and with interest and compassion, instead of reactively going to war with what is happening.

Try this meditation to experience the power of positivity to broaden and build your resources for meeting and overcoming the difficulties and challenges of life.

BRIEF PRACTICE #15

When you notice yourself caught in a negative emotional state—feeling upset, helpless, hopeless, afraid, or angry, for example—as soon as you can, step away from the situation, take some time for yourself, and pause for meditation.

Find a comfortable position, relax, and let yourself drop into awareness. Put your attention on your body sensations or your breathing for a few moments, letting some ease and calm arise in you, and trust yourself simply to notice the changing sensations. Let your thoughts go, or be, and make room for any experience, letting all things come and go. From time to time, return attention to your breathing or body sensations patiently in order to anchor your attention in the present moment.

Paying full and compassionate attention to your experience, trust your own creativity to bring about something beautiful as you direct attention to one or more things you are grateful for in your life. You might be grateful for your heart beating, or for a part of your body such as your hands, teeth, lungs, or eyes. You might be grateful for your circumstances—having a job, having loved ones or friends, or living where you do. You might be grateful, thankful, for so many things. Let yourself be surprised at the things that come to you when you ask, "What am I thankful for?"

Breathe mindfully, noticing any feelings, even feelings of anger, fear, or upset, meeting all of your experience with kindness and care. Quietly repeat your question from time to time: "What am I thankful for?" Breathe mindfully, listening and being open to any response.

Relax and let the breath come to you. Relax into any softening and ease in your body. Breathe mindfully and let yourself notice any positive feelings such as joy, pride, serenity, inspiration, or love that may appear. You don't have to be analytical—just notice thoughts and sensations, and let yourself feel any peace and warmth that may be present as you reflect on the things you are grateful for. Rest in that positive feeling. Breathe with it. Let it fill and support you.

End your meditation when you are ready. If you have any new ideas or insights about the situation that troubled you in the beginning, reflect and act on them only if it would help. If not, don't. In either case, know from your own experience that you can touch the strength of positivity in yourself whenever you need to.

EXTENDED PRACTICE #15

As a Longer Formal Meditation Practice

Take a comfortable position in a place where you will not be disturbed. Give yourself some time for this practice to deepen your exploration of positive emotions.

Begin by gathering attention in your body, feeling the sensations. When you are ready, put your attention on the sensations of your breathing. Let the breath come to you. Let yourself feel the peace and ease that comes as you simply watch and allow the breath sensations to come and go.

When you like, shift attention to any one of the qualities of positivity that you would like to explore more deeply. As you continue to breathe mindfully, reflect on the quality with a simple, quiet question.

You might ask, for example, "What brings me joy?" After asking your question, patiently listen mindfully for anything that comes back in response. Not becoming lost in thoughts, just ask and listen. Resting in awareness and breathing mindfully, include your body sensations in your noticing. From time to time, quietly repeat your question, listening with curiosity.

This is a practice of patience, acceptance, and trust of your own inner wisdom and goodness. It is not so much about thinking, but it is about being present with sensitive attention and an open heart. This practice invites you simply to be present fully for yourself, to ask, and to listen. You might be surprised by what you learn by remaining mindful and listening deeply.

In this same meditation period if you like or in a later one, you might explore any or all of the other qualities in a similar way. For example, after steadying yourself in awareness and becoming very present yourself, you might drop a question very quietly into your heart and mind: "What am I grateful for?" *or* "What brings me peace?" *or* "Who and what inspires me to live more fully?" "When do I feel awe, or a sense of the grandeur, beauty, and mystery toward this world?" "What am I proud of?" "When and with whom do I feel loved?"

Let your inner wisdom guide you. Choose questions and phrases that resonate most deeply within. Let any wisdom that comes to you carry over and support you in your life.

Into Daily Life

Extend this practice of reflection on positivity in your life by choosing one of the qualities and commit to being mindful of it for a day, or a week, or longer if you like.

If it helps, write the quality on a note or post it someplace where you will see it. The note will remind you to notice how that quality manifests in your life—as a feeling inside, in a moment or aspect of a relationship, or somehow in the world around you, possibly in the actions of others or as beauty in nature or art.

When you notice any moment of positivity, pause and let yourself feel it deeply, letting it saturate your being, even for a single breath, and let the goodness contained in that positive moment carry you on.

KEEP IN MIND

- Any strong emotion, including anger and hatred, is made of elements that are not that emotion.

- Learning to use mindful and compassionate attention to look more closely at the elemental conditions required to form the cloud of anger or to create and sustain such powerful rivers of emotion in your life can empower you to escape them and to change the conditions in yourself so you won't be so vulnerable to these destructive emotions in the future.

some common questions

and concerns about

calming your angry mind

It is important that students bring a certain ragamuffin, barefoot irreverence to their studies. They are not here to worship what is known, but to question it.

—Jacob Bronowski

One of the central themes of this book is that, as a human being, you have the capacity to utilize meditative practices based in mindfulness and compassion to discover a larger sense of identity beyond constantly changing emotional states such as anger. If you learn to strengthen and trust your ability to be more mindful and compassionate, then you are actually using your mind to change your brain, and you are broadening and building your resources for greater resilience and wiser emotional intelligence related to anger and other intense and burdensome emotions.

Over these first seven chapters, you have been learning more about the territory of your inner life through a variety of meditative practices based in mindfulness and compassion. You have also been offered some challenging and (hopefully) empowering and freeing perspectives on anger and its cousins, such as ill will and aversion.

Now that you have had a chance to engage in some meditation practices and contemplative reflections, it is likely that you have some questions and possibly even some concerns about your experiences of practicing mindfulness. If you do, that is very good! It shows you have actually been practicing and have been noticing what comes up for you as you become more mindful of your inner life and the life around you.

It is good to have questions, also, because they can help you establish a daily mindfulness practice and help you make mindfulness a way of living your life. In fact, you will have the most success with your practice when you learn to make mindfulness a part of all of the moments of your everyday life, and not just think of the practice as a "tool" to use only when you are angry or upset. The process of living a more mindful life will almost certainly evoke questions about how to practice mindfulness in different situations and about what you notice in yourself as you practice. Seeking answers to your questions as you build your mindfulness practice is an important way to make your practice as strong and steady as it can be.

From the perspective of neuroscience, it will probably be your regular daily practice, including periods of formal meditation and the times that you pause for mindful moments (with those frequent and repeated influences of mindfulness, kindness, compassion meditations), that will promote the changes in your brain and nervous system that will prepare and protect you in overcoming the challenges of controlling anger and other destructive emotions. Much like regular exercise strengthens your muscles so that when you really need them they are strong and ready, if you have gotten into daily habit of being intentionally more mindful, kind, and compassionate, then when you do have a "storm" of anger or rage, you will find it much easier to manage.

The questions and concerns you are about to read are common ones. You will probably recognize your own experience in some of these questions. People usually have some variation of these questions and concerns whenever they take up, or continue, mindfulness meditation and the other practices we have explored in this book. Questions like these reflect the universality and basic human experience of self-doubt, the tendency to be self-critical, the wandering mind, desire for pleasant things, and aversion and ill will toward unpleasant things. The commonness of these concerns is more evidence that we human beings are actually more alike than we are different.

QUESTIONS ABOUT MINDFULNESS

What is the difference between mindfulness and meditation practice?

This is a very good question, and one many people ask. A simple way to put it is to say that mindfulness is a capacity for nonjudging, welcoming, reflective awareness that each of us can access. Mindfulness is a quality available to us as human beings.

Even if you do not meditate, you can have mindful moments. Mindfulness occurs naturally, such as when you suddenly notice the coolness of a breeze against your face or when you realize that your mind is racing with worried thoughts. Mindfulness is the awareness that notices what is happening here, now, in the present moment. Mindfulness can be developed and made brighter by systematic training of the mind using various reflective practices that we also call "meditation."

Meditation is a term that refers to many, many practices, but a simple way to think of meditation is that any meditation practice is about cultivating stronger attention, brighter awareness, and greater understanding. Practicing meditation helps you train your mind (and change your brain!) in skills of intention, attention, and the attitudes of acceptance and nonjudgment. So, we could say that mindfulness meditation is a way of practicing meditation to intentionally strengthen and sustain your natural capacity for being aware in each moment—being "mindful". If you wish to be more mindful in your life, then you'll find, as most people do, that it is crucial to bring meditation into your life in both formal and informal practice.

You can learn more about mindfulness and meditation in chapters 1, 3, and 4. And, of course, there are many different meditations offered for practice throughout this book.

I don't have much time to meditate. What should I do?

There is really no magic number about how much time you should meditate. What is vitally important is that you make a commitment to being present—paying attention on purpose in a nonjudging and friendly way—in as many moments as you can.

It can help to remember that life always happens in *this* moment, the present moment. So, cultivating mindfulness means knowing something about what is happening now, including if you are feeling rushed or like you don't have much time for something, like meditation.

It is also true that by setting aside time for what we call "formal" meditation—even a few minutes one or more times each day—you will, over time, build your skills of intention, attention, and the crucial attitudes that support your mindfulness practice. Making at least some time for formal meditation practice is crucial.

So, instead of being stuck on the idea of not having much time to meditate, a good way to bring more mindfulness meditation into your life might be to ask a different question: "When can I meditate today?" If you can give yourself permission for that answer to be any amount of time and find the discipline to actually practice in the time you have, then your mindfulness practice will probably take care of itself.

Is one time of day better for my meditation practice than another?

Probably not. The most important thing is to see for yourself what time of day will be the best time for you. That could include the times when you are most likely to have some uninterrupted time for formal meditation, and when you are most likely to be at least somewhat awake and alert. Many people find that doing even a brief period (ten to twenty minutes, for example) of meditation first thing when they get up and just before they go to bed can be very helpful for how they experience and respond to their entire day.

Is one place better than another to be mindful?

If you are asking about formal meditation, the answer is that it totally depends on you. Important characteristics of the place where you practice might include a comfortable way to sit or a room where you can lie on the floor or move around; some degree of privacy from interruption; and, if possible, not too many distractions nearby. Many people also like to have a few inspiring objects around them when they meditate. This is purely a personal matter, and the object could be anything that holds meaning for you. For example, you could choose photographs, statues, meaningful keepsakes, beautiful flowers, or stones, to name a few of the kinds of things many people use.

It also can help to remember that you can be mindful anyplace you are! So, you may want to explore practicing mindfulness wherever you go, and also discover that mindfulness really is not limited to any location nor does it require any special conditions.

Could you say some more about those five hindrances in meditation? I'm not sure what you mean by "sense desire," or how ill will and aversion, especially, are hindrances. I kind of understand sleepiness and restlessness, and I think I have a lot of doubt sometimes.

Excellent question, and excellent noticing. If you are like most people, you can have a lot of doubt as well as frequent encounters with the other hindrances too. It seems to be part of the human condition! Let me talk about the hindrances in a slightly different order than you name them, and give desire a bit more attention near the end of this response. We'll start with sleepiness and restlessness.

You don't have to get too analytical about this, in my experience. Sleepiness, restlessness, and doubt can often be demanding and relatively easy to notice. If you notice doubt and feelings of sleepiness or restlessness, then they are here. You can trust that you are noticing those hindrances and look more closely in order to understand them better.

Calling any of these energies "hindrances" is just a way of acknowledging that they can be very distracting and can "hinder" your ability to notice what is here, now. The hindrances can also interfere with almost anything else you try to do, from daily chores to enjoying time with your family.

So, it helps most people to know about these five energies, and to have a name for them when they arise. It can be very empowering simply to become more mindful when each one comes into a moment or situation of your life. Knowing they are here instead of being unconsciously stuck in them can make all the difference if you wish to escape their distorting influence in your life. At times, if you recognize the hindrance is present, you may be able to make a choice or take an action that frees you from the hindrance or weakens its power over you in a particular moment.

Now let's return to your question about desire. "Sense desire" simply means that you want something that is pleasant (or very pleasant) to come to one or more of your senses. By recognizing that the desire for a pleasant experience (sense desire) is present, you can make a better choice about how to relate to it. For example, if you are mindful when the desire for a rich and sweet snack arises, you might just practice mindfulness of the desire and observe if you are hungry or if something else is happening. You don't have to become angry with yourself (or anyone else!) or be self-critical. You might just say something like "Desire is visiting me now. What does it feel like? What does it want?" and then watch mindfully.

Also, please remember that you are only human! The hindrances are a part of life for most of us human beings, and feeling desire, ill will, sleepiness, restlessness, or doubt is not a mistake or a failure of some kind. Meeting any hindrance with mindfulness, compassion, and understanding about what it is can help you look more closely at the conditions that support it as well as the responses you might choose to disentangle from it.

I am sorry, but I just cannot sit still to meditate. What should I do?

Cannot or won't?

Perhaps you are not satisfied with what happens when you actually pause, sit, and pay closer attention to your own thoughts, feelings, and embodied experience.

If this is the case, then I suggest you let go of any expectations or agenda with your meditation, and just sit and watch what happens. Can you bring curiosity to what is happening? Is there any underlying fear or a set of ideas that you carry about yourself or about meditation that need closer inspection?

Many people I have known have a self-constructed identity based on a belief that they cannot sit (or something else, like they cannot meditate, for example), and the practice of becoming aware/mindful of those beliefs can be very instructive and freeing. So, I suggest you make a commitment, summon the discipline, drop any expectations, and simply bring compassionate attention to your experience each time you choose to sit and meditate. See for yourself what might be going on inside of you!

You said somewhere that it helps to slow down when you practice mindfulness. What does that mean?

Mindfulness actually does not have a speed limit. However, attention, for most of us, seems to. What I mean is that usually the faster something happens, the less our attention can take it in, or the more easily attention is distracted.

So, as a simple aid to practicing mindfulness and to developing steadier and more penetrating attention, I often suggest that you deliberately slow down any activity you are practicing mindfulness with. Some examples are stepping very slowly in walking meditation, or putting your utensils down between bites when eating a mindful meal, or mindfully washing the dishes without music or other distractions as you place attention on the sensations of water temperature, the hardness of the dishes, and the changing visual patterns as food is slowly cleaned off of dirty plates.

When your attention is steady on a focus (such as your walking or cleaning the dishes), it can be fun and instructive to change the speed of activity on purpose. As you continue observing mindfully, intentionally increase your speed (walking, for example) and notice what happens. Be sure to pay close attention to what happens in your thoughts as the speed of your movements increases. You may learn something interesting about the relationship between your mind and your body!

There are different mindfulness practices in this book. I am feeling a bit confused. How and when should I use the different ones—for example, how do I decide between mindful breathing or observing sensations in different parts of my body or walking meditation?

Very good question! I have had the same one. I can recall going on retreats early in my meditation practice and hearing different teachers give instructions that seemed different to me for similar methods of meditation. I felt confused, until I realized that there was no right way that I had to rigidly follow. When you can relax about doing it "right" and trust yourself simply to notice and to pay attention, doubts and questions have a way of fading or being answered by your practice experience. The confusion is a good thing in these cases if for no other reason than it shows you are taking the practices seriously and paying careful attention to what is being offered and to your experience as you try them on.

Actually, mindfulness is really about relaxing and paying attention to what is happening here and now. That is it. Mindfulness is definitely not only about breathing, or walking, or eating. It is about awareness in this moment. Different methods or practices are usually about different points of emphasis, ways to steady attention, or cultivate a more compassionate, open heart, for example. All aim at helping you to be more present and more aware in the changing moments and conditions of your life.

Having said that, most people find some combination of practices helpful. For example, you might choose your practice for formal periods of meditation, or informal ones, to emphasize strengthening and steadying attention (like mindful breathing or walking), to increase body awareness, or to cultivate qualities of kindness, compassion, and wisdom about the changing nature of emotions and other experiences in life.

It is good to practice with different methods, and it is also good to stick with a particular practice for a period of time or through multiple sessions. You can even combine the two. For instance, you might make awareness of breathing your main practice daily for a week or several weeks, and you could begin each session of that mindful breathing with a few moments of a loving-kindness or compassion practice. Staying with a particular practice (like awareness of breathing) for a period of time empowers you to better understand the range of challenges and the benefits that practice offers.

So, it is really up to you. You might also find it helpful to join a mindfulness class or go on a retreat, even for a few hours or a day, to get a sense of how the different practices can support each other over time. As you practice more, you may also recognize that the points of emphasis in any one practice are also present in the other practices—for example, steady attention is present in the compassion practice, just as kindness and friendliness is a part of mindful breathing.

How will I know if I am getting anywhere with my meditation, and how hard should I be trying when I meditate?

Well, the paradox is that you should practice mindfulness with *no* agenda or expectation about getting anywhere at all! The core attitudes of nonjudging and nonstriving are related to this perspective.

Mindfulness is really about not trying to fix anything or get anywhere, but it is about becoming more aware of what is actually here. It is about knowing what can be known.

So, if you find yourself feeling impatient or bored, look deeper. There is a good chance that some judgment or voice in your head has decided you are not getting anywhere or not trying hard enough and is causing you discomfort. In that moment of recognizing the distress and the angry or impatient thoughts, try simply naming what is here—judgment, striving, impatience, for example—continue to breathe mindfully with it, allowing and observing with curiosity. What happens next to these demanding thoughts and feelings?

My mind races with thoughts when I do these practices. Should I be trying to blank my mind or control those thoughts so I can become more peaceful and better at meditation?

No. In mindfulness meditation, we take a friendly and inclusive approach to all experiences, including when the mind is racing or worried. A key instruction in mindfulness practice is the one that advises us how to work with any thoughts—racing, angry, desire filled, worried, sad, or something else. The instruction is this: "In this meditation, you don't have to blank your mind or control your thoughts; you can let them be. And you don't have to feed your thoughts or argue with them; you can let them go."

One of the paradoxes of mindfulness practice is that when you stop trying to control your mind to make it become more peaceful and just let things be, then the peace you seek is more likely to find you.

Meditation is too boring. Is this the only way?

Is life too boring? Meditation is basically about growing awareness of the unfolding experience of your own life. Mindfulness is about knowing something about how things are in this moment, including when unpleasant feelings like boredom are present. We benefit from meditation by learning and knowing more about our deeply habitual reactions to any of our experiences, even difficult or boring ones. Deepening understanding about ourselves and our reactions by becoming more mindful of them is the source of much of the healing power that mindfulness practice brings.

If you feel bored, you can make that feeling, and the thoughts that feed the feeling, the object of mindful attention. Instead of seeking to escape the feeling of boredom, you can turn attention toward it. Similar to the response to the question about getting someplace in meditation, the response to noticing feelings of being bored is to become more curious about what boredom feels like, and to investigate the thoughts, expectations, or beliefs creating the judgment that the meditation is boring.

Usually when people complain about feeling bored, they are not happy with how things are in this moment. They long for distraction or something to take them away. Mindfulness gives you the opportunity to choose a different response. The constant pursuit of feeling different can be more a source of pain and stress than a relief, yet most of us spend a lot of time trying not to feel bored or otherwise dissatisfied. With mindfulness practice, you don't have to depend on external circumstances to help you. You can make the feeling of boredom itself an object of curious and compassionate attention. What you learn from that focus on boredom might surprise you!

QUESTIONS ABOUT MEDITATIONS ON KINDNESS AND COMPASSION

When I meditate, I don't like the feelings of anger and fear that I feel, and I want to get away from them. You talk about "turning toward" difficult emotions like anger with kindness and compassion. I don't understand exactly what you mean. Could you explain more about how I can do this?

This is a very good question, and an important one too.

It is especially important because the learning and healing available through meditation practice seems to happen when you are able not to turn away (or run away), but remain present and observe with compassion any experience, including painful feelings like anger and fear.

So, when we say "turn toward the difficult," we literally mean resist the impulse to look away or go away. With an intention to watch this difficulty with compassion and curiosity, turn your attention toward the difficult experience that is here now. This can seem very strange at first, and it can also be frightening or confusing in itself.

Turning toward the difficult may seem strange because we have been taught for so long and from so many others that we should respond to difficult or painful feelings and situations by turning away from them, or, if we cannot do that, ignoring or denying them, or distracting ourselves. And, of course, sometimes these strategies do help, at least for a time. It is good to know about them as one response. But turning away or denying pain or unpleasantness is not always possible, does not always help, and, for many reasons, can actually be hurtful, if it becomes your only response to any pain that comes to you. In the case of angry feelings, for example, chronically denying them or pretending they are not there has little impact on the destructive effects of those feelings upon your inner life and health, or how they are expressed in your words and behaviors, which are easily visible to others.

So, turning toward the difficult is a crucial element of the healing and transformation that mindfulness and compassion practices can offer you. It can be as simple as understanding the importance of developing your skills for paying attention to everything, including unpleasant things, and believing, and eventually truly knowing, that you—and others who need you—can really benefit from your staying present. It also helps to remember that you already have all you need. And, if you decide to do it, you will discover that turning toward the difficult does become easier, more rewarding, and more natural as your meditation practice grows.

What if I cannot feel anything in these meditations? I am not sure I know what kindness and compassion actually feel like! Does that ever happen to anyone else?

It is an act of kindness and compassion to remain open to whatever you are feeling in this moment—even not feeling anything. Indeed, by acknowledging when you do not feel something could be the beginning of a voyage of deeper self-discovery and healing. The practices focused on kindness and compassion are so powerful, in part, exactly because they can awaken you to deeper levels of feeling—even blocked feeling.

Many people also report that—rather than feelings of kindness or compassion—they feel sadness or anger, confusion or fear, or other intense feelings when they do these meditation practices. If that happens to you, never fear! You are okay. The arising of strong emotions during or following periods of meditation focused on qualities of compassion and kindness is a sign that something is happening in you, and it deserves your attention, your kindness toward yourself, and your self-compassion.

Doing the loving-kindness practice, I realize I need to do something with forgiveness for some people. Can you say more about that?

Thank you. That sounds like a deep personal insight.

And, yes, it is very common for people to recognize the need for forgiveness when they take up the practice of cultivating feelings of friendliness and loving-kindness. In fact, this is one of the ways this type of meditation can promote deep healing. It reveals places in the human heart that have hardened and need care.

A simple and practical definition of forgiveness I like is this: forgiveness is the end of resentment. It is easy for hurts of all kinds to stay with us. Carrying any hurt can be the breeding ground for resentment. The resentment carried this way can color and provoke strong, angry feelings, even years after the initial hurt. So, recognizing the need to practice forgiveness is definitely a step in the right direction if you wish to heal old hurts, end resentment, and become less angry.

In meditation practice #9 in chapter 6, you will find a basic forgiveness meditation practice. Of course, it is not the only way to practice forgiveness. This practice can be very powerful, however. It invites you to offer forgiveness in the "three directions"—to those who have harmed you (first direction) and to ask forgiveness of those you have harmed (second direction). The third direction of the practice is to offer forgiveness to yourself for any harm you may have caused intentionally or unintentionally.

When I first learned this meditation form, the teacher emphasized two points that I have found very helpful over the years. First, the harm that causes pain, in us or in others, may be either intentional or unintentional. Whether intentional or unintentional, resentment can build and forgiveness is needed. Second, we can only offer forgiveness. We cannot force anyone to take it.

Finally, it is good to remember that memories run deep, and mind habits of resentment can be very strong. It can take real patience to work with forgiveness. Knowing this, you might relax a bit and not be in a big hurry. Just bring curiosity and clear intention to your practice, and trust mindfulness and the goodness of your own heart to reveal what you need to know and do at just the right time you need to know and do it in order to heal any resentment in your life.

Sometimes the loving-kindness and compassion phrases and those meditations feel phony to me. I feel like I am just a dumb Pollyanna pretending things aren't so bad. Am I missing something?

That is an excellent question, and it reflects some excellent mindfulness of what is happening for you in the meditation practice! There is absolutely nothing wrong with you.

It sounds as if you are noticing that you have some doubts, some self-critical thoughts, and a sense of not being connected in an authentic way to what you are doing. Yes?

These are very common feelings that can arise when you begin to practice the meditations on kindness and compassion. Your natural mindfulness is helping you to notice these conditions, and because of that greater self-awareness, you have a good opportunity to deepen the practices of loving-kindness and compassion.

These practices based in kindness and compassion are basically about connecting (or reconnecting) with qualities that you already have. Kindness and compassion are in everyone. If you have some difficulty feeling them, you are not alone. It is very common.

The habits of inattention and absence that interfere with mindfulness can also block your capacity to connect with the innate goodness of your own heart. They also may keep you from realizing your connection, through compassion, with others. Further, emotional habits of meanness, ill will, aversion, and chronic anger run deep and are often fed by even more basic feelings and beliefs about separation, hurt, and abandonment. Such deep emotional habits and distorted or false beliefs and ideas can continue to feed the very doubts you express.

One thing you might try is to settle on a single phrase or just a couple of phrases to use to practice loving-kindness and compassion. In this book, I offer a variety of different phrases to give you an idea of the possible range of language you might use. The most powerful phrases are usually the ones that resonate most deeply with you. In some cases, especially if you are not feeling any feeling, a helpful phrase might invite the possibility of feeling the feeling. For example, you might offer this wish for yourself: "May I experience the possibility of deep peace and ease." Let the sense of authenticity of and resonance with your chosen phrase guide you.

And, as your meditation practice deepens, you will likely find that the words and phrases will speak more completely and meaningfully to you. You will probably begin to use different phrases too. And don't be surprised if, in that process of deepening, more feelings of anger or sadness appear. The deep listening and open-heartedness of these practices makes possible a fundamental release of strong feelings and the healing of long-carried hurt. Whenever intense feelings appear, never fear! Healing and transformation is happening in you.

Sometimes doing the loving-kindness and compassion for myself, I don't feel worthy. I feel like I am being selfish. It's like, deep down, I know I don't deserve to be happy. Is something really wrong with me?

Of course not! You are a beautiful and valuable human being. And, as we like to say in the mindfulness-based stress reduction classes, "No matter how much you think is wrong, we believe there is more right than is wrong with you."

A very good thing that is right with you is your capacity to be mindful. It sounds as if you have become mindful that you have some strong inner feelings of unworthiness, self-doubt, and perhaps dislike of yourself. Yes?

If that is so, then join the club! One of the most common things people practicing mindfulness in my classes notice is just how mean and critical they are toward themselves—a lot of the time. After a while in the class, we are all able to laugh knowingly whenever someone tells their latest example of being hard on themselves. "We certainly can be our own worst stressors," we will say.

So, noticing the deep habits of meanness to yourself and feelings of unworthiness offers you a real opportunity for life-changing healing and transformation. You can begin by bringing more mindfulness and compassion to yourself and any feelings of self-doubt or unworthiness when you notice them. Allow them to be just as they are and to reveal themselves to you as you observe and welcome these feelings with curiosity and kindness. What you discover about yourself might change your life in beautiful and powerful ways.

For a long time, I have thought of myself as maybe not so kind a person. I think I am an angry person, mostly. I don't like it, but I think that is how I am. Do you think I can change?

Probably, the truth is that you are a whole person who has many different ideas about yourself and a wide variety of feelings, like other people. You may notice that you have certain feelings, like anger, more often, but that doesn't mean you aren't, or couldn't also be, kind or compassionate, or wise and tolerant.

And we know that our mental habits and brain function develops and strengthens (or withers) depending on how we use our minds.

So, you can definitely change and be less angry and more kind, if you want to change. To do this will take some work on your part. That work will begin as you recognize and understand your anger and learn how to care for it better. Caring for your own anger with kindness and compassion is a powerful step toward becoming more kind and compassionate in other places in your life. The work continues as you intentionally bring more mindfulness, kindness, and compassion into your life and relationships with others.

Anger thrives on our inner narratives, the stories we tell ourselves. When you are more mindful of mental habits and critical narratives targeting self and others, you can begin to question and let go of those narratives. You can replace them with other intentions, like growing understanding and building kindness and compassion toward yourself and others. You can change—your mind, your brain, and your life—by taking on the mental training of particular meditations, like those in this book.

So, yes! If you can start to bring mindfulness to your anger and more kindness and compassion to yourself and to others, I know you can change.

I have been doing some of these meditations, and realize that, even though I don't want to be an angry person, I have felt that way for so long it feels kind of comfortable to me. I wonder if maybe I am actually afraid to let myself find out who I might be if I am not really an angry person. Do you think I am crazy for thinking like this?

Not at all. I think you are probably onto some very important insights about yourself.

It is widely said that people are more comfortable with the known than the unknown, even when the known is not very pleasant. You may be sensing a variation of this theme in yourself when it comes to recognizing some fear about not making an identity out of being angry.

Anger serves many purposes, including the purpose of creating a (false) sense of control and safety through a more limited view of ourselves and our relationship to others and the world. Such a limited view—"I am an angry person"—can start to feel comfortable, like an old pair of shoes, but it is very restrictive too.

So, if you could begin to explore the possibility that who you are beyond the anger is actually much more complex, much larger, and very much more interesting and alive than you ever imagined, then you might find that this thought about not being an angry person is not crazy at all, but perhaps the wisest thought you could have.

QUESTIONS ABOUT MANAGING ANGER USING MEDITATION

I have tried some of these meditations and am still pretty angry. And sometimes I can't focus or I fall asleep. I don't think meditation will work for me. Should I move on to something else?

Well, of course, that is your choice. But why would you stop trying to help yourself feel less angry because things aren't what you expected?

Like most emotions, angry feelings are very deep habits in mind and body, and it is usually not realistic to expect them to disappear quickly. Likewise, difficulty focusing attention and feeling sleepy in meditation are very common experiences. When these things happen, you have not made any mistakes.

Instead of judging your meditation or yourself by whether or not you feel any anger, or can focus attention in every session, or may fall asleep, what if you shifted your attention away from the outcome and simply made the experience—whatever it is in this moment—the focus for your mindful and compassionate attention? That is, after all, really what mindfulness is about—watching and knowing something about what is here in this moment, including your reactions and thoughts about what is here.

If you notice anger is here, instead of getting caught in more thoughts or doubts about still being angry, you might try just paying closer attention to the thoughts and feelings of anger. Breathe mindfully with the experience and watch it. Remembering the structure of anger model (see chapter 2), let your attention include body sensations of arousal or fear, and any thoughts or beliefs beneath the angry feelings. What do you notice then? Or, if your attention wanders, perhaps naming "restlessness," or if you are sleepy, naming "sleepiness," and watching that condition to better understand its influence over you.

You could stop practicing mindfulness if you choose, but from your question, it sounds like things are really just getting interesting!

I realize that maybe I don't know when I am angry. My friends tell me I am angry sometimes, but I thought that feeling was me being anxious or maybe excited. What do you think?

You might be surprised by how many people have similar experiences. One of the main obstacles for people healing and becoming free of chronic feelings of anger is that they don't know what anger actually feels like inside.

It is very good insight that leads you to ask this question. You could build on this sense of curiosity and gently bring mindfulness to your body and thoughts more often. When you think you may be feeling angry, or when someone tells you that you seem angry, you might pause and bring mindful attention to your body and your inner life in that moment. Breathe mindfully and allow yourself to notice what is happening. You may be able to feel the places in your body where the emotion is. You may actually be able to hear the tone of voice in your thoughts and know if the thoughts are angry or judgmental, or critical and disliking.

And, very importantly, remember to practice patience and compassion with yourself. It is not a failure to feel angry! Anger is a basic human emotion and experience. By learning to turn toward the feeling and to investigate your own experience of it by using mindfulness, you will learn exactly what you need to know.

Sometimes when I am doing a meditation, I start to feel more angry and upset. What am I doing wrong?

Actually, nothing. It sounds as if you are getting somewhere.

In the orientation session for the mindfulness-based stress reduction classes, we warn people by saying, "It will probably get more stressful before it gets less stressful." What we mean is that as we grow our mindfulness in daily life through meditation and informal practice, we very likely will become *more* aware of the difficult and stressful things as well as the more enjoyable and pleasant moments.

For most of us, difficult feelings like anger actually come and go daily, but we learn many (sometimes clever) ways to prevent ourselves from noticing or feeling them. Becoming more mindful means you will notice your feelings more accurately and more often. This is exactly as it should be for those who seek to better manage their stress and their difficult emotions. Increased awareness leads to increased understanding of the causes and the conditions that support difficult feelings like anger and resentment.

Remember how in chapter 7 we said that the cloud is made of non-cloud elements and that anger is made of non-anger elements? Well, when mindfulness makes the feelings of anger and upset more visible and palpable, you are better able to focus on them and observe the elements that form and sustain them. That understanding will help you heal and transform any chronic feelings of anger, resentment, ill will, and upset.

I grew up being told that being angry is a form of weakness. It is a defect you have to correct. So, I have learned not to let myself feel anger. Is that a problem?

How is that working for you so far? Has not letting yourself feel anger created any problems in your life? (Many people know, and much research indicates, that anger is easily misunderstood, and that chronically ignoring angry feelings is actually quite harmful to your health and to your relationships.) If you believe anger is a form of weakness, how do you feel about yourself if you have an angry feeling?

You are very insightful to identify that you were taught at an early age to reject anger, and that you carry a deeply rooted belief that anger is a defect and a form of weakness. The core beliefs we carry about so many things are the basis for so many reactions we have in the present moment toward others and ourselves. It is very empowering to identify one's core beliefs about things.

So, what if you questioned that belief? What if you opened yourself to the possibility that feeling anger is not a form of weakness at all, but it is something that practically every human being experiences and must learn to understand and to cope with?

What if you tried on a different view of anger? Could you perhaps relax a bit with anger and become more curious about what it is and what it means in you? If you could try that, then the meditations in this book might help you explore the territory of anger in more depth. Then you can decide for yourself if anger is a form of weakness—as you have been taught—or if anger is actually a powerful vehicle for understanding more about the mystery and meaning of this human life.

A long time ago, I decided that if someone makes me angry, it is their problem, not my problem. I have a right to be angry, and it's their fault. They'll get what they deserve. What do you think about that?

I think there is some wisdom in your position, but I also think you may be selling yourself a bit short too.

The wisdom is that other people will do what they do, and that is pretty much out of our control. So, when they do what they do and you feel angry, it is good not to take what they did personally. For example, when someone reaches in front of you in the grocery store and takes the item you were looking at, that person probably did not mean any harm to you personally, so don't take it that way.

But when you say, "They'll get what they deserve," it indicates that on some level a part of you feels hurt or disrespected, has some resentment, and the situation actually has become a problem for you. So, can you let that thought about them getting "what they deserve" become a reminder to you to look more deeply, to become more mindful, and to watch and listen more compassionately to the parts in you that feel hurt or resentful? When you can do that, any situation in which someone "makes you angry" can become an opportunity both to grow in self-awareness and understanding and to embrace the possibility of transformation and deeper peace in your life.

When I am caught up in the storm of anger, what should I do to escape?

It can be a difficult moment, for sure. Here are some basic principles for responding to that storm of anger. Recognize and name what is happening. Protect yourself as much as possible. Use a mindfulness practice—mindful breathing or walking, for example—to stop and disentangle from the streams of angry thoughts and sensations in mind and body. As you breathe or walk mindfully, remember what anger is and what it is not: anger is temporary and made of non-anger elements; anger is *not you. Then* turn mindful and compassionate attention to your unfolding experience. You could experiment with meditation practices based in kindness and compassion to help you stay present, keep anger in focus, and manage any upset. Please remember not to beat yourself up. It is natural to be angry at times. Practice the core attitudes of patience and trust, allowing yourself to look deeply, resting attention on your body or sounds, breathing mindfully with the experience, watching.

Finally, it can help to shift the basic intention of your response from escaping the "storm" to understanding it. If you try to escape, you probably feel some aversion and perhaps even anger at the storm of anger. This is, of course, quite natural. It is also a very unpleasant experience. And, if you feel some aversion to experience in this moment, bringing mindfulness and compassion to that feeling of aversion is very helpful.

By shifting to an attitude of kind curiosity about the anger that is here and about any reactions you notice in yourself, you give yourself more space and opportunity for understanding. It could prove very informative. What will you notice with a deeper look?

Can I expect that these meditations will eventually protect me from ever feeling any anger, and is it a sign of progress if I feel less anger?

His Holiness the Dalai Lama once said that, of course, he feels angry, but it doesn't have to be a problem. I have also heard many meditation teachers tell their own stories about how anger visited them, and how they learned to work with it in meditation. So, I would not expect that you will never feel anger if you practice these meditations (or any meditations). Feeling anger seems to be part of our lot as human beings. In fact, it can be a real obstacle and the source of much doubt, and possibly more anger, if you create an unrealistic expectation that if you learn to meditate "correctly," then you will not feel anger. Please don't think that way.

Instead, a more useful approach is to pay attention to how you treat the feelings of anger when they arise. The response you choose is where healing and the real learning can happen.

It can be very important, as any psychotherapist can attest, for each of us to learn to recognize our feelings, including angry feelings, accurately. Many people, as we have mentioned in this book at times, don't actually know that what they are feeling is anger. How can they hope to free themselves from the toxic effects of chronic or unmanaged anger if they don't even know when it has taken them over?

No, these meditations are not so much insulation against ever having angry feelings as they are skillful means to help you recognize and manage any anger that comes your way. As you learn to do that, and to better understand the roots of anger in yourself and in your life, there is a very good chance that you will actually experience less anger and more happiness. If you notice this is happening over time as you build your meditation practice, then it could very well be a sign of progress.

But it is also a good idea to be careful about any notions of progress in meditation. Again, there is the paradox. The true progress is most likely to occur when you stop trying to gain or attain anything. So, you can relax. Allow the anger to be there, and bring mindful and compassionate attention to it, using any of the many ways we have been exploring in this book.

Being curious, mindful, and steadily observant of your anger when it appears probably will change your relationship to the anger and ease its power over you. However, it is probably not realistic to think you will never again feel angry, and maybe it is for the best if you remain capable of anger at times so that mindfulness and anger together can continue to teach you about the mystery of this human life.

PART 3

beyond your angry mind

CHAPTER 9

you have not fallen

out of the universe

Nature loves man, beetles, and birds with the same love.

—*John Muir*

Anger can be a master illusionist. Angry, hostile, or scornful feelings can fool you into believing that you are permanently and unalterably isolated from other human beings or any life around you. Thoughts filled with resentment and dislike for others can convince you that you are not being respected, or seen, or heard by them. To make matters worse, the belief that you are isolated and not being seen or heard can lead you to project your angry reactions onto others when they mean you no harm—with the result that you are very likely to drive them away, worsening your sense of isolation.

In increasingly painful ways, the insistent voices of anger inside you—voices that are sulking, steaming, feeling bored, irritable, or visited by any of the rest of the family of feelings united by ill will and aversion—can deceive you into forgetfulness and obscure your recognition of your true place and role in the web of life. The distortions of an angry mind can block your conscious perception of connection with others, breath by breath, and cloud your sensitivity to the interdependency of all living things as they coexist moment by moment.

The lesson of mindfulness is the opposite of the isolation and alienation of anger. Mindfulness reminds us that we all do belong in this life, and it invites us to befriend our own feelings of self-doubt, unworthiness, alienation, and the anger that drives them. Mindfulness opens the possibility in this very moment that you might actually touch what is here for you deeply and accurately. Resting in steady, mindful awareness, noticing and including any changing thought or feeling of separation or isolation as simply another thought, frees you from its spell and reminds you that you have not—and cannot—fall out of the universe!

In this chapter, we will look more closely at the ongoing reality of belonging and interdependency that mindfulness practice illuminates as well as how that reality can be obscured by flashing and burning moments of anger and ill will. We will finish the chapter with more brief mindfulness meditations and reflections to help you overcome anger's illusions of disconnection from and misperception of others.

BELONGING AND INTERCONNECTION

Whatever their source, feelings of isolation and loneliness are distortions and misperceptions of our deeper reality and situation as human beings, which is actually a dynamic reality marked by continuous interaction, interrelatedness, and interdependency. Here are a few examples of the many different views speaking to this perspective of belonging and interconnection in each moment of each human life, offered as food for thought.

A Scientific and Mindful View of Relationships

Modern neuroscience has concluded that humans actually evolved systems in brain and body that are constantly interacting to promote understanding, empathy, and concern for one another. According to this research, humans needed to cooperate in order to survive—and cooperation was more important to survival than aggression.

Daniel J. Siegel, MD, is a noted authority on the science of the mind and has a particular interest in what is increasingly being called *interpersonal neurobiology*. This term refers to studies and research into the connections among your mind, your brain, and the relationships in your life.

Here are some of Dr. Siegel's perspectives on the nature of human interactions: "**Relationships** are the sharing of *energy and information flow*. **Integrative communication** involves the sharing of energy and information in which each individual's internal world is respected and allowed to be *differentiated* and then *compassionate* connection is cultivated. Integrative communication promotes the *development of healthy* relationships as it honors differentiation and *linkage*" (Siegel 2012, 125; emphasis Siegel's).

For example, if you see someone who is sad and crying, your various brain circuits related to emotions, memories, and self-awareness might become activated. As you experience similar feelings inside yourself from these activated circuits, you would begin to feel a deeper sense of connection and identification with the other person. Very soon after that, you might notice tears on your face or sensations of heaviness in your chest. Your experience with this other person has become more subjectively rich and information filled, and probably more empathetic as well. This is due to these amazing circuits of interpersonal neurobiology present in human beings, neural mechanisms and circuits that promote the sharing of energy and information about and between the internal worlds of each partner in the relationship.

From the perspective of mindfulness and the ever-unfolding present moment, we have already explored the idea that your sense of a solid "me" that is always here and unchanging is not accurate. Simply witnessing in meditation the changing nature of thoughts and feelings in your inner life can raise questions about how fixed the sense of self—of I, me, mine—actually is. Interpersonal neurobiology also suggests that one's sense of "I-me-mine" is not fixed, but is co-arising with the information and energy flow in the relationships between each of us and our surroundings, moment by moment.

Dr. Siegel points to this interdependent view of our sense of self when he notes, "The 'self' is both embodied and embedded. These are not two separate domains of experience, but instead are the essence of how the mind emerges from the *energy and information flow* within and between us" (Siegel 2012, 134, Siegel's emphasis).

You might say that in any given instant, the subjective sense of who we are—that sense of "I, me, and mine," which can feel so solid or be so intense, as when anger is present—is actually arising and changing at speeds so great that it creates the impression that "I, me, and mine" is a substantial and permanent reality. In fact, according to the science of relationships and the awareness that practicing mindfulness brings, the sense of self is located in the changing experience, information, and energy flows arising from bodily experience (the "embodied" self). It is also dependent upon and changes with the stream of information flowing among us, others, and the world around us—is "embedded" in that stream.

In other words, applying this scientific understanding about what constitutes our sense of self can be very helpful, especially when anger or ill will have hijacked you. Whenever your own emotions are painful and distracting and your thoughts about being isolated and alone have become loud and believable, just remember that—according to current neuroscience—the "you" that feels so much pain, loneliness, and isolation is not permanent at all. That "you" is constantly being formed, upheld, and even made to feel more solid by energy and information streams, feelings and thoughts, that are arising, briefly present, flowing, and changing inside you and outside of you—literally breath by breath! So, if this is the case, some reasonable questions might be these:

- Who is the "you" that is so angry, so sad, so indignant, and so hurt?

- Where does that one go when "you" are not angry, sad, indignant, or hurt?

- What are the energy and information streams that keep that feeling of the solid, angry "you" feeling so large and intense?

Looking deeply and mindfully can help you transform the pain that sustains the angry "you." When that "you" is angry, afraid, stuck, and feeling alone, perhaps mindfulness, compassion, and wise understanding can help that "you" recognize and rest in the experience of belonging in this moment, and know deeply and personally that no one can fall out of the universe.

Faith and Wisdom Perspectives on Belonging and Interconnection

Of course, faith and wisdom traditions have long spoken to this truth of relatedness, belonging, and interdependency—the continual and necessary give-and-take among us—in each unique, unfolding life. Here are a few selected examples from the many possibilities offered in various faith traditions:

Give, and it will be given to you ... for the measure you give will be the measure you get back.

—Luke 6:38

Those who act kindly in the world will have kindness.

—Qur'an 39:10

Even as a mother protects with her life her child, her only child,
So with a boundless heart should one cherish all living beings.

—Buddhism's Metta Sutta

It is only when one does not have enough faith in others that others will have no faith in him.

—Tao Te Ching 17

Who is honored? He who honors mankind.

—Mishnah, Abot 4:1

A Poetic Perspective on Belonging and Interconnection

If you look closely enough and deeply enough, you might notice—in the changing, rich, and complex fabric that forms reality in each moment of your life—the long threads of countless other people and relationships, and numberless moments of experience, all alive and contributing to the beautiful particularity that makes you who you are moment by moment. If you are mindful and your attention is steady enough, you may be able to distinguish some of these threads and observe how the impact of long-ago people and places arises and impacts your lived experience in this moment.

For example, the smell of a particular food cooking might bring back memories of holidays with your family growing up. Depending on many other factors, the memories evoked by the smell of that special food might be warm and nostalgic, or the food smells in this moment could summon painful memories and feelings of anxiety, or even fear and pain. Either way—pleasant memories or painful ones—the reactions in your mind and body that follow contribute to and perhaps shape your experience as you relate to the people with you and to the food you are preparing now. How you manage that relationship to the here and now, knowing that it contains and is being impacted by the totality of who you are and who you have been, is a crucial question if you wish to heal, transform, and live a happier life. As human beings, we all carry and are influenced by this long body of our own lives—present, adding to, and informing the changing texture of our experience in the unfolding present moment. In his poem "Call Me by My True Names," Buddhist monk Thich Nhat Hanh poignantly describes how we carry the complex human condition of interconnection and interrelatedness:

Call Me by My True Names

I am the twelve-year-old girl, refugee on a small boat,
who throws herself into the ocean after being raped by a sea pirate,
and I am the pirate, my heart not yet capable of seeing and loving.

I am a member of the politburo, with plenty of power in my hands,
and I am the man who has to pay his "debt of blood" to my people,
dying slowly in a forced labor camp.

My joy is like spring, so warm it makes flowers bloom in all walks of life.
My pain is like a river of tears, so full it fills the four oceans.

Please call me by my true names,
so I can hear all my cries and laughs at once,
so I can see that my joy and pain are one.

Please call me by my true names,
so I can wake up,
and so the door of my heart can be left open,
the door of compassion.

In the wholeness of who we are as human beings lies the deep threads and impact of many others' pain and fear as well as our own. In us also rests the capacity for great wisdom, goodness, and compassionate, life-affirming response.

These varied perspectives on belonging and interdependency are probably not new ideas to many people. The challenge for most of us as we go about our busy daily lives is in moving from noble ideas and inspiring words to a direct lived experience in which we apply these principles and build a world of thoughts, words, and actions that reflect them.

Later in this chapter, to help you make this crucial shift from good ideas to liberating experience and informed action, you will find some brief mindfulness practices that are designed to shift you out of the distortions and obscurations of belonging and interconnection that anger and ill will create. To set the stage for those meditations, let's briefly revisit some of the common ways anger and ill will reinforce their false message of separation.

ANGER AND ILL WILL
OBSCURE CONNECTIONS

In a moment, feelings of anger and other expressions of ill will and aversion can blind you to the connections, relationships, and reality that is present and supporting you, here and now. Such was the case for Don:

• Don's Story

Don is a man who has felt much of life's pain in his forty-six years. He had some happy early memories, especially of being outside in nature, playing with his dog, Jake, and of going on fishing trips with his father. Unfortunately for Don, his parents divorced when he was fourteen, and he lost touch with his father, who moved to another state to take a job and was killed in an auto accident there. Don was frequently in trouble in school after that, and he struggled to graduate. After high school, Don joined the military to "start a new life, one where I only worry about me and my buddies." Don had some incidents in the military related to anger and frequent fighting, but he finished his contract and received an honorable discharge. After that, he attended college, graduated, and eventually found a good job. He was successful, and advanced over the years based on his intelligence and hard work and his strong desire "to help people and to support my family." In his workplace, however, Don occasionally had "anger problems" with supervisors and was at times reprimanded for being too harsh with his subordinates. These things usually happened when he was under a lot of stress or when there were deadlines and heavier workloads than usual.

Don and his wife had a family, a boy and a girl, and as the children grew older and more independent, Don began to feel increasingly isolated and angry even at home. He eventually began talking to a therapist, who taught Don to practice mindfulness. The therapist also offered Don a safe place to share his deepest fears and doubts. In that healing space, Don began to become aware of old feelings of mistrust and anger, and the grief he had carried for his parents since his own teenage years. Don began to see how the life experiences of his teens had become the basis for an ongoing interior narrative that he repeated to himself, especially in stressful times, about feeling vulnerable, unlovable, and not good enough. He began to touch an old and deep fear inside that he lived in a world where he couldn't really trust anyone. As his therapy and mindfulness practice progressed, Don began to realize his angry outbursts and fighting, and the "problems" with supervisors and subordinates as well as with his own wife and teenage children over the years, were defenses against the pain of these distorted views and feelings and not truly based in reality.

With his growing self-awareness through mindfulness and counseling, Don began to practice greater self-compassion and self-forgiveness, and he found courage to seek forgiveness from others. He came to understand how, in being driven unconsciously by anger and pain to speak and act with blame and judgments, he had lost touch not only with himself but also with the sense of trust and belonging in the world he had known as a child. In time, Don began to touch and trust those positive feelings again, and to experience and return the love of his family more completely.

Anger and ill will can blind you to connections, with damaging consequences, in several ways. With Don's story in mind, let's take a closer look at some common distorting effects of anger and ill will.

Anger Distracts and Blinds You

Feeling angry sustains a reaction in mind and body—the freeze-fight-or-flight reaction—that produces a state of hyperarousal that is very attention getting. The resultant inner perceptions and thoughts fueled by anger—the blaming and judging—can distract and even create an external focus or target for the anger, which in turn, can strengthen and sustain the subjective feeling of being isolated and alone. Such complex, anger-driven experience distracts you from and blinds you to what is also here for you in each moment.

For example, in Don's story, it is easy to imagine that when he felt stressed from work, upon returning home to his family, he was lost in his anger and the memories and imaginings that fueled it. As a result, he was not fully present or available for the love and affection that his wife and children felt and expressed for him in the present moment.

Anger Distorts Your Perception of Others

When you are angry, sulking, steaming, or otherwise filled with ill will and aversion for what is present in this moment of your life, it is very easy to misunderstand someone else. For instance, let's say you're sullen and fuming about an incident at work. When you return home, your teenager goes out the door with a friend and you overhear a remark about how adults "just don't get it!" Do you immediately think they are talking about you? Are they showing disrespect for you? How do you feel when your spouse tells you later that your teen's friend was grounded, and the comment was made about someone else?

Or, filled with anger, you can also be supersensitive to a simple request from someone to do something. For example, your spouse asks you to take out the trash, or your colleague at work asks you to cover for him for a few minutes at the end of the day. If you feel angry at the time, you might fall into a self-focused narrative about how no one respects you or how everyone takes you for granted, when your spouse and your coworker only needed some help themselves. Can you think of an example in your life when something like that happened?

Anger Isolates

How do you feel when an angry person yells at you? Or when someone, even someone close to you, raises his or her voice and is critical of something you have said or done?

Most people probably would want to get away from that person as soon as possible, and may even feel some anger toward that person in reaction—anger not felt before that outburst of yelling.

There are good reasons that people who are chronically angry and who are often critical and judgmental of others feel more isolated socially. Most likely, they have pushed others away with their (sometimes unconscious) persistent and rejecting hostile words and behavior.

Anger Distorts Your Awareness of Yourself

Anger projected onto others can also serve as an effective, if not very healthy or skillful, defense against painful feelings you carry inside. As we have seen, beneath anger can be feelings of fear as well as harsh and untrue thoughts and beliefs about yourself and others. When angry feelings rage and scornful narratives direct the blame outward onto others or onto situations, your experience and awareness of yourself in that moment, including your own internal reactions— thoughts, feelings, and embodied life—is likely to be distorted or ignored.

Chronic feelings of anger and ill will are inevitably turned on oneself as well as on others. Many people say they are their "own worst critic." When the inner voices and narrative are frequently critical, there is little room left for self-compassion or self-care. When criticism and denial of fatigue, pain, and upset are the first response to those painful feelings, the result can be a damaging blindness and disconnection from your own body and your own feelings.

Don, as we saw in his story, suffered for years, and others who loved him suffered too, because he held the inner belief that he couldn't trust the world and that he was unlovable and unworthy of affection. When he began to understand this belief of unworthiness upholding the fear that he would never be safe in a relationship, Don could see the roots of much of the anger in his life. With that understanding, he could begin to heal and let himself trust again in the basic truth of his own value and his connections to life.

CORRECTING ANGER'S DISTORTIONS

Any of these distortions can be corrected. You can disentangle from the delusion of isolation and feelings of alienation and experience the reality of interconnection in any moment. The sections that follow offer some brief meditations that you might try for working with the distortions that anger, ill will, and their relatives bring to your relationships and your life.

When Anger Distracts You in This Moment

Life is available only in *this* moment. Yet, because anger thrives on habit energies of critical thoughts, pain-filled inner narratives, and negative meanings, it distracts from the present moment and your sense of belonging to life. Anger and feelings of ill will and aversion operate effectively by taking you into the past and the future with the narratives and critical thoughts that accompany them. Anger often uses "shoulds and should nots" and blaming judgments in order to survive. In effect, anger hijacks you when it fills the present moment with the memories and fears about past and future, and evokes intense reactions in your mind and body, reactions that also add to your lived and felt experience in the here and now.

I once heard a famous meditation teacher tell an inspiring story. During a retreat, the teacher was the target of a series of angry questions and comments from a retreatant. The teacher said that he asked for time to reflect on the questions, and he took two full hours and practiced walking meditation in order to touch more deeply his own pain as well as the pain of the other person before giving his response to the questions. After those two hours of walking meditation, the teacher said he was able to offer a response that came from a much wiser and better place of compassion and understanding.

One of my lessons from this story is that if such an accomplished teacher at times needs to practice mindfulness and compassion for as long as two hours to step back from the grip of anger, why wouldn't I? Why shouldn't I practice to be as patient and wise? Habits of anger and judgment can be very deep and strong. Qualities of patience, wisdom, and the intention not to be controlled by them can take real commitment and courage. Here is a brief mindfulness meditation that may help.

A BRIEF MEDITATION PRACTICE WHEN YOU FEEL AGITATED OR DISTRACTED BY ANGER

When you feel angry or irritated in any way, pause and name what is happening: "This is anger. It is in me now."

Practice mindful breathing or mindful walking, and bring attention back to this moment. Make room in your heart for any angry thoughts, hearing them without judging or blaming yourself or anyone else. It is enough to listen, and keep breathing or walking mindfully. Practice patience with yourself, not trying to get rid of the anger or to fix it, allowing it simply to be, noticing more and more closely the thoughts and sensations in your body, and perhaps how anger moves through the present moment in your body and in your thoughts.

Conclude your meditation by offering yourself compassion with one or two phrases that help: "May I take care of my anger with compassion." "May I find the resources to remain present and open in this moment."

When Anger Distorts Your Perception of Others

It is said that among some native peoples there is a greeting. When you approach someone, you say, "I see you." That person responds, "I am here."

If you are stuck in anger or resentment during a difficult moment in a relationship or a situation when you disagree with another, "I see you" and "I am here" will probably *not* be your greeting or response! When we are totally absorbed in a narrow, self-centered perspective, holding tightly and defensively to a particular idea or opinion, we become very limited in our ability to see a larger context or to better understand the position of others with whom we disagree. However, learning to practice mindfulness can help you interrupt this limiting, defensive, and reactive habit energy of anger in your heart and mind, and create the possibility for different and better outcomes to arise. With the support of mindfulness, perhaps you will be able to see more accurately who is there, what they are about, and what you need to do next. Being more mindful, you may also be better equipped to be there for them when you are needed. Here is a brief mindfulness meditation for those challenging relationship moments.

A BRIEF MEDITATION PRACTICE
WHEN ANGER DISTORTS YOUR
PERCEPTION OF OTHERS

When you notice that you have an angry or aversive reaction to another person, step back, pause, and focus mindful attention on the sensations of your body and your breathing.

Steady your attention patiently and repeatedly on your focus, gently listening and allowing any angry thoughts to be without adding to them or trying to control them in any way. Breathing mindfully with this unfolding experience, let thoughts be, let sensations go, return your focus patiently to body sensations or breath sensations, and simply observe.

When you are ready, shift your practice to focus on qualities of kindness and wisdom. Breathing mindfully between phrases, silently repeat phrases of kindness, compassion, and wisdom: "May I be filled with peace and protected from harm." "May this situation teach me about the true nature of life." "May I see clearly what is here, and respond wisely."

After a few mindful breaths and phrases directed toward yourself, silently shift attention to the other person and imagine the person as a child who is in pain. Imagine that the pain causes them to speak and act the way they do. Can you send them compassion? "May you find peace, and be free of pain." *Know that wishing them well, even for a few breaths, does not have to make you more vulnerable or mean you hold a weaker position. Practice for as long as you like. What do you notice?*

When Anger Isolates or Alienates You

One of the traditional phrases used in the loving-kindness meditation focuses upon feelings of safety. One may say, for example, in the meditation practice, "May I be safe, or may you be safe." Teaching this meditation once, I asked for comments after the practice, and someone said, "Dr. Brantley, I have never felt safe in my life!"

There are so many ways that each of us can be hurt. And we easily remember and carry that hurt so that, sadly, the feelings of safety or the experience of being loved and cared for can be scarce or even absent in many lives. Such deep hurt can be a cornerstone of anger that continually builds feelings of isolation and alienation.

But even old hurts can be healed. They do not have to be obstacles to experiencing joy or safety. Sister Lou worked in an orphanage in a war-torn country. She told this story at a mindfulness meeting.

• The Orphans' Story

The children who come to our orphanage have been so traumatized in so many ways that many of them have had no experience of any goodness from any adult. They come to us very shut down. This is often because either their parents abused them, or because they cannot remember their parents and all the other adults they have known brutalized and terrorized them. I have learned to approach these children very gently, especially in the beginning of their stay with us. I know that I am literally trying to help them come back to life. When I ask them to touch the goodness and happiness in themselves, they often don't know how at first.

Well, we have some beautiful flowers growing in the back behind the building that is our kitchen and dining room. So I take them outside and we walk around in and among the flowers growing there, and look at those flowers. We smell the flowers, and gently touch them. I tell the children that they can let that beauty and any beauty in nature be their inspiration and their comfort. Nature's beauty can be a place of peace, and a reminder, whenever they see something beautiful in nature, that they, too, belong and are beautiful in this world. After that, some of them usually began to draw pictures of their families, to cry, to reach out to me and the other staff, and to heal.

Learning to change the relationship to these feelings of deprivation and neglect will greatly reduce the power of anger to create a sense of isolation and separation in you. This meditation may help.

A BRIEF MEDITATION PRACTICE
WHEN YOU FEEL ANGRY, ALONE,
OR ALIENATED

Any time you are caught up in feelings of anger, isolation, unworthiness, loneliness, or similar intensities of ill will and aversion, pause as soon as you notice these feelings, and breathe or walk mindfully for a few breaths or steps.

Let your thoughts simply be, or go, and patiently bring attention back to your body. Bring mindful attention to the world around you, and let any beauty in nature you see remind you of the beauty in yourself and your good deeds. Let this beauty support you.

Send yourself kindness and compassion with one or two phrases: "May I be protected from inner and outer harm." "May I notice beauty around me and remember the goodness in me." If you like, look around at any beauty you see, or remember a good deed you have done for someone.

Breathing or walking mindfully, conclude your meditation wisely, perhaps noticing how the feelings of anger and isolation can change, how they are not a permanent condition or identity, and how you cannot fall out of the universe, despite what your inner thoughts tell you.

When Anger Distorts Your Experience of Yourself

There is an old story of a child who asks his mother an interesting question. Here is one version of the story.

Child: Mom, imagine you are surrounded by monsters, really scary monsters, and you don't have anyone to help you or anything to fight them off with. What would you do?

Mom: (*after pausing a bit*) Wow, I don't know what I would do. What would you do?

Child: I would stop imagining!

Angry feelings can be like those monsters. Fueled and fed by imagined or perceived hurts and threats, angry thoughts feed more angry feelings, and those feed more thoughts that take your focus away from your own body and take you out of the present moment.

Filled by feelings being fueled by the imaginings of continued hurt, of what might happen, or what could have happened, over time you can literally be so out of touch that you are surprised when your body collapses or when you realize that all you feel is numb. The really good news is that it doesn't have to be that way.

A BRIEF MEDITATION WHEN YOU FEEL ANGRY, DISCONNECTED, OR NUMB TO YOURSELF

When you notice you are having difficulty feeling anything, even the sensations in your body, stop and take some time for yourself.

Take a comfortable position, and let go of trying to change or fix anything. Remember the key attitudes of nonjudging, nonstriving, trust, and patience, and let yourself drop into awareness.

Begin with gently noticing any sounds. Let them come to you, flow over you, and flow out of the present moment. Relax and simply notice the sounds. When you notice thoughts about the sounds, just let them be, or let them go, and come back to the sounds.

When you like, shift attention to your body, and notice any feelings that come to you—perhaps noticing the feeling of heaviness in some part or region, or a sensation of air or clothing touching your skin. You can relax. Trust yourself to notice what you can, and let that be good enough for this meditation.

SEEING WITH NEW EYES

Our experience of being alive in this present moment results from the continuous interplay between our interior life, including our body sensations, memories, ideas, perceptions, beliefs, and consciousness as well as the incoming steams of new information from others and the world around us, breath by breath.

Similarly, other people's experience of being alive in this moment includes us and our interaction with them. What they see, hear, and feel in the fabric of their unfolding experience in the present moment includes threads made up of our actions and words.

In amazing and countless ways, we constantly interact with each other in the ever-changing present moment—contributing to and shaping the unfolding reality of being alive, shaping and being shaped by each other. From the exchange of oxygen and carbon dioxide with each breath, to the ways we consume and generate energy, to the production and distribution of our very ideas, images, and feelings across various mediums—physical, electronic, digital, or otherwise—each of us is inescapably, deeply, and undeniably interconnected with others; we have an impact on one another and our world.

The French novelist Marcel Proust once observed that having new eyes, rather than seeking new landscapes, is the critical element in any voyage of real discovery. What if you could bring new eyes to each moment of your life? What might you see?

Just because we do not perceive multiple layers of connection, or because we subjectively feel alienated and alone, does not mean the reality of multiple connections is not here. The problem—actually, a problem that everyone has quite often—is viewing the world selectively through a filter of anger, fear, sadness, or pain, which obscures all that is present in addition to those feelings.

Because selective perception and seeing with "old eyes" of anger, blame, and pain is so very common, an important and useful question to help bring you back to here and now when those intense feelings threaten to blind you is always "What is also here now?" Two additional important and helpful questions are "What is blocking me from seeing?" and "Does it need my compassionate attention?"

All We Are Makes Us Who We Are

To help you remember that you have not fallen out of the universe, there is another understanding about connections and belonging that is worth noting: all we are makes us who we are.

It is easy, and often fashionable, to view our own painful past or hurtful words and actions as somehow "not me," as in no longer part of who we are. People often go to great (and sometimes dramatic) lengths to distance themselves from embarrassing, painful, or unwanted aspects of their behavior and past. But selectively owning some facets of yourself while discarding others is not an accurate or truthful perspective, and attempting to hide or deny a part of yourself that you regret or feel shame or guilt about always has consequences.

As you know from mindful observation of the flow of your interior life, every thought, every action, and every word is temporary. Each one has causes, and each one has some form of consequence that shapes and impacts the next moment, and so on, through all the days of your life. It is like that for each of us.

One might say that wherever you are in this moment, whatever is your reality, the wholeness of you in that instant is the sum total of your life experience, including the full tapestry of your inner life, with all of its thoughts, feelings, memories, and associated meanings. That means everything! Who you are in this moment is the result of your mistakes as well as your successes. You are here as a result of your insights and your blind spots, your beauty and your warts. All of these and more, along with the people and events of your entire life have brought you to this moment. If it were not for all of those things, you would not be what and who you are now. Looking at yourself this way could be both an awesome and a disconcerting view—and it's definitely food for thought!

Let's go back to Don's story as an example. Without his painful childhood and his ongoing beliefs concerning his unworthiness and the untrustworthiness of others, he would not have experienced such difficulty in his life—nor would he have been motivated from feeling such pain to seek therapy. And without the love he shared with his family and the courage and intelligence already present within him, Don would not have been able to act on getting help. Could Don have arrived at this moment of healing without any of those conditions?

Seeing this totality of ourselves with mindfulness and wisdom, we might have found the "new eyes" that Marcel Proust speaks of—"new eyes" for ourselves. If you think deeply about it, what does it mean for you to become more open and accepting of all that you are? What are the implications for you, if you begin from that perspective of immense wholeness already present inside?

Heart and Mind

If you think about it at all, how do you usually think about your heart? Or your mind? There is a Sufi saying that goes, "The mind is the surface of the heart, and the heart is the depth of the mind."

In this way of speaking, the heart is not the physical organ any more than the mind is limited to the brain in your skull. This view suggests that the mind and heart are deeply interconnected, not actually separate, and the depth is the awareness that includes the qualities of kindness and compassion, wisdom, and joy. Together the mind and the heart can help us both connect with and understand the mystery of this life and our relationship to it.

Practicing mindfulness means not suppressing any pain, anger, or fear. Mindfulness is inclusive—it can hold anything that comes into awareness. Your capacity for mindfulness rests in both heart and mind. Trusting yourself to rely on the intelligence and goodness of your heart-mind can be very revealing of connection and belonging.

I had a touching reminder of the supportive and informative power of the heart-mind during a difficult time in my own life. Let me tell you about it.

• *The ICU Story*

Late one evening a few months ago, I found myself with several close family members in a medical intensive care unit at the bedside of another dear relative, who was on the fence between life and death. Of course, I was filled with many intense emotions, including fear, doubts, and even anger. I began to breathe mindfully and pay closer attention to those feelings, and also to what was happening in the room around me. As I became more grounded and present, I noticed more fully the anguish on the faces of my loved ones, and I could feel my own inner upset, even as I heard the electronic sounds of monitors and the rhythmic pumping noises of the ventilator. In the midst of all that input and emotion, a single thought came into my mind: "These are the ones I travel through this life with. We have been in many other moments together—moments that included a wide range of emotions and love. We are here now in this moment, together, on the edge of life and death, facing the reality of life and death." With that realization, instantly my focus became steadier, I could feel my heart soften, and strength from some other place filled and supported me.

The beauty of our human intelligence and goodness, acting through the heart-mind dimension, empowers each of us to look at anger, or fear, or any difficulty, with new eyes; to embrace ill will and aversion with curiosity and compassion; and to transform through greater awareness the fear and distorted beliefs separating us from a deeper understanding of connection and belonging in this moment.

KEEP IN MIND

- Feelings of anger, ill will, aversion, and their relatives can easily create an illusion of lonely separation or build on old memories and hurts to blind you to the amazing reality of interconnection and belonging that unfolds in each moment.

- Practicing mindfulness, compassion, and wisdom for yourself and others can help shatter the illusion of separation and make the truth of belonging a realized experience in every moment of your life.

CHAPTER 10

many possibilities—which will you choose?

Hatred can never cease by hatred.
Hatred can only cease by love.
This is an eternal law.

—*the Buddha*

Each moment holds an amazing number of possibilities. Something happens, and you respond. Suddenly that response becomes the manifestation and embodiment of one possibility from a universe of possibilities that could have happened—and the other possibilities remain unexpressed and not visible.

What does manifest enters and becomes part of the unfolding tapestry of experience flowing through the present moment, and a cause or condition evoking next responses, manifestations, and expressions in you as well as in others who are touched by the conditions emerging now, in this moment. And so it goes, on and on—continually changing conditions flowing through the now of the present moment.

In this chapter, we will look more closely at the freedom that comes with the possibility to choose in each moment, and the ways our freedom to choose can either be increased or limited by the degree of awareness and the qualities of kindness and compassion—or fear, anger, and blame—that we bring to this moment and what is present here and now with us.

CHOICES, ACTIONS: A LIFE OF THEIR OWN

The degree of awareness and the quality of heartfulness that you bring to the process of life flowing and unfolding within and around you makes all the difference as to what response you make and to which universe unfolds next. By practicing mindfulness, one can begin to see the many ways in which each person, indeed each living thing, is constantly both receiver and contributor, beneficiary and benefactor, in the beautiful, frightening, awesome, interactive, and interconnected unfolding process of life.

For example, when you stand in a line or walk on a crowded street, perhaps feeling angry or irritable, and someone bumps into you by accident, what do you do? Do you ignore the person, and walk on, but get angrier still—steaming and sulking inside? Do you say something harsh or bump the person back? Can you let it go, or do you carry it with you, perhaps for many steps or many minutes longer? Whatever choice you make in response (or reaction) to someone or something that happens, your words and actions immediately become not only a part of, but also help to shape, the larger fabric of life that continually appears in, changes expression, and flows through and out of the present moment.

When you reflect on it, you might also recognize how the conscious or unconscious choices you make in words and actions, here and now, also become pieces of the evolving reality of others—impacting them inside and contributing to the actions that they, in turn, take with others besides you. For example, imagine what might happen if you angrily curse or push back physically when that person accidentally bumps into you. How different the ensuing universe might be—for both of you—because of your reaction. The universe might appear in a very different way if you did not respond outwardly and aggressively.

Yet, even when you don't respond outwardly, you might carry the bump and your angry reaction to it forward on the inside. If you continue fuming, blaming, steaming quietly, and lash out at someone else later, you might say that the new person now feels some of the bump you felt when the first person bumped you. If you are really angry, it could be a bigger bump! At any rate, this new person still gets bumped because anger and irritation, briefly suppressed, have smoldered inside of you and finally erupted.

This scenario of bumping into each other (or you might say of passing the bump from one person to another) is another example of the deeper view of interdependency and connection we can take in each moment of our lives. How many accidental bumps (physical or verbal or otherwise) have fed angry feelings that eventually became angry actions that "bumped" against someone else sometime later? How many kindnesses have opened the way for someone else to be kind?

With mindfulness, you can actually observe the forming of complex networks of connection. You can watch as they flow into and out of every interaction, becoming visible in their unfolding, infusing each moment of our lives with the rich poignancy often called "the ten thousand joys and the ten thousand sorrows."

A word of caution and humility is in order: None of us has or could have anything like total control over what life is or how it unfolds—either in ourselves or for others. Obviously, life is simply far too complex for that to be true, even though our egos or personalities try mightily sometimes to act like they have total control! But it's important to remember that we are all deeply connected and interactive, and personal choices and the actions embodying those choices touch and impact others in complex and ongoing ways.

LIFE: GIFT AND CREATION

You may have heard the popular expression that goes "We have two lives—the one we are given and the one we make." When we become prisoners of anger, ill will, aversion, and hostility—directed either toward ourselves or toward others—we literally make a life for us and others that is more painful than it has to be because of our choices driven by anger and aversion. We may also fail—being limited by ill will and hostility—to see what else is here with us, to recognize the possibilities, and to make a life that could be more beautiful and courageous than we possibly have ever imagined. Here is a remarkable story of adversity, courage, and possibility:

• Joshua's Story

Joshua A. Miele was only four years old, a child living in Brooklyn, New York, when a disturbed neighbor threw acid in Joshua's face, blinding and disfiguring him for life. As reported in a New York Times *story about Joshua (Jamieson 2013), he underwent many reparative operations, but he never regained his vision. The trauma he suffered extended to his family and contributed to his parents' divorce after the attack. Doctors wanted to try more procedures in an attempt to restore Joshua's face as much as possible. Finally, Joshua said, "Enough."*

As reported in the New York Times, *Joshua told his family that "it was time to start accepting his blindness and his face, and for him to start living his life." Joshua was about twelve years old at the time.*

From that time on, Joshua excelled in school, and went on to earn a degree in physics and a PhD in psychoacoustics from the University of California at Berkeley. He has worked for NASA, is a scientist at the Smith-Kettlewell Eye Research Institute, is married, and has two children.

In addition to these accomplishments, Joshua has contributed in important ways to the quality of life of others with blindness and visual impairment. He helped develop tactile maps in braille for the (San Francisco) Bay Area Rapid Transit system. These maps are in every station of the transit system. He has developed software to help blind people use computer programs based on graphics. He is currently working on a project to make narrated versions of videos and movies available to anyone who cannot see them. Joshua also has been an influential advocate for improving museum experiences for blind people.

Stories like Joshua's serve to remind us that the relationship we take and the choices we make, moment by moment, to any set of conditions present here and now, make all the difference in our lives. We can choose to be rejecting or accepting. Either choice leads into entirely different lives and experiences. Knowing our choices matter so much can empower us to become more aware, more in touch with our deepest values, and to accept ourselves, no matter who we are, as a significant element and thread in a universe that couldn't be the way it is without us and who we are.

How do we decide what relationship to take to the circumstances of our life? What determines our freedom to choose one path over another? How can we find the resources to overcome the challenges and obstacles?

Tigers in the Heart

There is a popular story told about the wisdom of a village elder. Here is one version:

In a certain village, there was a beloved and wise old man who was the most respected elder in the entire region. One day a small group of strangers came to visit, offered gifts of food, and asked if they might pose a question to the elder.

"Of course," said the old man. "Ask whatever you like of me."

"Honorable one," they said, "you are famous far and wide for being so kind and happy. You are wise and respected by all who know you. How did you come to be this way? What is your secret?"

The old man smiled and replied, "Very simple, my friends, but not always easy. Long ago I realized that I carry two tigers in my heart. One is the tiger of anger and hate, and the other is the tiger of caring and love. How I am all depends on which tiger I feed each day."

Remember the skills of mindfulness—skills developed and strengthened directly through meditation practice that we discussed in chapter 3? They are the skills of intention, attention, and attitude. In this story, we can imagine that as the elder became mindful of the two tigers in his own heart and noticed the effects of feeding each one, he was able to decide and intend which one he would choose to nurture and grow. His entire life unfolded differently when he saw the two tigers. Once he set his intention on nurturing the tiger of caring and love, his attention settled and returned there, and the acts of nurturing that tiger, directed by his intention and guided by attention, nourished and grew the qualities and forces of caring and love that people came to identify with him.

In mindfulness-based stress reduction classes, we like to say "we practice being, not doing." This means we learn to stop, to step back from the busyness and habit energy of doing, doing, and more doing, and instead relax into awareness, observe, allow, and be with whatever we are experiencing in the present moment.

In those same classes, we also like to say "being informs doing," which is another way of saying that mindfulness helps you move from (hurtful and ineffective) patterns of *reacting* to stress and into (more effective and healthy) patterns of *responding* to stress. In other words, if you become more mindful, you may not be able to do much about tigers in the jungle, but it is easier to choose which one gets fed!

HARDSHIP: CHALLENGE AND OPPORTUNITY

From the point of view of mindfulness practice, everything depends upon our degree of awareness of the conditions present in this moment and the relationship we take to those conditions when they appear. How we sustain attention on the changing conditions (or not), and remain in the open heart of kindness and compassion (or not), and how we are able (or not) to continue observing and opening when hardship and challenges are present or intensifying are skills that will determine whether we actually get to the other side of anger (or not).

Acknowledging Hard Times and Difficult Moments

Polly Young-Eisendrath is a respected psychoanalyst and also is an experienced practitioner of mindfulness meditation in both the Zen and Vipassana traditions. Here is her perspective on the idea that we should always try to avoid or eliminate the suffering in our lives:

Hardships are the major catalysts for change and development in our lives; they wake us to how we create suffering through our own attitudes and intentions, our actions and relationships…. Much of our suffering originates with our own discontent, emanating from the evaluations and attitudes that arise in protecting ourselves and separating ourselves out from the context of our own engagement (Young-Eisendrath 2009, 117–18).

What often blocks us from clearly seeing the lesson a hardship offers can be our own fears, our own desires, or our own stress and exhaustion. In fact, the lesson itself can be learning to acknowledge such distress inside of us. The following example illustrates the high price of self-neglect and exhaustion.

• Monica's Story

Monica is a fifty-two-year-old woman, married with two teenage sons, who has a busy job working as an emergency department nurse, and whose parents live nearby in a retirement community. Besides being with her family and her good relationship with her husband, Tom, Monica's outlets for self-care and stress management have been to exercise faithfully and to spend "quality time" with some of her girlfriends after work or at lunch several times each month. Because her father has some health issues, Monica has been spending more time helping her mother care for him. And, in the last few months, Monica's older son has been busy looking at colleges, and Monica and Tom have been increasingly worried about the cost of college and how they will be able to meet those costs for each of their sons.

Because of these increased time demands and worries, Monica felt more obliged to make things right and put all of her time and energy into the problems of her parents and her son's college choice. Since then, she has found herself sleeping poorly, not eating as well as she would like, and feeling more stressed and even overwhelmed at times. On a particularly busy shift at work, Monica surprised herself by snapping at a patient and later by responding in a loud, angry voice to one of the emergency department physicians. Because her work was the one place where Monica prided herself as never being "rattled," as she put it, she found herself afterward beset by angry inner voices criticizing her for "losing it" and demanding that she "get hold of herself." After those incidents in the emergency department,

Monica realized how stressed and exhausted she felt and decided to change it. She made an appointment to meet with a person in her hospital's employee assistance program. From there, with the support of her family, she enrolled in a mindfulness-based stress reduction class and began to learn how to recognize her stress and manage it with more awareness and compassion. She made her own "personal time" for a few hours each week a priority again. Over time, Monica began to view her own self-care as just as important as the care she gave to others. Later she told a friend, "Mindfulness and self-compassion have changed my life!"

When you feel exhausted or overwhelmed can be precisely the time when it is most important—and most difficult—to move with clear intention toward the difficulty you face. But as you turn toward any difficulty, it will help if you trust and allow compassion and awareness to help you.

Finding the Opportunity in Hard Times

Monica could be anyone. Becoming caught in a web of increased demands, loss of self-care and support, and beset by an internal "Supreme Court" of judges eager to deliver a verdict of failure and unworthiness is an all-too-common situation in today's busy world. You might say that these challenges and demands led Monica to habits of isolation and feelings of exhaustion in mind and body that ulti-mately fed the tiger of anger and hate rather than the tiger of caring and love!

When Monica paused to recognize and acknowledge exactly how difficult her life had become, she could take steps based in awareness and compassion to respond to her difficulties, beginning with herself. By first stopping to "be" and look more closely at herself, Monica was able to recognize and choose new opportunities and possibilities for growth and transformation that also were present in the hard times she was going through.

Hard times offer both challenges and opportunities. Rather than becoming a victim of anger, ill will, exhaustion, and related conditions, take advantage of the lessons and wise choices present in any situation as you build your capacity to remain present and turn toward the chal-lenges you face in this moment, and in each moment after that.

THE ONLY RESPONSE THAT MAKES SENSE

But, after all, we are only human! It is natural and easy to lose our way in difficult times and make poor or harmful choices.

You might find that it is very helpful to remember this: you *are* only human, so keep a reserve of patience, forgiveness, and kindness available for yourself, because the process of healing and transformation is not easy. You could start by remembering that any mindful moment you have is also a moment of kindness and compassion. Practicing mindfulness *is* an act of generosity and love—expressed in caring attention—that nourishes the heart.

Mindfulness brings you back to this moment, which is the only moment where you can actually choose your response to the difficulty that is present. Perhaps learning to remain present and open to what is happening—to what Polly Young-Eisendrath calls the "context of our own engagement"—could help. Perhaps staying present and observing can be a wise reminder of the larger context of life and death that is always present in each unfolding moment.

The poet Naomi Shihab Nye, in her popular poem "Kindness," has observed that sorrow is the "other deepest thing" besides kindness (1995). She beautifully suggests that upon realizing the pervasive extent of sorrow in this life, how sorrow touches us and others alike, the only response that makes sense in the face of such pain is kindness—not the frequent reactions of rejection, distraction, or numbing.

You might call such attention a form of self-care, or *self-fullness.* Such attention is not selfish or self-indulgent. Including yourself in mindful, self-attention will take intention, and it could require some energy—energy that naturally grows from acts of self-care and self-compassion.

That energy could come from appropriate self-care expressed in rest, exercise, and personal time for yourself and with loved ones. Including yourself in mindful attention could demand the courage and willingness to see accurately all of who you are, including your capacities and powers for helping and hurting, for succeeding and failing, for strength and for weakness and vulnerability, and the wisdom to face more compassionately the fact of your eventual death.

Seeing the size of the cloth of sorrow and pain that can be present in our lives also involves seeing the complex causes of pain in others. As difficult as it can be to witness pain and suffering in another, even a perfect stranger, it can be even more difficult—and take real courage, determination, and understanding—to turn to compassion as a response in those moments when we are confronted by people who offend, threaten, or challenge us.

In those situations with others, it can help to recall that turning toward this moment with compassion does not mean condoning or consenting to their hurtful words and actions. Choosing compassion simply and immediately makes possible a different relationship to pain and suffering in ourselves and, through our wise and kinder response, a different external expression from us and a different experience for others.

Recognizing and Befriending Ourselves

The voices of poets like Naomi Shihab Nye come from a rich tradition in literature and artistic expression that reflects awareness of the two tigers—one of anger and hate, and one of caring and love—that reside in the human heart. Besides artists and poets, others including psychologists and therapists, theologians, philosophers, and spiritual teachers also point to the importance of becoming aware—not remaining in denial—and owning, understanding, and embracing the full range of our desire, fears, and ill will as human beings. His Holiness, the Dalai Lama (2009) put it this way:

> In reality, we have to live together. We cannot destroy all the other beings. Even if we do not like our neighbors, we have to live together. In the field of economics, also, we have to depend on others, even hostile nations. That is a reality. Under these circumstances it is always better to live harmoniously, in a friendly way, than to maintain a negative attitude. The globe is becoming much smaller and more interdependent. Empathy and altruism are the keys for happiness (14).

Attempts to deny or ignore the pain we carry from our past inevitably lead to more pain. Here we see how attempts to ignore or deny pain impacted one man's life.

• Jerry's Story

Jerry is a thirty-two-year-old man who works as a fireman in a large city and frequently faces life-threatening situations. He is a courageous and reliable fireman, and has received numerous awards and public recognition over the several years he has been in his job. Before being a fireman, Jerry served two combat tours in the military, and has always believed he constantly had to prove he was a "real man" in a world "that is out to get you." Jerry's childhood was marked by frequent moves, always to "tough" neighborhoods, and a home life with an abusive alcoholic father, who physically punished Jerry and his two siblings whenever anything in the house went wrong. When Jerry was about twelve, his mother divorced his father and took Jerry and his younger brother and sister to live with her parents in a working-class neighborhood of a small town. Jerry finished high school there and joined the military soon after.

Since then, Jerry has been through two marriages that ended in divorce largely because of his tendency to isolate himself, bury his feelings, and explode into violent behavior marked by hitting the wall or smashing furniture when he feels very stressed. Now, with a wonderful woman, Sandy, in his life, Jerry has decided to take a different path. "I don't want to lose anyone else who loves me!" he told Sandy soon after they became serious about each other. He meets with a counselor provided by the human resources department of the city he works for, and is enrolled in an anger management class. After a few weeks of sessions and classes, Jerry told his counselor that "for the first time in my life, I realize the anger I feel inside is not something that I have to push down or push away. I know now that letting myself feel the anger and pain will not kill me. Feeling it does not make me more vulnerable. Fighting what I feel hurts me. I need to pay attention better and learn how to control my anger by understanding it. If I can do that, then I will finally be the man I want to be."

It can be very hard to acknowledge and accept our long-carried inner pain, and to own the deep habits, capabilities, and perhaps our own history of harming others and the world. It can also be very hard to find the courage and mercy needed to heal ourselves. And yet the world goes on, turning and turning, always generating a huge cloth of pain and suffering but also manifesting—in beautiful ways and countless moments—possibilities and expressions of a vaster and deeper cloth of kindness and awareness in every moment and in each life. If we truly want something better for ourselves, for our loved ones, and for our world, then why not begin by bringing mindful attention, compassion, and understanding to the only life we can save—our own?

COURAGE, WISDOM, SAFETY, AND PRESENCE

Any and every difficult moment, situation, or relationship offers you a choice: do you respond with kindness and compassion or with rejection, scorn, and hostility? Any moment of confusion, anger, or sorrow invites you to respond with curiosity and mercy, listening and observing mindfully in a way that includes your own reactive pain as well as the pain present in the other person or in the situation. Choosing to respond with compassionate attention, breath by breath, can become a gateway for entering into a vastly different world in the very next moment or breath.

Radical, positive transformation and change around anger and ill will can happen in any moment. It is also true that it almost always takes determination, perseverance, and energy to remain present to enable and to experience the transformation. Nourishing your humor, patience, and forgiveness (including self-forgiveness) can be a big help too.

When you fall into old habits of anger and hostility, you have not failed. You are only human. Remember that mindfulness is about not judging and not striving. Mindfulness recognizes what is here, now. Mindfulness practice empowers you to better understand, and that understanding becomes the basis for authentic and enduring healing, change, and transformation.

It helps if you can relax enough not to become discouraged or blame yourself in those times when you do not feel mindful, or compassionate, or kind. If you remain filled with anger and rejection, mindfully noticing it and naming the feeling you have *is* practicing mindfulness of the anger.

The most important thing you can do to calm the anger and feed the goodness in your life is simply to stay on the path of awareness and to keep at the work of growing mindfulness. Here are more brief meditation practices to help you choose new possibilities built upon mindfulness, kindness, and compassion in difficult moments filled with anger, dislike, and blame.

Courage and Wisdom Support Kindness and Compassion

Let courage and wisdom help you choose kindness and compassion, as it did for Brother David Steindl-Rast. Adding his voice to the response by spiritual leaders to the 9/11 attack on America, Brother David, a Benedictine monk, wrote this:

> Violence has its roots in every heart. It is in my own heart that I must recognize fear, agitation, coldness, alienation, and the impulse to blind anger. Here in my heart I can turn fear into courageous trust, agitation and confusion into stillness, isolation into a sense of belonging, alienation into love, and irrational reaction into common sense (Steindl-Rast 2001, 257).

Through the lens of his own life experience, Brother David reminds us that we have the potential to transform the fear and pain in ourselves if we choose to look into our own hearts with awareness.

In the face of any difficulty or challenge, especially when anger fills you with its insistent demands for action, to restrain yourself from acting impulsively out of anger takes real courage and wisdom. It requires courage to face the intense distress of pain and anger and the internal demands to escape from or remove that pain. Such courage is supported by understanding that the anger and pain is not permanent, and that acting impulsively on it will likely bring much more pain.

In that moment of a mindful pause generated by courageous restraint, greater clarity can arise. Looking deeply, you can see for yourself and act on the wisdom of Brother Steindl-Rast—"It is in my own heart that I must recognize fear, agitation, coldness, alienation, and the impulse to blind anger." Remember your tools of courage and wisdom when facing anger, fear, and related feelings.

BRIEF MEDITATION TO NURTURE COURAGE AND WISDOM

Anytime you feel or face anger and upset, pause, acknowledge the unpleasant feelings, and breathe mindfully for several breaths.

As you continue to breathe mindfully, kindly offer yourself support with phrases of courage and wisdom: "In this moment, may I find the strength I need." "May I have the support I need to make the most helpful response in this moment." "May this situation teach me about the true nature of life."

Safety and Protection for Kindness and Compassion

Let safety and protecting yourself help you choose kindness and compassion. A common misunderstanding about compassion is that being compassionate or kind means we must become somehow passive and more open to abuse. This is not true. Compassion can have a fierce and protective dimension that can actually help you stay present for the difficult and painful moments in life.

The meditation teacher Sharon Salzberg tells a story about herself and her growing understanding of compassion. Sharon recalls a time in India when she was studying and practicing meditation focused on kindness and compassion. One day in a local village, she was approached and grabbed by a large, drunken man. She escaped when her friend fought the man off. Later Sharon describes the advice her teacher gave her upon hearing the story. "Oh, Sharon, with all the loving-kindness in your heart, you should have taken your umbrella and hit the man over the head with it!" She goes on to say that this experience helped her learn the strength in compassion and how compassion "allows us to name injustice without hesitation, and to act strongly, with all the skill at our disposal" (Salzberg 1995, 103).

Sharon's story reminds us that any of us can act with kindness and compassion in response to a threat and still protect ourselves. Her teacher did not tell Sharon to keep hitting the man angrily or to hurt him. Instead, he instructed her to hit the man over the head with a spirit of kindness. In that instruction, the teacher opened her (and us) to the possibility of responding to a threat with sufficient force to deter it, without becoming hijacked by anger and fear to the point we overreact and cause more harm.

BRIEF MEDITATION TO TOUCH FEELINGS OF SAFETY AND EASE

When you feel angry, afraid, or upset, pause and breathe mindfully for several breaths.

As you continue to breathe mindfully, patiently offer yourself well wishes for safety and protection: "May I be safe and protected from inner and outer harm." "May I find the wisdom and courage I need to act and be safe in this moment." "May I value myself and protect myself in this moment."

Mindful Attention Includes Kindness and Compassion

Let mindful attention help you choose kindness and compassion—in this moment. Life is happening in the present moment. Life is happening in each of us in this moment.

In any moment, perhaps *this* moment, are you practicing anger and confusion, or can you stop, disentangle from, and stop nourishing those habits, and shift? Can you nourish your practice of awareness, caring, and compassion through closer and steadier attention? The Buddhist teacher Joseph Goldstein puts it like this:

> It's not enough to simply think love is a good idea. There's some work to be done, attention to be paid. We need to express it in the way we relate to people.... All of this requires practice. We need to notice those times when we are not being straightforward, gentle, or easy to speak to. And, on the other

hand, we need to notice what happens when we let down the walls of defensiveness and fear, let go of the tension of separation, even for a few moments." (Goldstein 2002, 109)

Many possibilities! In any moment, which will you choose? What will that choice reveal? Where will that choice take you? How will others and the world around you be different by each choice you make?

Shifting attention to the intelligence, goodness, deeper values, and purpose in your life can strengthen and increase your capacity for choosing kindness and compassion and taking the positive actions that can mean so much.

BRIEF MEDITATION TO REFLECT ON GOODNESS AND YOUR DEEPER VALUES

Anytime you are not feeling angry or upset, take time to pause and breathe mindfully for several breaths.

Reflect on your deepest values and the source of meaning in your life. What is your deepest wish for yourself?

As you continue to breathe mindfully, offer yourself kind phrases that support your deepest wishes for yourself, wishes that resonate with you: "May I be happy, healthy, peaceful, and safe." "May I grow in understanding and live with ease and well-being." "May I discover the true purpose of my life."

KEEP IN MIND

- In each moment, we have the possibility of choosing how we will respond and relate to what is present with us. Old habits of anger and fear arise quickly and drive us in one direction. Mindfulness and compassion, practiced moment by moment, situation by situation, even breath by breath, offer the possibility of changing our relationship to the difficult in our lives.

- Being more mindful and compassionate takes work. It does not mean being passive or becoming more vulnerable to harm.

- Tapping into the strength of mindfulness and compassion as a practice and way of relating to your life and yourself can be the basis for radical transformation and healing of the power that anger, ill will, and aversion have over your life and in your relationships.

the gift of no fear

You must be the change you wish to see in the world.

—*Mahatma Gandhi*

Throughout this book, we have been exploring the relationship between your mind, brain, and body, and your life. We have been looking in detail at the nature of strong emotions like anger, hostility, and fear, and the many ways these emotions can distort and impact your relationship to yourself, others, and your experience of life itself.

Through the lens of mindfulness, we human beings can witness the ever-shifting nature of experience flowing through our senses in the present moment and actually observe the appearing, disappearing, changing fabric of our life, breath by breath. If you have experimented with even a single mindfulness practice, then you have likely witnessed the flow of thoughts and emotions within you, and have also perhaps noticed how strong emotions like anger can take control of you and color your life. You have also probably experienced a power within, perhaps unsuspected, to calm the storm of anger, and see and make different choices in any moment.

By bringing more mindfulness and understanding into your life, and observing the lives of others with more compassion and forgiveness, perhaps you have also recognized that no one acts alone. The actions each of us takes have consequences; they impact others and our world. In a very real sense, each of us is a dynamic factor in the unfolding present moment of changing conditions that is the web of life we all share. This final chapter reflects on the implications of our interconnectedness and the powerful positive possibility of offering others and our world the gift of no fear as we organize ourselves and our lives around practices of mindfulness and compassion.

VIOLENCE BELONGS TO US

The poet Rilke once said of our world, "If it has terrors, they are our terrors." And, sadly and painfully, we humans fill our world with terrors and violence every day.

The World Health Organization (WHO) defines violence as "the intentional use of physical force or power, threatened or actual against oneself, another person, or against a group or community, that either results in or has a high likelihood of resulting in injury, death, · psychological harm, maldevelopment or deprivation" (World Health Organization 1996). The authors of the WHO's *World Report on Violence and Health* (WHO 2002) noted that violence can also occur when the perpetrator uses force but does not know or intend to cause harm— as when an upset parent shakes a crying child to quiet the child and causes brain damage. And, they point out, this definition includes all acts of violence—public or private, reactive or proactive, criminal or noncriminal.

The WHO recognizes three categories of violence: violence toward self, interpersonal violence, and collective violence, which is committed by larger groups to carry out particular political, economic, or social agendas. According to the data of these categories of violence, violence toward self makes up the largest percentage of mortality from violence globally, estimated at almost 50 percent of all violence in a survey in 2000. Homicides make up approximately 31 percent, and war-related deaths from violence are estimated at almost 19 percent of global deaths by violence (World Health Organization 2002). The report goes on to say that these estimates on worldwide mortality from violence are almost certainly underestimated, and that worldwide data on nonfatal violence—physical and sexual assaults, for example—is said to be very incomplete due to a variety of social, cultural, resource, and other reporting limitations.

Despite these staggering numbers about the incidence and cost of violence, the authors of the report are hopeful. They write, "Violence can be prevented and its impact reduced.... The factors that contribute to violent responses—whether they are factors of attitude and behavior or related to larger social, economic, political, and cultural conditions—can be changed" (World Health Organization 2002, 3).

VIOLENCE BEGINS WITH US

The public health understanding of the sources of violence, not surprisingly, aligns with the views of mental health and other professionals. Both sources point to the factors present in each individual, to the nature and quality of interpersonal and social relationships, to the level of community contexts—neighborhoods, schools, and workplaces, for instance—and to larger societal factors such as cultural norms about violence, parental and child rights, norms about the role of women and children, and the presence and expression of political or other forms of institutional conflict. These views of violence also align with the wisdom that comes from bringing mindfulness into your life and into situations where anger and disapproval flower into overt expressions of force against what is here in this moment.

Violence, Aversion, and the Inner Life

From the perspective informed by mindfulness, we could say that the behavior that is labeled "violence" actually is deeply interconnected with the inner life of the person behaving violently. That inner life can be the home of a calculated intention to harm, or a form of violence can occur when the person using force does not intend to harm the victim, as in the case of the parent, as we noted earlier, who—driven by inner upset—shakes a child, resulting in brain damage.

By looking deeply, mindfulness practice can reveal—even in the latter example where the person using force does not intend to harm the victim—that it was the deep and compelling feeling of aversion to the unpleasantness of what was present that fueled the physical expression of force that harmed the victim. In this view, there are two victims: the victim of the forceful act and the person who committed the act—the person ablaze with aversion to feelings deep within and to the situation without. The two are deeply interconnected in the present moment, and feelings of unpleasantness, reactive anger, and the forceful expression of aversion, dislike, and rejection of the conditions present in this moment all reflect the interconnections and interdependency between the two victims.

The forms of violence can be almost unlimited, but they all arise from the dynamic interplay of internal beliefs, feelings, and interactions with the external world and others in it. Besides obvious extreme forms of violence involving threats or actual gross physical violence, there can be less visible, yet very harmful expressions of the impulse and intention to do harm that are driven by inner fires of anger and fear.

For example, as the WHO analysis points out, a large category of violence is violence toward oneself. Such violence doesn't come from nowhere. When anger, pain, and self-loathing feed a thought like *I hate myself and I should die*, it should come as no surprise that the thinker of that thought may later try to commit self-harm. Indeed, how could people act violently if their inner lives, including their thoughts and emotional lives, weren't already consumed with the intention to harm, arising from beliefs of danger or threat that come from others and resultant fear and anger toward them? When anger and fear feed thoughts like *Those people are so stupid and greedy. They are not really like me at all. They are not even really human!* it should not be surprising when those thoughts lead to more violent actions against the targeted group.

From a mindfulness perspective, when looking deeply, one can observe that the energy behind an intention to harm arises most likely in anger built on some fear or fears fueled by strong beliefs. From that structure of anger, an elaborate world of thoughts and plans can arise in support of the intention to harm violently. With the structure, intention, and plan to harm in place, the target of those thoughts that intend harm can be almost anything—oneself, another person, types of other people, or even things not alive like buildings or flags that symbolize something the strong belief system disapproves of.

As an outward expression of the layers of fear and strong beliefs below anger, we might say that any resultant violence both belongs and has begun with us. To better understand this perspective, let's look more closely at the relationship between the inner life and outwardly directed actions, especially aggressive or violent ones.

Inner Pain and Outward Violence

From the view of mindfulness, it might be said that the intention to be violent or do harm rests on one's inner self-absorption and single-minded goal either to remove one's own pain and/or to remove an external factor that one believes causes the pain or blocks one's own pleasure, or both.

Being lost in an inner world filled with pain, urgency, irritation, doubts, or a myriad of other unpleasant thoughts, emotions, and body sensations, the outer world can literally disappear in a moment, and the actions arising in the next moment can be something to later regret, especially if they bring fear and rejection to someone we care about. Consider this example.

• The Grocery Store Story

Kenny is a busy, hard-working married man in his midthirties. He has a six-year-old son, Derrick, who worships him and longs to go everywhere Kenny goes. One afternoon Kenny took Derrick with him on a trip to the grocery store. Kenny was feeling very stressed and was in a hurry, and feeling irritable and annoyed about many things at work. In the soft drink aisle, while Kenny was looking for something else, his little son, Derrick, wanting to help his dad, tried to bring a big plastic soda bottle to the shopping cart. It was too heavy for Derrick, and he dropped the bottle in the aisle, where it bounced and rolled around loudly before bumping against the shopping cart. Hearing the commotion, and already filled with impatience, irritation, and a mind full of critical comments about many things, Kenny turned and saw the bottle vibrating against the cart. His anger had a focus.

He looked at Derrick angrily and spoke in a loud voice, "See the mess you made," he said. "Now that soda bottle is all shaken up and will probably explode when we open it. I should have left you at home." What Kenny did not see was his son's love and desire to help his father. What he did not see was that Derrick needed his father's help to do things he wanted to do for himself. What he also did not see was what Derrick felt and would carry as a memory: he had disappointed his father, his father was angry, and his father did not want to be with him.

Of course, our actions and words can do harm, and perhaps be experienced as a form of violence by another, even when we do not intend to do that person harm. If we are perceived as capable of lashing out or doing harm, we may burden others with fear when they are in our company. Our angry words and actions threaten others and they feel fearful. Instead of fear, how could we learn to give a gift of no fear instead?

GIVING THE GIFT OF NO FEAR

When you feel afraid, it is likely that you sense a threat of some kind. Something has happened, and you do not feel safe in that moment. When you feel safe again, it is because you no longer feel threatened.

For most of us, feeling safe is related, very basically, to being in circumstances and relationships that are life affirming and life respecting. Our essential needs are being supplied, and others are not threatening or abusing us. This affirming and respectful way of being and experiencing life in the world and in relationships includes how we are with ourselves as well. You could say that feeling safe begins at home!

Because of the interactive and interconnected nature of our lives, outward actions—which always reflect our inner lives—whether they be life affirming and respectful or life denying and rejecting, have the power to evoke in others and ourselves a sense of being safe or in danger. The remarkable "gift of no fear" appears when we cease making ourselves or others feel less safe by speaking or acting in ways that deny or reject life. The gift of no fear appears whenever we align closely with the deep values of affirming and respecting life. We then speak and act in ways that naturally promote feelings of safety and well-being in this very moment, here and now. You might even think of yourself as a "peacemaker" when you offer the gift of no fear, and you might find that you can approach any moment or situation of your life that way.

It can be very helpful to bring mindfulness, compassion, and understanding into a difficult situation and to recall that the gift of no fear goes in two directions. The first direction is toward yourself. Learning to hold and care for your own fear means you have come to understand it and are no longer afraid of it. You can give the gift of no fear to yourself in any moment; it begins with compassionate, unshakable mindful attention to yourself and to your own fear and its causes. The second direction for the gift of no fear is toward others and the world, and it depends on the first. When your inner life and your actions are no longer driven by the fear that underlies so much anger and hostility, then the gift of no fear to others comes in the form of your powerful life-affirming and life-defending presence in the world.

Finding Meaning, Acting with Purpose

What gives our lives meaning? What gives our acts purpose? Of course, we all must answer these questions for ourselves.

For many people, it may take a tragedy or a life-threatening experience to awaken in them the curiosity to formulate such questions. But once brought to consciousness, questions about meaning and purpose in our lives can become an unfailing compass and a reliable companion on the journey of discovery that mindfulness and compassion support.

How do you embody your values and intentions? While thoughts and views may be the basis of all intentions, the actual action you take is important.

Ayya Khema was born in Germany, educated in Scotland and China, and later became a United States citizen. After a rich and busy secular life, she was ordained as a Buddhist nun in Sri Lanka in 1979. She established a training center for Buddhist nuns and other women of all nationalities wishing to lead a contemplative life in Sri Lanka in 1982. Ayya Khema speaks clearly about action related to the quality of loving-kindness:

> Loving-kindness conduct—we all know what that means: looking after someone who is sick, inquiring after somebody's

health, visiting them in hospital, giving them some food when they're incapacitated and can't look after themselves, being concerned about other people and trying to help them.... That is loving-kindness conduct. Loving-kindness conduct should not only be confined to a small group, but it should show itself everywhere." (Khema 1987, 73–74)

When your actions and words are linked to your deepest values, the experience of integrity arises. This can be felt deeply in one's response to difficult situations and challenging times.

Richard Strozzi-Heckler is a sixth-degree black belt in aikido and holds a doctorate in psychology. He was an All-American in track and field at San Diego State University, and is the president of the Strozzi Institute, the Center for Embodied Leadership and Mastery. For the last thirty years, Dr. Strozzi-Heckler has taught awareness disciplines and principles of embodied leadership to business, government, military, nonprofits, health care, and education.

In his book *In Search of the Warrior Spirit: Teaching Awareness Disciplines to the Military,* he recounts an exchange about deep values between a group of Green Beret Special Forces soldiers and Brother David Steindl-Rast. One of the soldiers challenged Brother David with a question: "What do you mean by God, anyway? How do you know you're leading a spiritual life?"

Brother David defined spirituality as a sense of belonging or connectedness—with a person, with nature, with a community, with an inner feeling. "Do you feel any of these things?" he asked.

When the soldier replied that he felt connected to his newborn son and to his fellow soldiers, Brother David said, "From my point of view, this is a spiritual life. In fact, it sounds like you have a wealth of spirituality."

To the assembled group of elite soldiers, he went on to say that "your profession can be a vehicle for worshipping that which is sacred. If you wish, your chosen profession can be an expression of your highest spiritual values" (Strozzi-Heckler 2007, 271–72).

What do we stand for in our lives? How could we act in ways that are more life affirming and life respecting? How do those actions become the gift of no fear to us and to others?

Perhaps doing the hard work of growing self-awareness, with mindfulness and compassion as vital allies, is a good way to proceed toward the goal of giving no fear. And doing that work of awareness could be viewed as a warrior's path. To understand what this means, let's hear what Richard Strozzi-Heckler has to say about warriors. From his experience and perspective working with military in combat theaters worldwide, Richard Strozzi-Heckler states, "We must envision the warrior beyond our preconceived notions of gender, physical size, strength, or earning honor through combat. The battlefield of the warrior must expand beyond the literal interpretation of war and destruction to include every moment of our lives. In order to live authentically with integrity, we must have a certain kind of courage.... When we're no longer afraid of being who we are we act from integrity and authenticity" (2007, 243).

To Know What Can Be Known

Years ago on a long, silent mindfulness retreat, I found myself for a time preoccupied with thinking about questions and theories focused on the meaning of life, my purpose on this earth, and related philosophical and theological ideas. Hungry for answers to my questions, I went eagerly to my interview with the monk who was leading the retreat. After telling him my thoughts and questions, I waited expectantly. He answered very kindly, and wisely.

"All of that is very interesting," he said gently, "but I suggest you put your attention on knowing what can be known. Pay attention more closely, and directly observe what is present, here and now. That is what the meditation practice can do for you. It can help you know what you are capable of knowing for yourself by direct experience. If you can do that, then you will probably find the answers to your questions."

I will be forever grateful to that monk for his response. In a moment, kindly and with patience, he pulled me out of my tendency to be lost in ideas (even inspiring ones!), and brought my attention back to the present moment. By encouraging me to trust my innate capacity to know what I could know—paying attention with interest and being open to and allowing my own experience—he reminded me that I already had what I needed to answer the important questions I was so preoccupied by.

Broaden and Build Beyond Fear and Negativity

Faith traditions and spiritual teachers of all ages and perspectives have emphasized the importance of mastering our impulses toward violence and harm, and have pointed to ways for doing that. Mindfulness, kindness and compassion, and understanding are widely recommended meditation approaches to master the force of anger and the impulses toward harming—whether it be harming ourselves or others.

These contemplative practices can actually cultivate positive emotions in us, and the positive emotions can change us in important and lasting ways. Positivity points toward the life-affirming and life-enriching elements of emotional experience. The positivity "palette" consists of joy, gratitude, serenity, interest, hope, pride, amusement, inspiration, and awe. "Positivity opens us. The first core truth about positive emotions is that they open our hearts and our minds, making us more receptive and more creative" (Fredrickson 2009, 37; 21). Positivity, awareness, and presence are also an ancient wisdom, as reflected in this statement:

> *Blessed are the man and the woman who have grown beyond their greed, and have put an end to their hatred and no longer nourish illusions. But they delight in the way things are and keep their hearts open day and night.*

—Psalm 1

EVERYTHING IS WAITING FOR YOU

As this book draws to a close, it may be helpful to recall our view of anger: Anger is not you, but is a temporary condition that depends on many other conditions, much like a rainbow or a cloud depends on other conditions in order to appear. Anger does not actually come from "out there" but arises when a stimulus or situation that you meet triggers a complex set of conditions that live in you—conditions such as beliefs, fears, perceptions, and physical reactions. And by growing a more accurate awareness of your anger and its causes, you can broaden and build your resources for choosing to respond to angry feelings with the strength that arises from understanding, compassion, and knowing how to care for any pain that angry feelings mask. Turning toward anger and pain with steady attention that is based in kindness and wisdom can then become your wisest, most trusted, and most effective response whenever anger arises.

Trusting that you already have all you need for this work, you can begin to approach anger and other intense emotions mindfully and skillfully, and in the process, radically shift your understanding of these emotions and the power they hold to distort your life. As the poet David Whyte reflects, great benefits can come through such change:

Everything Is Waiting for You

(After Derek Mahon)
Your great mistake is to act the drama
as if you were alone. As if life
were a progressive and cunning crime
with no witness to the tiny hidden
transgressions. To feel abandoned is to deny
the intimacy of your surroundings. Surely,
even you, at times, have felt the grand array:
the swelling presence, and the chorus, crowding
out your solo voice. You must note
the way the soap dish enables you,
or the window latch grants you freedom.
Alertness is the hidden discipline of familiarity.
The stairs are your mentor of things
to come, the doors have always been there
to frighten you and invite you,
and the tiny speaker in the phone
is your dream-ladder to divinity.

Put down the weight of your aloneness and ease into
the conversation. The kettle is singing
even as it pours you a drink, the cooking pots
have left their arrogant aloofness and
seen the good in you at last. All the birds
and creatures of the world are unutterably
themselves. Everything is waiting for you.

May mindfulness in its most universal expression flower in your life. May you discover the boundlessness, dignity, and courage of your own heart.

May you find presence, compassion and kindness, and unshakable joy and wisdom, and may those qualities support and inform you all the days of your life. When you put your voice and action into this world, may you always offer the gift of no fear to yourself and to others.

references

Baer, R. 2003. "Mindfulness Training as Clinical Intervention: A Conceptual and Empirical Review." *Clinical Psychology: Science and Practice* 10: 125–43.

Baer, R. A., G. T. Smith, J. Hopkins, J. Krietemeyer, and L. Toney. 2006. "Using Self-Report Assessment Methods to Explore Facets of Mindfulness." *Assessment* 13: 27–47.

Baer, R. A., G. T. Smith, E. Lykins, D. Button, J. Krietemeyer, S. Sauer, E. Walsh, D. Duggan, and J. M. Williams. 2008. "Construct Validity of the Five Facet Mindfulness Questionnaire in Meditating and Nonmeditating Samples." *Assessment* 15: 329–42.

Barbour, C., C. Eckhardt, J. Davison, and H. Kassinove. 1998. "The Experience and Expression of Anger in Maritally Violent and Discordant, Non-Violent Men." *Behavior Therapy* 29: 173–91.

Barefoot, J. C., W. G. Dahlstrom, and R. B. Williams. 1983. "Hostility, CHD Incidence, and Total Morbidity: A 25-Year Follow-Up Study of 255 Physicians." *Psychosomatic Medicine* 45: 59–63.

Bateson, G. 1941. "The Frustration-Aggression Hypothesis and Culture." *Psychological Review* 48: 350–55.

Baumeister, R., E. Bratlavsky, C. Finkenauer, and K. Vohs. 2001. "Bad Is Stronger than Good." *Review of General Psychology* 5: 323–70.

Benson, H. 1975. *The Relaxation Response.* New York: William Morrow.

Berkman, L., and S. L. Syme. 1979. "Social Networks, Lost Resistance, and Mortality: A Nine Year Follow-Up Study of Alameda Residents." *American Journal of Epidemiology* 109: 186–204.

Biaggio, M. K. 1980. "Anger Arousal and Personality Characteristics." *Journal of Consulting and Social Psychology* 39: 352–56.

Boorstein, S. 2007. *Happiness Is an Inside Job: Practicing for a Joyful Life.* New York: Ballantine Books.

Brown, K. W., and R. M. Ryan. 2003. "The Benefits of Being Present: Mindfulness and Its Role in Psychological Well-Being." *Journal of Personality and Social Psychology* 84: 822–48.

Brown, K. W., R. M. Ryan, and J. D. Creswell. 2007. "Mindfulness: Theoretical Foundations and Evidence for Salutary Effects." *Psychological Inquiry* 18: 211–37.

Cardaciotto, L., J. D. Herbert, E. M. Forman, E. Moitra, and V. Farrow. 2008. "The Assessment of Present-Moment Awareness and Acceptance: The Philadelphia Mindfulness Scale." *Assessment* 15: 204–23.

Carlson, L. E., M. Speca, P. Faris, and K. Patel. 2007. "One Year Pre-Post Intervention Follow-Up of Psychological, Immune, Endocrine, and Blood Pressure Outcomes of Mindfulness-Based Stress Reduction (MBSR) in Breast and Prostate Cancer Patients." *Brain, Behavior, and Immunity* 21: 1038–49.

Carson, J. W., K. M. Carson, K. M. Gil, and D. H. Baucom. 2004. "Mindfulness-Based Relationship Enhancement." *Behavior Therapy* 35: 471–94.

Crockenberg, S. 1987. "Predictors and Correlates of Anger Toward and Punitive Control of Toddlers by Adolescent Mothers." *Child Development* 58: 964–65.

Davidson, R. J., with S. Begley. 2012. *The Emotional Life Of Your Brain: How Its Unique Patterns Affect the Way You Think, Feel, and Live—and How You Can Change Them*. New York: Hudson Street Press.

Dalai Lama, H. H. 2009. "Looking Deeply at Despair." In *In the Face of Fear: Buddhist Wisdom for Challenging Times*, edited by Barry Boyce and the editors of the *Shambhala Sun*. Boston: Shambhala Publications.

Deffenbacher, J. L., M. E. Huff, R. S. Lynch, E. R. Oetting, and F. Natalie. 2000. "Characteristics and Treatment of High-Anger Drivers." *Journal of Counseling Psychology* 47: 5–17.

Dentan, R. K. 1968. *The Semai: A Nonviolent People of Malaya*. New York: Holt, Rinehart & Winston.

Feldman, C. 1998. *Thorson's Principles of Meditation*. London: Thorsons.

———. 2001. *The Buddhist Path to Simplicity: Spiritual Practice for Everyday Life*. London: Thorsons.

Feldman, G., A. Hayes, S. Kumar, J. Greeson, and J. P. Laurenceau. 2007. "Mindfulness and Emotion Regulation: The Development and Initial Validation of the Cognitive and Affective Mindfulness Scale–Revised (CAMS-R)." *Journal of Psychopathology and Behavioral Assessment* 29: 177–190.

Fredrickson, B. 2001. "The Role of Positive Emotions in Positive Psychology." *American Psychologist* 56: 218–226.

———. 2009. *Positivity: Groundbreaking Research Reveals How to Embrace the Hidden Strength of Positive Emotions, Overcome Negativity, and Thrive*. New York: Crown Publishers.

———. 2013. *LOVE 2.0: How Our Supreme Emotion Affects Everything We Feel, Think, Do, and Become*. New York: Hudson Street Press.

Fredrickson, B., and R. Levenson. 1998. "Positive Emotions Speed Recovery from the Cardiovascular Sequelae of Negative Emotions." *Psychology Press* 12: 191–220.

Fredrickson, B., R. Mancuso, C. Branigan, and M. Tugade. 2000. "The Undoing Effect of Positive Emotions." *Motivation and Emotion* 24: 237–58.

Gentry, W. D. 1982. "Habitual Anger-Coping Styles: Effect on Mean Blood Pressure and Risk for Essential Hypertension." *Psychosomatic Medicine* 44: 195–202.

Goetz, J. L., D. Keltner, and E. Simon-Thomas. 2010. "Compassion: An Evolutionary Analysis and Empirical Review." *Psychological Bulletin* 136 (3): 351–74.

Goldstein, J. 2002. *One Dharma: The Emerging Western Buddhism.* San Francisco: HarperSanFrancisco.

Goleman, D. 2003. *Destructive Emotions: How Can We Overcome Them? A Scientific Dialogue with the Dalai Lama.* New York: Bantam Books.

Greenglass, E. R. 1996. "Anger Suppression, Cynical Distrust, and Hostility: Implications for Coronary Heart Disease. In *Stress and Emotion: Anxiety, Anger, and Curiosity*, edited by C. D. Spielberger and I. G. Sarason. New York: Routledge.

Grepmair, L., F. Mitterlehner, T. Loew, E. Bachler, W. Rother, and M. Nickel. 2007. "Promoting Mindfulness in Psychotherapists in Training Influences the Treatment Results of Their Patients: A Randomized Controlled Trial." *Psychotherapy and Psychosomatics* 76: 332–38.

Grossman, P., L. Niemann, S. Schmidt, and H. Walach. 2004. "Mindfulness-Based Stress Reduction and Health Benefits: A Meta-analysis." *Journal of Psychosomatic Research* 57: 35–43.

Grossman, P., U. Tiefenthaler-Gilmer, A. Raysz, and U. Kesper. 2007. "Mindfulness Training as an Intervention for Fibromyalgia: Evidence of Postintervention and Three-Year Follow-Up Benefits in Well-Being." *Psychotherapy and Psychosomatics* 76: 226–33.

Halifax, J. 2008. *Being with Dying: Cultivating Compassion and Fearlessness in the Presence of Death.* Boston: Shambhala Publications.

Hanson, R. with R. Mendius. 2009. *Buddha's Brain: The Practical Neuroscience of Happiness, Love, and Wisdom.* Oakland, CA: New Harbinger Publications.

Hansson, R. D., W. H. Jones, and B. Carpenter. 1984. "Relational Competence and Social Support." *Review of Personality and Social Psychology* 5: 265–84.

Hemenway, D. S., S. Solnick, and J. Carter. 1994. "Child Rearing Violence." *Child Abuse and Neglect* 18: 1011–20.

Herman, D. 1985. "A Statutory Proposal to Limit the Infliction of Violence upon Children." *Family Law Quarterly* 19: 1–52.

Jain, S., S. L. Shapiro, S. Swanick, S. C. Roesch, P. M. Mills, I. Bell, and G. E. R. Schwartz. 2007. "A Randomized Control Trial of Mindfulness Meditation versus Relaxation Training: Effects on Distress, Positive States of Mind, Rumination, and Distraction." *Annals of Behavioral Medicine* 33: 11–21.

Jamieson, Wendell. 2013, March 2. "The Crime of His Childhood." *The New York Times.* Retrieved from http://www.nytimes.com/2013 /03/03/nyregion/40-years-after-an-acid-attack-a-life-well-lived. html.

Jones, W. H., J. E. Freeman, and R. A. Gasewick. 1981. "The Persistence of Loneliness: Self and Other Determinants." *Journal of Personality* 49: 27–48.

Kabat-Zinn, J. 1990. *Full Catastrophe Living: Using the Wisdom of Your Body and Mind to Face Stress, Pain, and Illness.* New York: Delacorte Press.

Kabat-Zinn, J., and R. J. Davidson (eds.), with Z. Houshmand. 2011. *The Mind's Own Physician: A Scientific Dialogue with the Dalai Lama on the Healing Power of Meditation.* Oakland, CA: New Harbinger Publications.

Kabat-Zinn, J., J. E. Wheeler, T. Light, A. Skillings, M. J. Scharff, T. G. Copley, D. Hosmer, and J. D. Bernhard. 1998. "Influence of a Mindfulness Meditation-Based Stress Reduction Intervention on Rates of Skin Clearing in Patients with Moderate to Severe Psoriasis Undergoing Phototherapy (UVB) and Photochemotherapy (PUVA)." *Psychosomatic Medicine* 60: 625–32.

Khema, Ayya. 1987. *Being Nobody Going Nowhere: Meditations on the Buddhist Path.* Boston: Wisdom Publications.

Korbanka, J., and M. McKay. 1995. "The Emotional and Behavioral Effects of Parental Discipline Styles on Their Adult Children." Unpublished paper.

Lau, M. A., S. R. Bishop, Z. V. Segal, T. Buis, N. Anderson, L. Carlson, S. Shapiro, and J. Carmody. 2006. "The Toronto Mindfulness Scale: Development and Validation." *Journal of Clinical Psychology* 62: 1445–67.

LeDoux, J. 1996. *The Emotional Brain.* New York: Touchstone.

Lewis, H. K., and M. E. Lewis. 1972. *Psychosomatics: How Your Emotions Can Damage Your Health.* New York: Viking Press.

Ludwig, D. S., and J. Kabat-Zinn. 2008. "Mindfulness in Medicine." *Journal of the American Medical Association* 300: 1350–52.

Mann, A. H. 1977. "Psychiatric Morbidity and Hostility in Hypertension." *Psychological Medicine* 7: 653–59.

McKay, M., P. D. Rogers, and J. McKay. 2003. *When Anger Hurts: Quieting the Storm Within.* 2nd ed. Oakland, CA: New Harbinger Publications.

Morone, N. E., C. M. Greco, and D. K. Weiner. 2008. "Mindfulness Meditation for the Treatment of Chronic Low-Back Pain in Older Adults: A Randomized Controlled Pilot Study." *Pain* 134: 310–19.

Neff, K. 2011. *Self-Compassion: Stop Beating Yourself Up and Leave Insecurity Behind.* New York: William Morrow / HarperCollins.

Nhat Hanh, Thich. 1975. *The Miracle of Mindfulness: A Manual on Meditation.* Boston: Beacon Press.

Nye, N. S. *Words Under the Words: Selected Poems.* Portland, OR: Far Corner Books.

Peeters, G., and J. Czapinski. 1990. "Positive-Negative Asymmetry in Evaluations: The Distinction Between Affective and Informational Negativity Effects." In *European Review of Social Psychology: Volume 1,* edited by W. Stroebe and M. Hewstone. New York: Wiley.

Pradhan, E. K., M. Baumgarten, P. Langenberg, B. Handwerger, A. K. Gilpin, T. Magyari, M. C. Hochberg, and B. M. Berman. 2007. "Effect of Mindfulness-Based Stress Reduction in Rheumatoid Arthritis Patients." *Arthritis and Rheumatism* 57: 1134–42.

Ramel, W., P. R. Goldin, P. E. Carmona, and J. R. McQuaid. 2004. "The Effects of Mindfulness Meditation Training on Cognitive

Processes and Affect in Patients with Past Depression." *Cognitive Therapy and Research* 28: 433–55.

Rosenman, R. H. 1985. "Health Consequences of Anger and Implications for Treatment. In *Anger and Hostility in Cardiovascular and Behavioral Disorders*, edited by M. A. Chesney and R. H. Rosenman. Washington, DC: Hemisphere Publishing Co.

Rosenzweig, S., D. K. Reibel, J. M. Greeson, J. S. Edman, S. A. Jasser, K. D. McMearty, and B. J. Goldstein. 2007. "Mindfulness-Based Stress Reduction Is Associated with Improved Glycemic Control in Type 2 Diabetes Mellitus: A Pilot Study." *Alternative Therapies in Health and Medicine* 13: 36–38.

Salzberg, S. 1995. *Loving-Kindness: The Revolutionary Art of Happiness*. Boston: Shambhala Publications.

———. 2011. *Real Happiness: The Power of Meditation*. New York: Workman Publishing.

Schure, M. B., J. Christopher, and S. Christopher. 2008. "Mind-Body Medicine and the Art of Self-Care: Teaching Mindfulness to Counseling Students Through Yoga, Meditation, and Qigong." *Journal of Counseling & Development* 86 (1): 47–56.

Schwartz, G. E., D. A. Weinberger, and J. A. Singer. 1981. "Cardiovascular Differentiation of Happiness, Sadness, Anger, and Fear Following Imagery and Exercise." *Psychosomatic Medicine* 43: 343–64.

Seligman, M. 2006. *Learned Optimism: How to Change Your Mind and Your Life*. New York: Vintage / Random House.

"Seville Statement." *Psychology Today*, June 1988, 34–39.

Shapiro, S. L., K. W. Brown, and G. M. Biegel. 2007. "Teaching Self-Care to Caregivers: Effects of Mindfulness-Based Stress Reduction on the Mental Health of Therapists in Training." *Training and Education in Professional Psychology* 1: 105–15.

Shapiro, S. L., and C. Izett. 2008. "Meditation: A Universal Tool for Cultivating Empathy. In *Mindfulness and the Therapeutic Relationship*, edited by D. Hick and T. Bien. New York: Guilford Press.

Shapiro, S. L., G. E. Schwartz, and G. Bonner. 1998. "Effects of Mindfulness-Based Stress Reduction on Medical and Premedical Students." *Journal of Behavioral Medicine* 21: 581–99.

Siegel, D. J. 2007. *The Mindful Brain: Reflection and Attunement in the Cultivation of Well-Being.* New York: W. W. Norton.

———. 2012. *Pocket Guide to Interpersonal Neurobiology: An Integrative Handbook of the Mind.* New York: W. W. Norton.

Speca, M., L. E. Carlson, E. Goodey, and M. Angen. 2000. "A Randomized, Wait-List Controlled Clinical Trial: The Effect of a Mindfulness Meditation–Based Stress Reduction Program on Mood and Symptoms of Stress in Cancer Outpatients." *Psychosomatic Medicine* 62: 613–22.

Steindl-Rast, D. 2001. "An Early Attempt at Gratitude." In *From the Ashes: A Spiritual Response to the Attack on America,* collected by the editors of Beliefnet. Boston: Rodale.

Straus, M. 1994. *Beating the Devil Out of Them: Corporal Punishment in American Families.* New York: Lexington Books.

Strozzi-Heckler, R. 2007. *In Search of the Warrior Spirit: Teaching Awareness Disciplines to the Military,* 4th ed. Berkeley, CA: Blue Snake Books.

Tavris, C. 1989. *Anger: The Misunderstood Emotion.* New York: Simon & Schuster.

Wachs, K., and Cordova, J. V. 2007. "Mindful Relating: Exploring Mindfulness and Emotion Repertoires in Intimate Relationships." *Journal of Marital and Family Therapy* 33: 464–81.

Walach, H., N. Buchheld, V. Buttenmüller, N. Kleinknecht, and S. Schmidt. 2006. "Measuring Mindfulness: The Freiburg Mindfulness Inventory." *Personality and Individual Differences* 40: 1543–55.

Whitting, J. W. M. 1941. *Becoming a Kwoma.* New Haven, CT: Yale University Press.

Williams, R. B. 1999. "A 69-Year-Old Man with Anger and Angina." *Journal of the American Medical Association* 282: 763–770.

Williams, R., and V. Williams. 2006. *In Control: No More Snapping at Your Family/Sulking at Work/Steaming in the Grocery Line/Seething in Meetings/Stuffing Your Frustration*. New York: Rodale.

Wolff, H. S., and S. Wolf. 1967. "Stress and the Gut." *Gastroenterology* 52: 2.

Wood, C. 1986. "The Hostile Heart." *Psychology Today* 20: 10–12.

World Health Organization (WHO). 1996. WHO Global Consultation on Violence and Health. *Violence: A Public Health Priority*. Geneva, Switzerland: World Health Organization.

———. 2002. *World Report on Violence and Health*. Geneva, Switzerland: World Health Organization.

Young-Eisendrath, P. 2009. "What Suffering Teaches." In *In the Face of Fear: Buddhist Wisdom for Challenging Times,* edited by Barry Boyce and the editors of the *Shambhala Sun*. Boston: Shambhala Publications.

Zautra, A. J., M. C. Davis, J. W. Reich, P. Nicassario, H. Tennen, P. Finan, A. Kratz, B. Parrish, and M. R. Irwin. 2008. "Comparison of Cognitive Behavioral and Mindfulness Meditation Interventions on Adaptation to Rheumatoid Arthritis for Patients with and Without History of Recurrent Depression." *Journal of Consulting and Clinical Psychology* 76: 408–21.

Jeffrey Brantley, MD, DFAPA, has practiced mindfulness meditation for over thirty years, and his work in medicine and psychiatry has emphasized mindfulness and mindfulness-based interventions to promote individual health and well-being. He is a founding faculty member of Duke Integrative Medicine, and founded the Mindfulness-Based Stress Reduction Program at Duke Integrative Medicine in 1998. Brantley is the author of *Calming Your Anxious Mind* and coauthor of the *Five Good Minutes*® series and *Daily Meditations for Calming Your Anxious Mind.*

Foreword writer **Barbara L. Fredrickson, PhD,** is author of *Love 2.0,* and is Kenan Distinguished Professor of Psychology and director of the Positive Emotions and Psychophysiology Laboratory at the University of North Carolina at Chapel Hill.

MORE BOOKS *from*
NEW HARBINGER PUBLICATIONS

CALMING YOUR
ANXIOUS MIND,
SECOND EDITION

How Mindfulness &
Compassion Can Free You
from Anxiety, Fear & Panic

ISBN: 978-1572244870 / US $16.95
Also available as an e-book

30-MINUTE THERAPY
FOR ANGER

Everything You Need To Know
in the Least Amount of Time

ISBN: 978-1608820290 / US $15.95
Also available as an e-book

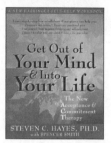

GET OUT OF YOUR MIND
& INTO YOUR LIFE

The New Acceptance &
Commitment Therapy

ISBN: 978-1572244252 / US $21.95
Also available as an e-book

MIND-BODY WORKBOOK
FOR STRESS

Effective Tools for
Lifelong Stress Reduction
& Crisis Management

ISBN: 978-1608826360 / US $21.95
Also available as an e-book

WHEN GOOD MEN
BEHAVE BADLY

Change Your Behavior,
Change Your Relationship

ISBN: 978-1572243460./ US $16.95
Also available as an e-book

THE CRITICAL PARTNER

How to End the Cycle
of Criticism & Get the
Love You Want

ISBN: 978-1608829276 / US $16.95
Also available as an e-book

 newharbingerpublications
1-800-748-6273 / newharbinger.com
(VISA, MC, AMEX / prices subject to change without notice)

 Like us on Facebook   Follow us on Twitter @newharbinger.com

 Don't miss out on new books in the subjects that interest you.
Sign up for our **Book Alerts** at **newharbinger.com/bookalerts**